Theorist-at-Large
One Woman's Ambiguous Journey into Medical Cannabis

Regina Nelson

ISBN: 1507664079
ISBN-13: 978-1507664070

Library of Congress Control Number: 2015901195
CreateSpace Independent Publishing Platform, North Charleston, SC

DEDICATION

Dedicated to ALL who have supported me and to all who may learn from my journey

Special Thanks to:

My mom, Billie Jo Holt, for her motherly devotion and encouragement that have kept me going and helped this book become a reality

My children, Daniel, Rachel, BreAnna, Stephanie, Timothy, and Bryan— You are the pieces of my heart and I continue forward hoping to make the world a bit better place for Jakob, Tyler, Aurelia, Skylar, Layla, Shane, Sophie, and those we've yet to meet of our future generations and the future generations of every family

The Cohort 10—Original and Adopted Scholarly Family Members—This project reflects a bit of each of you, it is because of you I came to Union Institute and University, and because of you that I continue to preserve

In loving memory of Ezekiel Dukes, Ph.D. (c)—A man who encouraged and challenged me and who inspires me still

Please note that throughout this book the terms *marijuana, medical marijuana* (MMJ), *medical cannabis,* and *cannabis* will be used interchangeably. While cannabis refers to the plant and whole plant medicines, and is the preferred term among patients and MMJ organizations, the terms marijuana and medical marijuana are directly associated with public policies, in each case this author is referring to the same substance.

TABLE OF CONTENTS

INTRODUCTION

This book, well, it's about my academic journey, at least a portion of it... a journey of a lifetime. Like nothing—NOTHING--I ever expected! I began this journey in 2011, a hopeful and totally unprepared doctoral student. My first term began in early January, so it truly was like a New Year's resolution in action. I'd been preparing, reading philosophy, considering my future studies and goals. The primary goal was to follow the ambiguous process of the Ethics and Social Justice Program in Ethical and Creative Leadership at Union Institute & University...follow it where it may go, learn a great deal along the way, gain a much greater understanding of research and methodologies, and eventually upon gaining the coveted "Ph.D." teach in a program much the same as the one I was entering. Not to be a renowned Professor or become some kind of Advocate or Global Leader but to venture further as a lifelong Learner, helping others do the same...and living life on my own terms while (hopefully) gaining a retirement plan!

To make this journey a successful one I needed an issue; some social injustice that needed exploring. Many options were considered but one thing kept coming back to me: cannabis...medical cannabis, specifically. Other than its illegality, the use of cannabis had always been a secret pleasure that helped keep my sanity—it kept me balanced and creative in the small doses I sneaked. And, considering that I have raised six (yes, 6) children to semi-responsible adulthood, while working in corporate Human Resources, business consulting, and often carrying a full-time student course-load...cannabis kept me sane.

At the time "medical marijuana" was becoming a hot topic, even in Texas, and I began to explore. What I found early in my research was astounding; not only would this plant be considered a "miracle" food and drug if discovered today, but in the good ol' USA, very few academics were following the social, political, and cultural changes it's "medicalization" was causing. And, virtually no one was conducting research with medical cannabis patients or sharing their plight so that others would understand that this is a vital issue in our society. After much searching, I found one article that by happenstance spoke of the habits of cannabis patients in Canada (thank you, Andrew Hathaway). Hathaway (2011) was looking at the "recreational use" of marijuana and by population in Canada, which has favorable medical cannabis regulations, some of his 'research participants' were cannabis patients simply by the default that he was seeking "regular" or daily users for this project. Other than this small glimpse, there was virtually no other reference to cannabis patients in research I could find at the time. (Thankfully, in the three years since small amounts of research here in the U.S. and more from other countries have begun to trickle in…someday soon, I hope we'll see much more).

I waited until my third class introduction before revealing to my Cohort (The Cohort 10) that I planned to focus my research and studies in medical marijuana (though I had no idea how this ambiguous plan would come together). The looks of astonishment—well, they're funny to remember, and I dare to venture, not one of this Cohort (not to mention Instructors), thought I was in my right mind. When I discussed my topic of interest with my Dean and Associate Dean, I was warned to "be careful" but not entirely discouraged. Instead, I was offered very safe ideas from which I might choose to explore under my Leadership studies and marijuana. Somehow the resistance and the observed lack of knowledge about cannabis and its medical usage made me more determined to follow this course of study, so the ambiguous process of this social justice program began with me venturing academically into new terrain that few have shown themselves brave enough to enter.

This book is an exploration of my academic adventures to date—they're not finished yet! Each section will cover a semester term, briefly providing an introduction as to my life at the time and then a few chosen articles, or rather papers, I submitted as coursework that I hope are article worthy. As you will come to see, I had no idea the direction—the twists and turns—this journey would take me as I followed this ambiguous process in interdisciplinary education. And, today, I still don't know exactly where it will end. As the character Dexter, a Showtime serial killer I used as an example of ethics, during the same day I announced my intent to focus my research on marijuana, once stated, "Some experiences are so big...they change your DNA." This isn't my life's story...but it's a portion of my life that changed who I am (or woke me to who I am) and hope you will find interesting enough to read.

Chapter One
January 2011 - June 2011

When I entered the doctoral program at Union Institute and University I was living in Texas, married to my best friend in an attempt to survive life after a painful divorce and deep-seeded empty-nest syndrome—and because I desperately needed medical benefits. After several lay-offs, a sojourn to South Korea to teach English, and several years trying to figure out what to do with the rest of my life, Bill pushed me to return to school. It made sense and quite honestly, I love interdisciplinary education—I am a nerd this way! The happiest times in my life have revolved around my return to school as an adult—first at Vermont College in 1996 to finish my Bachelor's degree (after many stops and starts—I hated traditional college) and then attending a liberal studies program a few years later at the University of Oklahoma beginning my studies in Leadership. (Note: My Master's studies were in progress when the WorldCom scandal broke. I was also a Human Resources Manager at WorldCom at the time—another book could be written about that time in my life, but for now I will spare you).

Union Institute and University is not a traditional college; one that requires you to attend classes several times a week, over many years, in order to earn a degree. Instead, it's a liberal studies program, a low-residency program that allows learners to attend residencies twice a year (about 9 days at a time in Cincinnati in my case) and then study at home. It's intense, both the residencies and the semesters! And, the path is ambiguous, even for those who doubt that fact when they enter the program, they soon learn each student loses control of their life and any plan they think they have for their educational journey. Each student who succeeds has simply been successful putting one thought in front of another and moving forward to the best of their ability each and every day until the program ends!

When I arrived in Cincinnati for the first residency

(six are required), I had no idea what to expect from my "cohort"—the other new students who would join me in "The Cohort 10". But, the one thing I did know is that these people—whoever they were—they would be instrumental to my success. Today, each member of "The Cohort 10" has a special place in my heart—and you'll begin to understand why soon, though words can never do justice to the feelings I have for each of these incredible humans who've become my scholarly family be they from Cohort 10 or not!

Let me just briefly explain that "residency" is required for all students, it consists of about nine days of classes, seminars, and workshops. Some days begin at 7:00am and often don't end until nearly 9:00pm—or later. It's grueling, the days are long, but it's also highly stimulating and the diversity of thought makes it an incredible place to be! The first semester all new students begin with three courses and remain together through the courses. My first term courses consisted of: Engaging Differences, Analytical Writing, and Ethics & Social Justice (Philosophy at the Doctoral level). The first two courses I was excited about, (I did say I am a nerd, you'll want to keep this in mind as you continue reading), the third class intimidated the hell out of me. Despite my liberal studies background, philosophy had not been an area of study for me—and was the one subject I feared I was not prepared for...and I wasn't. Dr. Chris Voparil was my instructor for this course, and bless him, as he was kind, encouraging, and his criticism took me farther down the road than expected—his feedback was priceless! Critical, but priceless! (Thank you Chris, for the time and thought you put into each and every paper's feedback).

It also helped a great deal that I made friends with a couple of men one term ahead of me during residency: Steve and Christopher. Steve would eventually (about an hour after we meet) become family, more like a slightly older brother than a friend. Each day I've spent in Cincinnati for school since, I've looked forward to the conversations Steve and I will have driving around Cincinnati between classes and seminars; having down-to-earth intellectual conversations, clearly sharing values and goals, and being able to talk freely about the use of cannabis with someone who understands and does not condemn my relationship with this plant. (By the way, Steve is a mental health expert who understands the valuable role cannabis has in mental health—and one who listens to the needs of patients. I love my brother). Steve's advice—personal, academic, and professional—has helped me navigate the maze of academics, cannabis, and my own inner demons. And, most was accomplished while listening to some incredible R & B and blowing smoke out the windows of a Honda while cruising the streets of Cinci!

During this first semester, besides the increasing tension with Bill, my only distraction from the enormous study load was a part-time teaching gig at a business college. My students began to learn more about cannabis than they ever anticipated given they were taking marketing or human resource courses in Texas. I was excited about my coursework and even more intrigued by the plethora of information I began to find on the endocannabinoid system and cannabis as medicine. I was off and running…though I had no idea where I was headed.

Despite the fears I had when I entered this semester, throughout the course of the term my self-confidence and knowledge both grew exponentially to critical feedback received. Dr. Tony Kashani quickly became my champion, encouraging me to dig deeper and look further. Dr. Kathryn Burnthoff and I—well, we just connected, which was helpful because I was really worried about the rust that had accumulated on my writing skills. She really helped me clean things up! And, like I said earlier, Dr. Voparil, proved not to be my nemesis but one of the most thoughtful instructors I have ever had the pleasure to work with. The feedback he provided was often disclaimed with a note that he did not expect me to implement the changes he was suggesting (many of which I didn't even understand yet), but to keep "these things in mind" as I proceeded through the program. His first term feedback helped me publish "Framing Integral Leadership in the Medical Cannabis Community" in my fourth term (Nelson, 2012). In looking back on the two papers I wrote at the end of the first term—one of which I was encouraged to revise and publish (major kudos for a first term Ph.D. Student) by Dr. Kashani and one of which Dr. Voparil let me know "was not the paper I was asked to write, but must be one I felt compelled to write"—I am proud and a bit surprised to see how my thinking about Care Ethics and Medical Cannabis began.

Marijuana Misclassification Calls for Declassification
April 2011

As noted by my professor, Dr. Christopher Voparil, this was a paper I "was compelled" to write—not necessarily the one I was instructed to write for my final assignment...but I managed to pull an A- out of a class I deeply feared. I learned more in this one semester than I had in all my formal education to date—about philosophy, critical thought, and myself. As I've described it to many, it was as if Chris opened up a fire hydrant and asked me to fill a cup full of the water with only what water I could manage to grab in my mouth (just like on Fear Factor or some other crazy reality show). And despite the odds, I did! This paper is not unlike articles I've seen from within the cannabis industry since, it seems all advocates have a need to explore the history of this plant and most, if not all, come to the conclusion it should not be on the list of Controlled Substances, but removed.

Historically, issues such as women's reproductive health rights, from birth control to abortion, have called upon care ethics to support their cause. For instance, even many who hold abortion to be morally wrong will concede that in certain circumstances it should be a legally available option; specifically, people care when an abortion will save the life of the mother. With care applied, health issues, such as women's reproductive rights, are no longer solely justice issues. Within an ethics of care when a moral judgment is made, it is always more than a simple expression of approval or disapproval, it is expressing a "commitment to behave in a way compatible with caring" (Noddings, 19) and asking the other, what their needs are and then listening intently to their reply. In the medical marijuana debate, the key is in not making a moral judgment before listening to the needs of patients and learning about their needs. Further, "The one caring is careful to distinguish between acts that violate caring, acts that she herself holds wrong, and those acts 'some people' hold to be wrong (Noddings, 19) ." Much as with abortion, citizens must care about medical marijuana, even if they hold its use to be wrong, not only because marijuana provides relief to fellow citizens, who are suffering from a variety of serious ailments and pain but because as humans we each have an endocannabinoid system—a major endocrine system that responds favorably to the plants phytocannabinoids.

Currently, marijuana is a rising social concern that many citizens have moral or social arguments with which to address their personal views, in relation to, whether or not, this drug should be made available for responsible adults to use "recreationally." When considered specifically as a legalization issue, marijuana is an issue of justice, an issue concerning the individual rights of citizens that many of us may never agree upon. Although many of us are aware that marijuana has been associated with reducing the suffering associated with chemotherapy treatments, few citizens have much knowledge about marijuana's particular value as medication or knowledge about recent research that suggests marijuana may be effective in fighting cancer or slowing the onset of Alzheimer's disease. Further, few doctors, much less citizens, understand that each and every mammal has an endocannabinoid system; meaning we each have a stake in cannabinoid medicine. Viewed with this knowledge, cannabis is more than a moral issue, to see it as such is seeing only one perception of a multifaceted picture. If we temper the perspective of justice with care, as Carol Gilligan (1987) encourages us to do, many citizens currently opposed to legalizing cannabis for medicinal use may come to view medical cannabis from a "care perspective," which is a much different picture than of marijuana when considered exclusively from a "justice perspective (Gilligan, 49)." However, as Joan Tronto elucidates we will be unsuccessful in merging care with justice if we fail to consider "compassion" as the "central value of caring (Tronto, 1993, 3)." Whereas justice often focuses on our institutions and systems of government and may even prompt us to repair some of the gaps that create unjust laws or situations that marginalize many citizens, compassion becomes the door way to justice when applied to the issues that cause suffering. It is essential to keep compassion central to our deliberation regarding the use of medical cannabis, just as we should do whenever we address any issue that causes suffering among our fellow human beings.

Either a social or a moral perspective may be equally legitimate when discussing the use of cannabis for strictly "recreational" purposes, as long as justice is the primary goal; although many of us will continue to disagree on our stances, as citizens we should have a voice, for or against. However, when we discuss the use of cannabis for medicinal needs, as Tronto contends, we must "place such an ethic in its full moral and political context." (Tronto, 105) I believe, what we will see with compassion placed in both a moral and political context will engage us in a different picture, one in which citizens, especially citizens who are suffering, should lend their voice. Specifically, this paper will concentrate on the medical marijuana debate as an issue of public health, requiring citizens to temper justice with an ethic of care, in order to find a solution that is both just and compassionate: reviewing the misclassification of marijuana as a Schedule I Controlled Substance. Further, this paper will discuss factors that relate to cannabis being considered an acceptable, sometimes preferable medication and question why the Drug Enforcement Agency (DEA) and the National Institutes of Health (NIH) have not taken into consideration the medicinal benefits of marijuana that require it to be declassified or entirely removed from the Schedule of Controlled Substances, providing federal protection, not federal prosecution, for its use. The misclassification of marijuana obstructs medical research and federally recognized access for patients and caregivers living in states with favorable medical cannabis legislation, placing medical cannabis as an essential public health issue.

Marijuana: The Need for Medical Recognition

As mentioned, issues viewed solely from a moral perspective often cause disagreement among citizens: the recreational use of marijuana, abortion, and stem cell research are but a few current topics that can always prompt heated debate. Because marijuana has been vilified as a 'recreational' substance of potential abuse during our lifetime, medical cannabis patients and caregivers are often met with skepticism because few understand how pain and suffering are alleviated by such a controversial plant. Others, typically those who are uninformed, assume medical cannabis is just a 'work-around' to legalizing marijuana; an illusion that 'stoners' are using to make their 'high' legal. However skeptical one may be, if cannabis has medicinal value, attested to by patients and caregivers, including doctors, nurses and medical researchers, shouldn't we investigate these possibilities? Cannabis is currently listed as a Controlled I Substance, which means in the U.S. it has been classified as having no recognizable medicinal value and as highly addictive; as we will discuss, both of these descriptions are false. Although Americans are becoming more informed about the medical value of cannabis, few are well informed, so It may help to begin by discussing why marijuana has been misclassified and is worthy of an argument to be recognized for medicinal use and thus, removed from the Schedule of Controlled Substances.

I will not delve into its long history, but cannabis has been used for thousands of years as a medicinal herb (Abel, 1943). Although never widely popular in the U.S. as a medication, "some 28 different medicines," both prescription and over-the-counter remedies, contained cannabis before it was prohibited in 1937, through The Marihuana Tax Act (Iverson, 122). Today, a number of us have personal stories usually of close family or friends that have drawn us into the cannabis debate; additionally, solid research studies validating the effectiveness of cannabis in treating a variety of medical issues that cause human suffering. In short, the therapeutic benefits of cannabis are derived from the interactions of cannabinoids and the human body's own endocannabinoid system. Studies have shown that cannabis can control pain, in some cases better than available alternatives (Aggrawal, 153 & Iverson, 59-61), in large part, this occurs because cannabinoids and opiates "act synergistically" in producing pain relief, but this effect is also enhanced by the fact that cannabinoids also outnumber opiate receptors (Iverson, 60). In one particular study, morphine was found to be "fifteen times more active with the addition of a *small* dose" of marijuana and codeine was nearly "900 times" more effective. (Shujaa, 1-my emphasis) What this means for suffers of chronic pain is that smaller doses of opiates are required to control their pain when combined with cannabis. In fact, many pro cannabis advocates, both patients and caregivers, speak of a reducing or ceasing opiate use for pain control once they began medicating with medical cannabis. (Grinspoon, April 22, 2011) For patients, this is very good news, because opiates are well-known to be addictive, warranting in most cases a Schedule II classification based on their high abuse risk. Americans have been led to believe that cannabis is also highly addictive and thus warrants a Schedule I classification. Moreover, anti-drug campaigns have for decades decried the addictive qualities of cannabis; for this reason, I think it is important to quickly address possible cannabis addiction before discussing toxicity and side-effects.

Many Americans admitted to drug treatment programs each year do list marijuana as *one of the drugs* they regularly consume. Most drug addicts engage in what is known as *polydrug* use, meaning "drug users do not consume a single drug, but rather multiple kinds of drugs" (Babor, 44). This fact is true for both adults and teens and currently in the U.S., diverted [black-market] pharmaceuticals are the most rapidly escalating trend in drug misuse and addiction (Babor 34-39). Any drug is potentially addictive; even caffeine is considered an addictive substance, so it is important for patients and caregivers to recognize the potential for addiction in any medication they consume. Dr. Lester Grinspoon, a professor emeritus and former researcher at Harvard Medical School and author of several books on the science of marijuana has found that cannabis a is, "far less addictive and far less subject to abuse than many drugs now used as muscle relaxants, hypnotics, and analgesics" (Grinspoon & Bakalar, 244; Grinspoon, April 22, 2011). In fact, Grinspoon found cannabis to be innocuous and therapeutic, so much so, that in the early 1970's he provided extracted cannabis oil to his young son orally to ease his suffering caused by cancer treatments. Although his son failed to survive cancer, Grinspoon has a great deal of compassion for cannabis patients, because he saw the relief it brought to his own child, making the last year of his life more tolerable (Grinspoon, April 22, 2011). Further, cannabis is well within the Food and Drug Administration's (FDA) range for approved medications and is far less addictive than many drugs classified much lower on the Schedule of Controlled Substances (Joy, et al 1), including Cocaine and OxyContin, which are both Schedule II Substances, codeine, which is a Schedule III Substance in its strongest forms, and Darvon and Valium, which are Schedule IV Substances (www.dea.gov). Each of these listed controlled substances is but one of many prescription medications that are known to be more addictive than cannabis (Joy, et al 115-135; Grinspoon & Bakalar, 201-214).

When it comes to healthcare, I believe most of us would agree that it is important to have reliable information so that we can make educated choices. In addition to the DEA, who oversees Controlled Substances and enforces U.S. Drug policies, the Food and Drug Administration (FDA) oversees the safety of nearly all consumable products, including most medications that Americans ingest. Safety, in the case of cannabis, dosing, toxicity, and side-effects, is critical knowledge for physicians, caregivers and patients to have access to and understand. Concerned citizens, patients, and caregivers want to be informed, it is their right to be informed; even large pharmaceutical companies have been made (forced) to disclose this type of information to consumers; however, cannabis patients or caregivers must privately search for this type of information online or rely upon members of the medical cannabis community in their state for information on cannabis. Because cannabis has become hybrid and grown into multiple strains, with no two strains quite alike, and more strains being developed, this leads to variations in medicinal value particular to differing ailments (Grinspoon & Bakalar, 117-118), as does the variety of forms cannabis can take from smokeables to edibles to extracts or concentrates.

Understanding this information can be overwhelming for patients who have no prior knowledge or experience with cannabis. Even in states with medical marijuana legislation, doctors are scrambling to keep up with new information that often comes from lay-people not scientists, since marijuana's Schedule I classification precludes marijuana-related human clinical trials and research in the United States. Fortunately, there has been reliable research making its way to the public, a small amount approved within the U.S. and the remainder from the global community. The good news is the toxicity of cannabis is so low that, "In layman's terms," according to an *The New England Journal of Medicine* article, "a smoker would theoretically have to consume nearly 1,500 pounds of marijuana within about fifteen minutes to induce a lethal response" (Annas, 4). In comparison, a lethal dose of caffeine is equal to about 100 cups of coffee (Degenhardt, et al, 322). Common sense conveys that based on these figures no one can ingest enough cannabis to induce a lethal response. Additionally, there are relatively few side-effects that are concerning beyond the euphoric or psychoactive properties in cannabis that can cause dizziness, fatigue, rapid heart rate, temporary and slightly decreased motor response; or paranoia in some. Like with many prescription medications, some patients should not drive after using cannabis. Yet, when compared to opiates, cannabis's side-effects are minimal; for many patients and caregivers the legal risks of using cannabis for medicinal purposes are far greater than either toxicity or side-effects (Grinspoon, April 22, 2011; Grinspoon & Bakalar, 269-270; Iverson 82-84).

What many people take issue with in regards to medical marijuana is not the product itself, but the fact that they believe marijuana must be smoked and at least smoking is commonly known to be harmful. Cigarette smokers will agree that smoking is bad for your health and, in fact, toxic to your body. Tobacco is, however, much more toxic to the human body than cannabis (Grinspoon & Bakalar, 211; Babor, 21-24). Even though cannabis is non-toxic, it is a reasonable assumption that even with medicinal value, smoking cannabis is not be the best delivery method for a terminally ill person—though there are no studies that indicate it's an unhealthy activity and millions of patients attest to its value in smoked form. Today, some cannabis patients choose to smoke cannabis in order to medicate themselves, but many others do not. In states that have approved legislation to recommend cannabis for medical use it can be delivered via tinctures, sublingual sprays, edibles, teas, or ointments. In fact, a wide array of small businesses have developed around this growing industry and are adding value to the cannabis industry by developing alternative delivery methods that at the federal level have been blocked through normal research methods because cannabis is a Schedule I Controlled Substance. If cannabis is declassified and this industry continues to grow and focus is placed on the medicinal good of cannabis, smoking is obviously not going to be the best option for ingestion for most cannabis patients; therefore, it is positive to see new delivery methods being developed by private entrepreneurs.

Cancer is certainly one of the diseases most feared by human beings; further, it is one of the diseases Americans are most passionate about finding a cure. The word, cancer, in and of itself, is frightening and associated with pain, suffering, and agonizing treatments. Many of us associate cancer with death. We assume a cancer diagnosis is at best a long battle for our health, a battle in which we would surely suffer great pain. For those of us raised during an era when cannabis has been considered primarily a recreational drug, not medicinal, is it possible to believe this plant can actually help relieve suffering, in cancer patients, at least as well as, if not better, than current pharmaceutical drugs? Testimonies of patients and caregivers suggest it can, as does medical research (and the patents our government retains or is providing to pharmaceutical companies for cannabinoid medicines). Further, cannabis has been approved by states to treat chronic pain associated with a variety of diseases and injury, muscle spasms associated with Parkinson's disease, multiple sclerosis and paralysis, inflammation accompanying rheumatoid arthritis, and many more medical conditions. States with medical cannabis legislation have recognized the medicinal benefits of cannabis and made it legal, at least on their level, for patients, caregivers, and dispensaries to provide safe access to cannabis for patients. Plus, patients can avoid criminal activity, should they decide to medicate with cannabis, at least on the state level. There is strong evidence that cannabis has medicinal value; with a growing number of states supporting medical cannabis for patients, it is time for the federal government to participate in this debate.

The Need for Declassification

To enter the medical cannabis debate the DEA must first address the misclassification of marijuana. Until it is reclassified as having medicinal value, it remains illegal for a physician to *prescribe* cannabis for medical use under federal law, although under the First Amendment they can *recommend* its use. The latest federal attempt to reschedule cannabis is pending before DEA Administrator, Michele Leonhart. In the United States the DEA oversees all controlled drugs, legal and illegal. These drugs are classified in a series of Schedules I through V. The scheduling system is a descending scale based upon the drugs addictive properties, side-effects, medicinal value, and safety, among other factors (www.usdoj.gov). Schedule I drugs are defined as having *no safe or accepted* medical use, *even under medical supervision*; further this classification also precludes research on the drug without strict licensing authorization from the DEA, which is rarely provided (www.usdoj.gov). The primary issues with the classification of marijuana as a Schedule I Substance are the failure by the DEA to acknowledge the safe and accepted medical use of cannabis, as well as their failure to review and understand the true abuse risk associated with cannabis; which is very low. As we've discussed cannabis is safer than the majority of our current pharmaceutical drugs and has accepted medical uses for patients under a physician's supervision. Further, not only does research support medical use, but in sixteen of our fifty states, the medicinal use of cannabis is acknowledged by law. However, regardless of their stance, if marijuana remains a Schedule I Substance, the DEA will continue to block the majority of research related to the medicinal use of cannabis and challenge patient's rights in states with medical cannabis laws; plus researchers, caregivers, and patients will remain subject to federal prosecution. The petition filed to request reclassification for cannabis is still awaiting DEA Administrator, Michele Leonhart's approval. It should be noted this petition has been pending since 2002 and remains at a standstill. It seems to me that the DEA is simply using the justice perspective in regards to cannabis, seeing it solely from their position leading the United States War on Drugs and not from a care perspective based on recent research and patient and caregiver testimonials. It also seems to be a conflict of interest that the same public institution that enforces drug policies, also determines what drugs physicians can prescribe to their patients.

If we are truly striving for a more compassionate society, we must temper justice with care in order to hear the voices of those suffering. Care helps us determine where we focus our attention, so that based on what we learn, we can respond appropriately. To understand why the cannabis issue is important we must listen to both those who suffer and those who care for the suffering, especially our primary caregivers: physicians and nurses. In 2009, The American Medical Association requested that cannabis "be reviewed with the goal of facilitating the conduct of clinical research and development of cannabinoid-based medicines, and alternate delivery methods" (www.ama-assn.org). In fact, organizations such as The American Academy of Family Physicians, the American Public Health Association, and numerous other caregiver organizations have supported medicinal legalization and further research on cannabis. If caregivers are willing to engage in moral scrutiny of the institutional structures that impede their ability to provide care to their patients, shouldn't the DEA be willing to engage in the debate with them? Compassion in care ethics focuses on people's pain and specific needs, but within a political context it also requires the recognition of human rights, and the realization of liberty, equality, and justice for those needs to be met. By failing to respond to the voices of the American people, primarily those who are suffering and their primary caregivers our government is acting without compassion. I propose we find a more compassionate view to consider the medicinal aspects of cannabis as seen through an ethics of care.

Compassion

The current climate in the U.S., as shown by the number of states adopting medical marijuana initiatives, strongly suggests that large numbers of Americans approve of medical marijuana and accept the beliefs of former DEA Administrative Law Judge, Francis L. Young, who has often been quoted as saying, that cannabis is "capable of relieving distress of great numbers of very ill people and doing so safely under medical supervision." Intrinsic to this particularity is a sense of connectedness, where the compassionate person recognizes his relationship as parent, family member, fellow citizen, or simply as human being in a wider societal context. Through his statement Young displays compassion for other human beings, particularly those who are suffering and are therefore, disadvantaged. Like Tronto, Martha Nussbaum makes compassion central to her ideas on human capabilities, which include being able to show concern for others by envisioning "the situation of another and to have compassion for that situation" (Nussbaum 1995, 84). All of us are aware that diseases and accidents, which can lead to pain and suffering, can occur in any of our lives, or of those we care about, at any time. In regards to cancer, we hope no one we know or love is ever diagnosed with cancer, but as life progresses we learn through lived experience that life is not fair and that people we love may become ill or suffer from great pain. When we are faced with this type of crisis our initial response is to resolve or at least improve the situation if we are capable. If you were faced with a medical crisis or chronic long-term pain and suffering, would you not want the best for yourself, or a loved one, or other fellow human beings; even if this help came in, what you might at first consider an unconventional plant?

An Ethics of Care, as espoused earlier by Tronto and Gilligan, conjoined with a perspective of justice, is in my opinion, the correct lens to apply to the cannabis debate. In the sense that compassionate co-suffering presupposes a sense of shared humanity; "the other person's suffering is seen as the kind of thing that could happen to anyone, including oneself" (Blum, 511). While there is inequality in suffering, compassion promotes the equality of possibility; in that, terminal or chronic illnesses could happen to any one of us or to any one we know or love; thereby, we must envision ourselves in the place of the one suffering. Compassion is an emotional and rational response to particularity; the compassionate person is after careful consideration, making a reasoned judgment about the needs of a specific person or group (Tronto 102-103); however, compassion can not only be applied specifically to cannabis patients, individually or as a group, but extends to sociopolitical concerns, such as cannabis's misclassification as a Schedule I Substance. If every human being is capable of suffering great pain, a compassionate response is required, for we recognize, as fellow human beings, we could be in their situation—after all we do each have an endocannabinoid system! In caring for our own health and the health of others, we must inform ourselves of public health issues, and consider those issues with compassion.

When a caring perspective is applied a compassionate person will respond to the suffering and needs of those suffering with empathetic practical wisdom. This practical wisdom is in the Aristotelian sense of *phronesis*, where there is thorough deliberation, examination of one's options, an awareness of appropriate feelings, and then the carrying out of good intentions through reasoned choices. Gilligan argues that justice and care are "two cross-cutting perspectives" that "cut across egoism and altruism," to help us arrive at our reasoned choice (Gilligan 34). Gilligan successfully argues that we're each vulnerable to oppression and abandonment; therefore, we must "not act unfairly toward others, and not turn away from someone in need" (Gilligan 32). In relation to public health issues, if we fail to consider the substance of the issue and respond in an informed manner, we are doing a disservice to ourselves and turning our backs on our fellow citizens. The disabled and the ailing are already marginalized, as people who care about others we should not further marginalize the infirmed in our society. Instead, we should listen to patients and caregivers, not feign care or neglect, but instead act within a framework that is both just and compassionate. We cut across the egoism when we listen and then contemplate what we have learned and we engage altruism when we behave in a manner appropriate to this new knowledge.

Compassion cannot be a substitute for the objectivity of justice; however, it is "intimately related to justice" and rights as asserted by Martha Nussbaum (Nussbaum 1996, 37). If a Schedule I Controlled Substance is found to have been misclassified because it has medicinal value, it seems logical to believe, at the very least, it should qualify to be reclassified to a lower level to facilitate further testing. Unfortunately, citizens realize that logic and government bureaucracy are not intimately related entities. I could argue cannabis has always met the qualification to be removed from the Schedule but how does it measure up to other drugs with higher mortality rates from use—drugs like cocaine for instance? As stated earlier cocaine is a Schedule II Controlled Substance, and open to not only prescribed use, but also to medical research; hence, cocaine is able to serve the needs of patients, based on its ability to do so, under the supervision of a licensed physician. Both cocaine and cannabis have been shown to provide pain relief to those who suffer, but cannabis has been shown to be far less toxic and addictive (Babor, 21-24) and it addresses far more symptoms of suffering than just pain relief because of our own endocannabinoid systems. Showing compassion toward cannabis patients through the ability to recognize the needs of those who are suffering and the ability to do so in the least toxic or addictive manner seems a preferable situation. If we fail to acknowledge the necessity to declassify cannabis, in some sense, we have made a reasoned choice to value the medicinal value of cocaine above that of cannabis. Not only does this not make sense from a drug safety standpoint, as cocaine rightly finds itself on the CSA, but it also fails to take into account the many suffering patients, who testify cannabis brings them pain relief or helps them turn away from cocaine or other drug dependencies.

If thirty-five states are either already engaged in, or have shown interest in, medical cannabis legislation, for the federal government to fail to reply to the petition requesting a review of the classification for cannabis, they must not understand what Americans care about and why they care for it. Tronto's theories regarding *caring about* and *caring for* are valuable in this debate. In short, she elucidates that, *caring about* refers "to less concrete objects: it is characterized by a more general form of commitment;" while *caring for* implies, "a specific, particular object that is the focus of caring." In this sense, in the medical cannabis debate, we must care about our nation's drug policies regarding the medical use of cannabis, because what we care for is our ailing relative suffering from cancer or another terminal or chronic condition. Tronto maintains that "the practice of care describes the qualities necessary for democratic citizens to live together well in a pluralistic society, and that only in a just, pluralist, democratic society can care flourish (Tronto, 1993 161-162)." In the example provided, that of an ailing relative, to assure our nation's policies address the demographic we care for, we must care about the policies our nation puts into place, and the specific inclusions the legislation incorporates. Until that time, we must care about the lack of attention our government provides issues like cannabis. Ignoring a public health issue doesn't make it go away; it seems to me, that almost a decade of waiting for a response from a government institution falls outside of both justice and care perspectives.

When we shift our attention from concerns about justice to concerns about care we change "the definition of what constitutes a moral problem" and this new perspective, combining justice and care helps us see the same situation in a new and different ways (Gilligan, 35). From this perspective we find a great need to investigate cannabis further; looking at it from simply a justice perspective does not provide sufficient information for many citizens to resolve their moral dilemmas with cannabis as a medication. I believe patients and caregivers in states that have enacted cannabis legislation find they are being treated far more justly, than those living in states that have not yet enacted medical marijuana laws, but they can also point out many ways policy and public opinion could support them better. As Gilligan elucidates, "...[care] modulates the strict demands of justice by considering equity...leaving the basic assumptions of a justice framework intact" (Gilligan, 36). Care perspectives are not, in any sense, inferior to justice perspectives; they expose additional dynamics to social issues (Gilligan, 32). Instead of considering only our moral stance on the use of illicit drugs, we begin to contemplate how we should respond to the situation as others who care. In this way, "these two perspectives are readily integrated or fused" (Gilligan, 43). I believe we have established that care theories support justice, whether in our families, communities, or a wider societal context. As well, by applying care theories, the cannabis debate is reframed as a healthcare issue to which compassion must be applied. The medical cannabis debate may be personal, in that your loved one might benefit from cannabis therapies. If the debate is personal, particular to someone you care for, you will react compassionately. If it is not personal, in that you know no one who can benefit from cannabis personally, then this debate can be viewed from the perspective of an American citizen, who is compassionate and cares for other citizens, specifically others suffering from illnesses for which cannabis might provide some relief. In either case, it seems reasonable to believe that citizens should have the right to choose to use cannabis, especially if their state has laws supporting their medicinal usage and, particularly if each citizen has an endocannabinoid system that reacts so favorably with the *cannabis sativa* plant.

Future Generations

We, of course, have close connections with and therefore obligations to our families, friends and communities, and it is arguable that in some matters, we have a responsibility to each of our fellow human beings, in a wider global context. Annette Baier recognizes that we also have a responsibility to consider "the next generation's" interest (Baier 55). As a mother of six and a grandmother of four (Note: now seven), I agree with Baier. As discussed previously, recent research is pointing toward cannabis as a possibility for treatments far less harsh than those cancer patients experience today. Future testing and research might lead to cures for certain types of cancer and for many other debilitating or deadly diseases. In just the past few months, the National Cancer Institute (NCI), attempted to acknowledge possible cancer-fighting properties in cannabis. The NCI, which is part of the National Institutes of Health (NIH), updated its website to include what appears to be the first federal recognition that cannabis indeed has cancer-fighting properties. NCI posted the following announcement to their website:

> The potential benefits of medicinal Cannabis
> for people living with cancer include
> antiemetic effects, appetite stimulation, pain
> relief, and improved sleep. In the practice of
> integrative oncology, the health care provider
> may recommend medicinal Cannabis not only
> for symptom management but also for its
> possible direct antitumor effect (cancer.gov).

This statement was retrieved online on March 21, 2011. Within days, NCI updated their website to reflect the following revision to the second sentence of the posting. That sentence was changed to the following:

> Though no relevant surveys of practice
> patterns exist, it appears that physicians caring
> for cancer patients who prescribe medicinal
> Cannabis predominantly do so for symptom
> management (cancer.gov).

Although updated to "clarify" their statement NCI, thereby NIH, continues to support the symptom relief effects of medical cannabis, although discarding the possible curative impact. Their website does state that there is indeed a possible antitumor effect, but that this effect has only been studied in animals, (cancer.gov) which makes sense, since human studies are not being conducted within the United States due to the misclassification of cannabis. However, the NIH website still reports the following:

> Scientific studies are underway to test the
> safety and usefulness of cannabis compounds

for treating certain medical conditions.
Currently, smoking marijuana is not
recommended for the treatment of any
disease or condition (nih.gov).

It seems our most preeminent government medical
institutions NIH and NCI are in conflict with the DEA and
each other. The NCI has information they believe citizens
would benefit from learning, but cannot posit it in a manner
that might require the DEA to resolve the misclassification of
cannabis, so that more studies about 'the safety and
usefulness of cannabis compounds' may be conducted by
NIH. Additionally, studies we've yet to discuss clearly state
cannabis helps patients suffering from AIDS, Multiple
Sclerosis, and other life-threatening illnesses (Grinspoon;
Grinspoon & Bakalar; Iverson).

This past week, I attended a conference in which Dr.
Lester Grinspoon passionately spoke about his belief that
treatments for not only cancer, but Alzheimer's disease may
be possible with further cannabis research. At the very least,
he tenaciously believes cannabis significantly slows the
progression of Alzheimer's disease and recommends it to
people he knows have a family history of Alzheimer's; in
hopes of helping them delay the onset of Alzheimer's
symptoms. As he explained, most family members who've
already watched a loved one, perhaps a parent or
grandparent, slowly lose their identity and suffer from many
other symptoms of Alzheimer's, are willing to do anything to
avoid a similar fate. If a *small daily dose* of medication delays
the onset of Alzheimer's, surely compassionate person would
have no moral dilemma with the fact that medication is
marijuana (Grinspoon). Imagine how angered American
citizens will be if any of these possibilities become a reality
and citizens learn that the DEA sat on the petition to
reclassify cannabis for nearly a decade and could have
rightfully declassified it while our citizens continued to suffer?
I, for one, am infuriated and exasperated because it appears
that no action is being taken to rectify the biggest obstacle to

further research: the misclassification of cannabis. As for my grandchildren and their future generations, I have the same hope as Richard Rorty, "that life will eventually be freer, less cruel...not just for our descendants but for everybody's descendants (Rorty 86)." Most people want to leave a better world for their descendants, but oftentimes it does not appear we will. If we fail to act justly and compassionately, what will our legacy to future generations consist of?

Conclusion

Now, imagine that your loved one is suffering cancer and also from chemotherapy treatments, perhaps, your parent, spouse, or child. After researching your concerns, and finding them amply satisfied, you may suggest that your loved one consider medicating with cannabis, to alleviate the pain and suffering they are currently experiencing, at the least—or perhaps as a treatment, if the knowledge and access to medical cannabis is legally available to your loved one. As stated earlier, in sixteen states you would have the right to do so legally, so you may choose this route, if you are not overly concerned with the fact that you remain in violation of federal law. In the remaining thirty-four states, you may find yourself torn between what you feel is right for your loved one and obeying state and federal laws. You may find yourself facing a moral dilemma much as Grinspoon did in the 1970s when his young son was suffering from cancer. Do you choose simply between right or wrong, legal or illegal, in this case, or does your loyalty and caring for your loved one present a more perplexing moral dilemma?

This is the same moral dilemma that all medical cannabis patients and their families have faced at one time or another. As stated earlier, Noddings (1984) believes that "one who labels moral statements as expressions of approval or disapproval, and takes the matter to be finished with that, misses the very heart of morality. He misses both feeling and content (19)." Through their silence on this issue, our federal government has expressed their disapproval of cannabis as a medication that can relieve the suffering of many of our ailing citizens. The review and removal of cannabis from the Schedule of Controlled Substances is vital for medical marijuana patients and caregivers, without it even those who comply with their state laws remain open to federal prosecution, for making healthcare choices in a manner acceptable to themselves, their physician, and their state—and in-line with their own endocannabinoid system. Further, removing cannabis from the Schedule would lead to additional research, which will lead to a clearer understanding of how the properties in cannabis works with our bodies own endocannabinoid system, as well we may find the means to prevent or treat cancer and other serious health conditions with processes that are far less painful, than those patients currently endure.

As one who cares and has compassion, when I see a more holistic approach to pain and suffering being addressed by citizen groups, in way of dispensaries or grow co-ops, who seek to inform the patient and assure properly grown medication, I see a care perspective in place. When I read about DEA raids on state legal co-ops, caregiver groups, or dispensaries, I see nothing but injustice. With a care perspective in mind, several states have at least reclassified cannabis to a lower level allowing private research teams to begin critical research within their states, but this legislation will still find researchers outside of federal compliance and subject to prosecution. Compassionate state lawmakers and citizens are taking action hoping that research will produce knowledge that may lead to further reduction of suffering for American citizens and future generations. As a society, the U.S. likes to consider ourselves the most just among nations; yet, if cannabis has proven medicinal value, then the necessity to remove cannabis from the Schedule of Controlled Substances must be recognized and addressed, so that resolutions for issues including: patient access, delivery systems, dosing requirements, and many more related issues can be found. As citizens, we can no longer simply express moral approval or disapproval for cannabis; we must rationally and compassionately consider the pain and suffering of others. Even if you believe the recreational use of cannabis is morally wrong, I ask you to compassionately reconsider the medicinal use of cannabis based on its potential to provide relief to millions of people, human beings who are terminally ill or in chronic pain. Further, if cannabis has the potential to treat cancer, reducing the growth of cancer tumors, or delay the onset of Alzheimer's disease, we owe it to future generations to show compassion today. Tronto states an approach to caring, "…needs to begin by broadening our understanding of what caring for others means, both in terms of the moral questions it raises and in terms of the need to restructure broader social and political institutions if caring for others is to be made a more central part of the everyday lives of everyone in society (Tronto, 112)." In my opinion, care and compassion must be a central part of our lives and integrated into our national institutions, especially those designated to support our citizens' healthcare, like NCI and NIH. By ignoring the citizens and states and failing to take action to rectify the misclassification of cannabis, our federal government shows disregard for both justice and care perspectives, failing to recognize the rights of American citizens who are suffering, and the possibility of providing better alternatives for future generations.

Note: In 2014, cannabis remains a Schedule 1 Controlled Substance, causing much confusion—and pain, for patients who choose to use it medicinally. Over the last three years, I've built a strong conviction of belief that this safe, non-toxic substance should not be regulated (or taxed) more than any other food or nutritional supplement. In other words, cannabis should not be labeled a "Controlled Substance" any more than any other food—Yes, I said Food!

Medical Marijuana by Eurocentric Means
May 2011

*This paper was written to satisfy the final essay requirements for
"Engaging Differences" led by Dr. Tony Kashani. Dr. Kashani had a
great deal of positive influence on me this first semester—he was my
champion and every Ph.D. student needs someone who believes in them!
(Thanks Tony—wishing that you were still at Union). Also leading
this course was Dr. Toni Gregory—it was during this term that she
became my antagonist all while leading me directly to Integral Theory
(her bailiwick at the time, now mine). Our first term began complicated
and that would set the terms for our on-going relationship. I could not
have worked with two instructors who viewed the theories and this
student more disparately.*

*Only two days before the end of the term, with one term paper fully
written and edited, I kept pacing the floors—I just didn't feel "done"
with this class. To pass time and 'think without thought' I perused the
internet late one night—and then I smoked a joint...and as you will see
I found a new topic and wrote a new paper over the next two days.
And, you can also see Tony's media influence in my work.*

*A few years later I am happy to see the inclusion of more minority faces
in the cannabis community in all realms, including commercials—
perhaps it was because I shamed some at MPP, NORML, and ASA
with my direct questioning...but I had to know—and I needed to assure
that they knew...*

In the United States, we have become accustomed to seeing
anti-drug public service announcements (PSA) intended to
curtail teen drug use. In the majority of these commercials,
until very recently, the message has been focused primarily on
marijuana, in an effort to reduce cannabis use among
teenagers. The intentions of these commercials are no doubt
good, but they relay a Eurocentric view of America's War on
Drugs. Anti-drug ads send conflicting messages to the target
market of adolescents and teens; for Black and Latino males,

it is a message of punishment; for white males, it is a message of making the wrong choice; and finally, when directed at females, regardless of race, the message is designed to frighten, not inform. For these reasons, and many others, anti-drug campaigns for youth have been largely unsuccessful; money poorly spent by our government that amused more than educated our youth (Feingold, 20-22).

What many of us are not accustomed to viewing are pro-drug commercials, in that the drugs are not over-the-counter or pharmaceutical remedies, but current illicit drugs, specifically marijuana. In the U.S., medical cannabis legislation first televised pro medical cannabis commercials in California in 1996. When Arizona passed a voter referendum supporting medical cannabis last year, shortly after Arizona voters also passed an extremely harsh immigration law, I became interested in how these commercials presented their case, as supporters of medical cannabis, to voters. I reasoned that from a marketing perspective, pro MMJ advocates certainly should endeavor to portray a less stereotypical America, than anti-drug commercials; so with that in mind, I was also hoping to find a less Eurocentric view of Americans and a dialogue that encompassed the heart of the medical cannabis debate: compassion. As this paper will discuss, I was at first encouraged by what I found, a discourse of compassion and care; in the end, after viewing pro medical marijuana commercials, anti- drug PSAs, and even pro legalization commercials, I was disappointed to find that cannabis commercials are every bit as Eurocentric as anti-drug PSAs, they just present the Eurocentricism in a different manner.

Within the U.S., I viewed twenty-two pro-medical marijuana public service announcements (PSA) or commercials that had run in various states with pro medical legislation initiatives in the past five years. A majority of the commercials are produced by Marijuana Policy Project (MPP), a national cannabis advocacy organization; several were made by other less prominent pro medical marijuana organizations, generally state-level organizations. As cannabis has taken on a new purpose, no longer used to 'get high,' but to 'medicate,' these commercials unveil a language of compassion, specific to the U.S. medical cannabis debate. This language of compassion is tucked within an ethic of care, primarily from the standpoint of "suffering seen as the kind of thing that could happen to anyone, including oneself (Blum, 511)." The commercials send a message of care and concern for one's fellow man, because none of us knows when we may suffer equally to the other. As Carol Gilligan elucidates, when considering a care perspective, the conflict between self and others recedes and places "the self as moral agent" able to perceive and respond "to the perception of need (Gilligan, 35)." Whether the viewer has suffered from pain or illness, or known someone who has, they are able to perceive the need of those represented in the commercial and empathize with their plight. Although these commercials verbally send the most suiting and desirable message for the medical cannabis campaign, it is my opinion, that these commercials also perpetuate Eurocentrism, in spite of its discourse of care ethics, because they fail to engage in a multicultural conversation.

The New Language of Medical Marijuana: Compassion

Within an ethics of care when a moral judgment is made, it is always more than a simple expression of approval or disapproval; it is expressing a "commitment to behave in a way compatible with caring (Noddings, 19)" and asking the other what their needs are, then listening intently to and thoughtfully considering their reply. In the medical cannabis debate, the key is not making a moral judgment before listening to the needs of patients and learning their perspective. "The one caring is careful to distinguish between acts that violate caring, acts that she herself holds wrong, and those acts 'some people' hold to be wrong (Noddings, 19)." Seeing the cannabis issue as a moral issue is seeing only one perception of a multifaceted picture. If we temper the perspective of justice with care, as Gilligan encourages us to do, what will come into view from the "care perspective" that is not seen from the "justice perspective (Gilligan, 49)?" Tronto believes it will be "compassion" and that compassion must be kept in the forefront of our deliberation (Tronto, 1993, 3). Further Tronto contends, "We cannot understand an ethic of care until we place such an ethic in its full moral and political context (Tronto, 1989, p 125)." I believe, what we see with compassion placed in both a moral and political context will engage us in a different picture; the medical marijuana debate, similar in many ways to how MPP portrays it dialectically in pro medical cannabis commercials: within an ethic of care. This shift in thinking changes the issue from a moral issue, toward which legalizing cannabis for adult "recreational" consumption would be considered, to a public health issue, toward which citizens in our society should show compassion. Pro cannabis organizations are attempting to enlighten the public of their individual responsibility to be informed, utilizing a language connected with their issue, a language based on compassion. The least amount of compassion would require the average citizen to inform themselves about cannabis before casting their vote in an election.

It was easy to find pro medical cannabis commercials online since sixteen states have successfully legislated for medical marijuana and nine more have pending initiatives. In looking solely, at those that support medicalized cannabis, for now, excluding those that are pro-legalization, in the sense they support "recreational" or adult use, as stated earlier, we start to see that cannabis advocates have developed a discourse of compassion. Each ad is a thirty-second slice of a real human being's lived experience: suffering or watching someone they loved suffer and cannabis alleviating the pain. As well, we see the inclusion of Tronto's theories regarding *caring about* and *caring for* within this discourse. Caring about referring "to less concrete objects: it is characterized by a more general form of commitment;" while caring for implies "a specific, particular object that is the focus of caring (Tronto, 1989, 103)." In this sense, these commercials send the message that we must care about voting on a specific proposition, because what we care for is our suffering fellow citizens, or more particularly, our ailing loved one.

If we've ever experienced a loved one suffering from chemotherapy treatments or chronic pain these messages were meant to speak directly to our compassion. Spouses and parents who've lost loved ones, patients suffering with horrific illnesses and treatments, who find cannabis alleviates pain and suffering, all offering their voice and personal narrative to this debate. Gilligan (1984) elucidates, "To have a voice is to be human. To have something to say is to be a person. But speaking depends on listening and being heard; it is an intensely relational act." These voices are human, they have something to say, and all viewers, whether the person plans to vote yes or no on the proposed legislation, can't help but be taken with their stories. The humans in the commercials tell you their personal story; each gives the viewer pause to think about the issue; in this sense, the ads are very successful. Advocacy organizations have tried to assure that the viewer will care about this proposition passing, because he relates to the suffering of the patients and caregivers. These are not the faces we're used to seeing in anti-drug commercials, these are older, more mature faces, and each human being is pleading with you to consider this issue one of compassion, of care, and of justice.

The overriding message in these commercials is, "Have compassion;" further, this is also the motto of many medical marijuana advocacy groups, including MPP. In these commercials parents and grandparents are using words and describing circumstances that include great pain, suffering, relief, ability to live life normally, or they've 'thanked God' for the relief medical marijuana provides. However, in about 30% of the commercials patients are also pleading "not to be treated like criminals." It seems they are disassociating their former or current illegal medical need against those 'others;'

the criminals who they otherwise have to rely upon for access to marijuana—the drug dealers. If viewers have no experience purchasing drugs, which may well be the case for many Americans, possibly the first images that come to mind will be similar to those portrayed in anti-drug commercials, on television shows, or in films.

Since anti-drug commercials portray drug dealers much the same as television and film, let's consider briefly, the images they portray. In every PSA viewed, from 1990 to today, with only two exceptions, drug dealers are portrayed by minorities, nearly always by a Black male. This stereotyping, "[reduces] people to a few simple, essential characteristics," that become fixed; it is also, "central to the representation of racial difference (Hall, 257)." In both cases that PSAs portray a White drug dealer, the actors were much less threatening in demeanor and the actor's tone of voice was almost friendly compared to the Black drug dealers, who were characteristically menacing and aggressive. If these representations are considered valid by viewers, then pro medical cannabis commercials may leave some viewers thinking grandma must drive to the ghetto for cannabis. In my opinion, is much more probable that grandma has some help from within her own family, but still, drug dealers do not verify their product is not tainted with chemicals, for this reason alone, the safety of cannabis is of upmost importance to patients.

Americans often prove to be quite compassionate and well-informed enough to have supported legislation in sixteen states, thereby, enacting medical marijuana laws and nine more states have medical marijuana legislation pending. To me, this seems proof that many Americans view the issue of cannabis from both a justice and a care perspective. Even voters in Arizona, who, in 2010, enacted one of the most controversial and potentially unjust immigration laws ever on record, showed compassion when voting to legalize cannabis for medicinal purposes. The aging baby-boomers, who retire and vote in Arizona, appear willing to listen to the experience of friends, family, and community and insist on compassionate care, regardless of the fact they are callous when it comes to immigration. *How can a state like Arizona take what appear to be, such opposing views, on two highly politicized issues, in the same year?*

The Face of Medical Marijuana

As a cannabis advocate, this is the question that prompted me to view Arizona's cannabis news coverage; honestly, I had heard and read enough about the immigration law by the time medical marijuana hit the Arizona ballot and thought the medical cannabis imitative would be easily defeated in a state that seemed to have such uncompassionate voters. However, when The Arizona Medical Marijuana Act passed, at first I thought I had reacted a bit judgmentally and may have been mistaken with my preconceived notion about Arizona voters, but then I viewed the six pro medical cannabis commercials that were running on television in Arizona leading up to the election in November 2010. After a quick run through of the spots, a trend was visibly apparent: the faces were all white; no ethnic minorities were represented in *any* of the commercials. It was evident; I was looking directly into the face of middle-class, white, grandparents, never before associated with cannabis use, all pleading what appeared to be legitimate cases for medical marijuana legalization.

In both the MPP ads and those by other advocacy groups, the dialogue of care and compassion was thoroughly ingrained in the Arizona commercials; in fact, I noticed this trend, after watching only two commercials. On the same ballot that Arizona voters re-elected John McCain to the senate with 59% of the vote, just over 50% of the voters made Arizona the 15th state to recognize the medicinal value in cannabis. Statistics show voters in this election were essentially white middle-class, conservatives with some compassion, at least when it came to citizens who represented their exact demographic: white, middle-class, retirees, suffering from illness and pain associated with aging (azcapitoltimes.com). Is Arizona an extreme Eurocentric example of trying to re-associate cannabis with grandma instead of grandson? Did cannabis advocates focus on ads with white patients and caregivers because they were concerned about possible racist views impeding their message of care in Arizona? At this point, I wasn't quite sure how explain this quandary so I began to dig deeper.

As I have already mentioned, in the same year of the cannabis campaign, Arizona also passed a very harsh, possibly unjust immigration law (I will refrain from delving into it in this paper). In political ad campaigns supporting that piece of legislation or supporters running for political office, the public was led to believe Arizona was being 'overrun' with 'hardened criminals,' visual graphics included long lines of illegal immigrants walking through the deserts or packed into trucks, dozens of arrests, and numerous acts of violence. A few of the ads were nearly identical to commercials for the television show *Cops*, except for the accompanying discourse, which in large part consisted of the message: 'Be afraid of others.' I naively thought, perhaps, MPP and other advocacy groups had recognized the voting demographic they were after in Arizona, realized they'd become afraid of others and played strictly to that audience. Cannabis advocates apparently thought no conservative, white, Arizonan wanted a possible family member, friend, or neighbor suffering *and* purchasing her marijuana from 'those' others. Possibly MPP and other advocates believed they were dependent upon these types of representation, all safe, sound, white, American, middle-class, grandparents, in order for Arizonans to attach specific meaning around the medical marijuana debate, in order to reach the demographic of voters at whom they were principally aimed. Since, I cannot understand why Arizonans couldn't understand the same message, from a Black, a Latino, or a person of any other ethnicity except white; I thought I would research a bit further.

Unfortunately, more investigation clearly showed that in all twenty-two pro medical marijuana commercials nothing changed. Not one patient or caregiver portrayed in the commercials is any race other than white; not one. Although they may well have come from a variety of socioeconomic classes, all were portrayed in middle-class settings. Do only white, middle-class Americans suffer in the United States? Certainly, not; all human beings suffer, though all may not need or choose to use cannabis to alleviate their suffering, they do all indeed have an endocannabinoid system which regulates the endocrine systems of their bodies.

Indeed, in the commercials, those who testified cannabis helps them, or has helped their loved one, state they believe it should be made available to *everyone*. Further, it seems reasonable to believe that those who suffer and do choose to use cannabis are not only white Americans, but of many ethnicities. However, cannabis advocates have chosen to position themselves and their message squarely on middle-class white Americans. They have succeeded in doing exactly what anti-drug campaigns do: provide the general public with information in an equally Eurocentric manner; only, they chose to do it through *exclusion*. Bryant Alexander's description of "presence of absence" seems to fit this situation well, in that "in the absence of color" the "presence of race and racism" is placed in the foreground (Alexander, 653). As a cannabis advocate, who participates in several advocacy organizations on a local level, I can assure you that although organizations such as MPP and NORML are dominated by white males, cannabis patients and caregivers are an ethnically diverse mix of people.

Eurocentricism

Eurocentricism is an ideology best defined as an Anglo-Saxon, Western perspective or 'what the white man thinks.' The medical cannabis commercials are political discussions that impact public health policies. However, the ads send a message of Eurocentric ideology by failing to incorporate an equitable demographic in their ads. Their message, while inclusive, is only delivered from dominant cultural signifiers, the patients and caregivers, although they may be disadvantaged due to pain and suffering, they all are overwhelmingly white. Sean Nixon states visual representation works through "interlocking...deep-rooted psychic processes," many of which we remain unaware of; but in our society even white, middle-class Americans, especially our elderly, also represent a "historical character of identities (Hall, 320-321)." These are representations and signifiers most Americans can recognize, even if the terms they describe them in are different. In short, these are the faces most closely tied to racism in our society; as well, as those most closely associated with white guilt as ascribed by Shelby Steele (Steele, 24), because a portion of their lived experience came before the Civil Rights Act.

It is impossible to fault one of these patients or caregivers, each appears genuine and sincere, they all have in fact suffered greatly, and their stories are real lived experiences. My parents fall into this particular demographic and while I surely trust the judgment of my parents, I also recognize that others may be leery of their intentions, especially when they fail to see other races represented. The obvious location for fault is with the cannabis advocates. For when we view only white faces in relation to an issue, any issue, many are prone to see a social construct in which "the social construction of identity" is linked with "access, worth and value (Alexander, 650)." The viewer is on an unconscious level told it isn't important to hear the voices of non-whites; others who may have similar experiences and perspectives and lend a great deal to this debate. If the viewer detects this trend, she may realize this is not the message of a compassionate organization that cares about representing American people equally, it is one of a perhaps compassionate organization that, in the words of Allen St. Pierre of NORML is in part of a social movement (pro-marijuana) that has been "too male and too White" for much too long (St. Pierre).

Anti-drug PSAs, produced with government funding,

are also political discussions, but about social issues. They differ from medical cannabis ads, in two ways. First, they present an equitable representation of most American populations, in that, their ads are ethnically diverse. However, while the PSAs recognize minorities, they tend to represent racial minorities in ways many would consider stereotypical. For instance, when PSAs represent minorities, such a Black or Latino teen males, they are situationally placed in low-income areas, typically inner cities, and if placed in a home environment, the viewer would no doubt assume the family was "working class poor (Hill Collins, 2000, 31)." The predominance of violence was much higher in PSAs with minority lead characters, as were weapons (guns, knives, and fists), robbery, destruction of property, as well as direct drug use. This type of misrecognition "shows not just a lack of due respect," but is able to "inflict a grievous wound, saddling its victims with a crippling self-hatred (Taylor, 26)." If we develop our identity "in dialogue" with others, (Taylor, 33) as well as through media portrayals that project "an inferior or demeaning image," to the extent that this image is internalized, it can also distort and oppress our identity (Taylor, 36). In contrast, white teen males are cast as characters not typically engaged in violence or theft, although there are a couple of exceptions: while, I only viewed one PSA with a black teen characterized as middle-class and non-violent, the vast majority of white teen characters have historically been and continue to be portrayed as middle-class and non-violent. Instead of being portrayed as drug dealers or gang members, white teens are more typically portrayed as 'losers' or 'stoners.' The message sent is that the white teens won't necessarily end up in jail, but it is highly probable they'll end up living in their mom's basement, if they don't stop smoking pot. After all, these teens are represented as living in upper middle-class homes, in suburban environments; they appeared to be rebelling, instead of engaging in crime. So, even though PSAs recognize the existence of minorities, they fail to engage or properly represent either white or minority teens (Feingold, 27).

If viewers take anti-drug PSAs to heart, we will
believe that Black and Latino teen males are frequently prone
to violence and crime, and are more highly probable than
whites to being drug dealers. One may in fact feel sorry for
the 'stupid' white kid who was led astray; after all he wasn't a
'bad' kid. Michelle Alexander would argue and her research,
as well as that by other researchers, supports that:

> People of all colors use and sell illegal drugs at
> remarkably similar rates. If there are
> significant differences in the surveys to be
> found, they frequently suggest that whites,
> particularly white youth, are more likely to
> engage in drug crime that people of color.
> That is not what one would guess, however
> when entering our nation's prison and jails,
> which are overflowing with black and brown
> drug offenders. In some states, black men
> have been admitted to prison on drug charges
> at rates twenty to fifty times greater than
> those of white men. (Alexander, M., 7)

Alexander argues that U.S. drug policies are as unfair
to minorities as Jim Crow Laws once were to blacks
(Alexander, M., 3). With this taken into account, PSAs should
acknowledge this disparity by representing whites engaged in
crime more often in their announcements. It is easy to see
why they portray more minority arrests, because minorities
are arrested much more frequently for the same crimes as
whites. In this case, they may have the statistics on their side,
but their representations of identities remain stereotypical
signifiers of oppression. Minority children, living in urban
settings and from low-income families, like those depicted in
PSAs, already know they are more prone to arrest and
violence and that these public misrepresentations "reinscribe
social hierarchies of race and gender (Hill Collins, 2000,
298)." Further, by producing PSAs in which nearly every
police officer is white, strengthens this already strong message

of racial intolerance and reinforces stereotypes and "negative characteristics opposite and inferior to those reserved for whites (Hill Collins, 2000, 97)."

Which is the greater wrong-doing: failing to acknowledge racial minorities in our society or representing them as stereotypes? In my opinion, neither is a good choice. By failing to incorporate minorities into commercials that highlight caring for one's fellow citizens, fairly representing a state's population of suffers and caregivers, and excluding the stories of others, cannabis advocates are utilizing "symbolic power" as described by Stuart Hall (Hall, 259). In this case, the symbolic power, of the white race, is representing the cannabis debate within a "regime of representation" (Hall, 232) that can be considered nothing short of "whiteness (Alexander, B. 652)." Further, by favoring the portrayal of white youth against minority youth, anti-drug campaigns send a message of racial intolerance. Both sets of ads are designed to educate, inform, or send a message to the viewer, in both cases they do, but unfortunately, it is a Eurocentric message, that whites believe they know what's best and that they have favor and power in U.S. Drug Policies, and minorities have no power or privilege in our society. In short, even when attempting to provide a public service, well-intentioned people and organizations continue to find ways to marginalize others.

Pro-Legalization Commercials

In the U.S., California is the only state yet to have run a full 'legalization' campaign meaning that lawmakers brought legislation before California voters to support decriminalization of marijuana for adult "recreational" use (Note: This was prior to ads being released in Colorado and Washington for 2012 ballet initiatives). In contrast to pro medical marijuana commercials, the commercials surrounding California's Proposition 19, target a variety of racial demographics and a wider socioeconomic range, working-class to middle-income, every day 'real people.' In fact, few were posed similar in nature to either anti-drug or pro medical marijuana ads. It seemed Prop 19 advocates wanted to separate themselves from the Eurocentric pack and offer a variety of messages: celebrities, police officers, and informational text set to a variety of ethnic beats, all clearly meant to draw the attention of the population they were seeking--everyone. The discourse in these commercials is focused on rights; the perspective provided is one of justice and individual freedom. Using verbiage strictly from a justice perspective, speaking of individual freedoms and rights, pro-legalization advocates repeatedly compared cannabis to more harmful legal alternatives, alcohol and tobacco (Babor, 21-23). Finally, other ads hoped to convince voters legalization would help curb teen cannabis use by regulating and taxing cannabis like cigarettes and alcohol. The primary message here was "Drug dealers don't ask for ID." However, drug dealers were portrayed by both white and minority actors relatively equally. The only commercial that fit into the same realm as pro medical marijuana and anti-drug commercials featured several 'usual suspects,' one by one having mug-shot photos taken following their arrest. In fairness, more of the 'criminals' were white than minority, but the last picture, is white, middle-class grandma admitting to smoking pot to get 'high'. In this case, grandma is obviously not a medical marijuana patient, because California has medical marijuana legislation, instead, she is an undercover pot smoker. It seemed to me, producers were spoofing MPP and other cannabis advocates, but at least they broke free of the Eurocentric hold on drug-related commercials and announcements.

Conclusion

As witnessed by strong Eurocentric messaging via visual media, including political or PSA-type commercials, "Eurocentricism maintains control over our society's political, economic, and cultural institutions (Schiele, 439)." As a cannabis advocate, I am distressed to find Eurocentric ideology and the exclusion of minority voices in pro medical marijuana commercials. In my opinion, the exclusion of minorities is, to some degree, a public pronouncement, by cannabis advocacy groups, encouraging the notion of white intellectual superiority. Even if the demographic these ads are designed to target is middle-class, white voters, to exclude minorities, sends the message that whites know best, they are the least associated with crime, and therefore, the most believable narratives in the cannabis debate. While each of patients and caregivers speak a clear message of acceptance and compassion for all, cannabis advocates chose to repress the voices of ethnic minorities, who have much to lend to this debate. After watching these ads, I couldn't help but wonder if MPP and other advocacy groups think the average white, middle-class, conservative, senior citizen is incapable of listening to others; if so, what does this say about average white, middle-class, conservative senior citizens in America? Certainly in the case of my own parents, who represent this targeted demographic, having experienced racial segregation, the enactment of Civil Rights, having worked alongside a diverse group of colleagues, and travelling abroad, has provided the lived experience that enables them and many like them to listen to voices of others. Certainly many white citizens recognize "our responsibility for every human being (Appiah, 7)," not just those who look like we do.

Cannabis advocates are excluding minority faces from their campaigns in order to reach white conservative voters, by having them view only one perspective in a multi-faceted discussion. Medical cannabis advocates are utilizing symbolic power, "to make people see and believe certain visions of the world rather than others (Bourdieu, 36)." Perhaps, advocacy groups would insist this was a strategic move—and one that worked in Arizona. In short, MPP and other advocacy groups have subordinated the need for accurate and equal representation to their desired agenda of legalizing cannabis. Further, at least to some degree, they are excluding minorities to distance marijuana with the racial stereotypes often associated with illicit drug use, including drug-related violence associated with minorities via television and film, including commercials. But, do the ends justify the means?

We have a number of taboo subjects in our society among those most pervasive are race, sexuality, and drugs. In talking about sexuality, Patricia Hill Collins states, "Under Eurocentric ideologies, normalized heterosexuality thus becomes constructed in contrast to two allegedly deviant sexualities, namely, those attributed to people of African descent and those applied to lesbians and gays, among others (Hill Collins, 2000, 140)." In much the same way, the producers of cannabis commercials have attempted to normalize cannabis use, in the eyes of those with Eurocentric ideology, in contrast to those they see as the 'criminal element,' by excluding minorities from their campaigns. Medical cannabis users have become white grandparents, often great grandparents, war veterans, conservatives, republicans, Christians, and middle-class folks, all verbally or non-verbally admitted from representations portrayed in cannabis commercials. Albeit they or someone they love has or had debilitating pain and much suffering; however, they are also the exact opposite of Black and Latino drug dealers in the eyes of white conservative voters. The exclusion of minority patients and caregivers, speaks poorly of the medical cannabis movement, for their dialogue was on track. The viewer understood that each person had experienced a clash in their own values (Appiah, 65), that they'd had to overcome in order to evaluate and determine medical cannabis was the best option for their circumstances.

The cannabis debate is an emotionally charged argument that was presented dialectically excellently; an ethic of care and true compassion encompassed the dialogue. In the spirit of the debate, the pro side focused on alleviating suffering, few can argue against relieving pain or helping someone in need, after all we may find ourselves in their circumstances; for even if we disagree now, how can we not listen to the pleas of our fellow citizens? But, if we have no narratives other than those of whites aren't we allowing dominate culture to once again oppress many of our citizens? When thinking from a care perspective, a compassionate person will respond to the suffering and needs of the sufferer with empathetic practical wisdom. This practical wisdom is in the Aristotelian sense of *phronesis*, where there is thorough deliberation, examination of one's options, an awareness of appropriate feelings, and then the carrying out of good intentions through reasoned choices. Unlike during the times of Aristotle, minorities and women are recognized as full human beings; so, although cannabis advocates chose to represent women, they failed to represent minorities perpetuating an ideology of white supremacy. As Charles Taylor elucidates, "Non-recognition or misrecognition can inflict harm, can be a form of oppression, imprisoning someone else in a false, distorted and reduced mode of being (Taylor, 25)." The dialogue of medical cannabis commercials got the language right, they underestimated the ability of their targeted audience, older, middle-class, white Americans, by believing they cannot recognize the obligation to show compassion for others. In the end, cannabis supporters prevailed in Arizona, and they will continue to do so in many other states and hopefully, eventually, at the federal level. However, does the end justify the means? I asked this question to about 50 people last week at NORML's (National Organization for Reform of Marijuana Laws) Annual Conference. Undoubtedly, my straw poll draws no conclusive evidence, but the overall sentiment expressed is best summed up by Allen St. Pierre, Executive Director of NORML, who said it best when, in a session addressing media relations and marijuana advocacy he stated, "Marijuana advocacy have been too male and too white for too long (St. Pierre)." He's absolutely right, it is long past time for female and minority voices to be heard in this debate.

Note:_As my first semester as a Ph.D. student came to a conclusion I was feeling confident of the direction I was moving, I just wasn't sure what direction it was in…the ambiguity was thick as pea soup, but it felt like the right path deep inside my gut. Unfortunately, Bill was not so confident—he like many, are not as comfortable with the process one follows in this type of study. He was also highly uncomfortable with my topic of choice, so my personal life was on fairly shaky ground as this semester ended. As well, at this time, I was also reintroducing cannabis back into my life after a considerable absence, in large part, because I didn't feel well. I was dealing with nausea and beginning to lose weight—I had no idea what was about to come…

Chapter Two
July 2011 – December 2011

The start of my second semester began in July 2011 and with a long car ride through Cincinnati with Steve. We processed the term and my personal life. I was excited about the scholarly path I was on, but my relationship was ending—this program had put too much pressure on an already fragile relationship. I sought advice and planned to rally certain that I could take on the world and still maintain my relationship with Bill. By late August, I was packing a few belongs into two suitcases and headed to Albuquerque, New Mexico. (It took a bit, but today, Bill and I are friends again—we don't talk often—but I do know he's proud of me, and that makes my heart happy! If he hadn't believed and encouraged me I may not have taken this path. I love you, Bill! You're a really good man who made an amazing difference in my life!).

My oldest daughter, Rachel and her incredible family, which includes three of my perfect grandchildren, live in Albuquerque, I'd lived there before, and my best friend, Yvonna still resides there—so I was off to New Mexico, knowing the "Lynn and Erin Compassionate Use Act" was about to have one more registered patient; and I was ready to live alone for the first time in my life. The first week of September I moved into a duplex near the UNM campus, close enough to 'everything I needed' that I could walk—which was good, because I had no car. No car, no money, no furniture, and because of the move, no job. I was drawing the last of an unemployment claim that would barely cover the $545 rent on the one bedroom apartment I began moving into...put together from furniture given by friends, bought on craigslist, and picked up off of local curbs. But, within a week I had a desk, internet, and a bed—and an awesome 50cc scooter! My priorities all in place; I was working hard to catch up on my studies, when I woke up sick at my stomach one morning, with what did and yet didn't feel like a terrible flu.

After thirteen hours of intermittent dry-heaves and puking, a friend carried me to his car and into the emergency room. God bless Greg, for he sat on the floor holding me in his lap for another six hours, while the nurses offered me Zofran in an attempt to stop the never-ending heaving. Long story short and several feet of small intestine later, I was still alive—not well, but alive. This would mark the beginning of a whole new journey for me—my journey as a medical cannabis patient—because once I survived a major bowel resection all I wanted was to get out of that hospital and go home to my pipe, so that I could begin to feel better and recover! I survived, it was on! I checked myself out of UNM Hospital on my 48th birthday sick as hell, less than 105 lbs. but also very determined—I figure there must be a reason I survived the nearly unsurvivable!

The next few months—the final two months of the term—took on a whole new meaning. Life revolved around daily survival, I slept when I slept, ate when I could, and tried to focus on my studies. Rebecca, a Cohort 10 peer and heart-felt sister really helped me survive the semester in terms of coursework. She checked in nearly every day after I came from the hospital and often sent me little to-do emails—respond to a post, read a small portion of text, etc. She kept me focused and helped me over one small hurdle at a time, while bearing her own crosses. And, the entire Cohort rallied around me— shocked that I was still going…and that I ended the term by deadline (well, give or take a day or two we can squabble over).

It also helped that during this time I was beginning to connect with other cannabis patients and learning how, besides simply smoking cannabis (which got my pain under control far quicker than dilaudid or morphine and without the terrible side-effect of making my nausea worse—and my skin crawl) to control my pain and nausea. A loving herbalist started me on tinctures—I'd mix a few drops in a hot cup of tea a few times a day. The difference was immediately amazing, my pain levels dropped and often an hour or so after the tea I could actually eat. The stomach ache I'd had leading up to the bowel resection remained and after losing nearly 30 lbs. during that experience and now having major malabsorption issues I was struggling to eat, much less gain weight...but I seemed to be onto something good, would it last?

Andrea Scarpino and Dr. Richard Couto were so wonderful during this time—laughing along with me at my early post-surgery ramblings and emails—but also trying to ease the Ph.D. burden while balancing course requirements so that I could also survive the semester, as I'd refused a leave of absence (I'm nothing if not hard-headed and persistent). Suggesting pieces of readings to "focus on" or encouraging me to do "less not more" when warranted (something this type A rarely does)...my surviving the semester became a community project—Cohort 10 and Instructors leading the way. While I only included one piece of my Creativity Portfolio this doesn't diminish the importance each piece played in my life and my studies. This course pushed me to self-reflection in a way I wasn't quite prepared for; perhaps I was also affected by the morphine and bed-induced state and later by the relief of having survived it all (though I was so naïve of the time healing would take). I was beginning to explore my own story and I knew that my life had shifted dramatically; I just wasn't sure how...the ambiguity was thick as pea soup.

In this chapter, I'm also including two of the three papers I submitted to meet the requirements of my Rhetorical Writing course led by Dr. Joshua Butts—a great guy, insightful instructor, and who's words of encouragement regarding my writing have helped me traverse this ambiguous path—and survive a peer-reviewed publication. Both of these papers were started before my surgery and revised during my recovery. I learned a lot about myself and how easily I get "married to my words"—and how wordy I really am—but I ventured into very uncomfortable places knowing Josh had my back. (Thanks Josh).

Jimmy Carter: Call Off the Global Drug War
October 2011

Note: Before we launch into the first article, I am
including a copy of *The New York Times* Op-Ed by
Jimmy Carter discussed so as you read this analytical
analysis you can follow my logic…or lack thereof.

June 16, 2011 *The New York Times*
Call Off the Global Drug War
By JIMMY CARTER
Atlanta

IN an extraordinary new initiative announced earlier this
month, the Global Commission on Drug Policy has made some
courageous and profoundly important recommendations in a
report on how to bring more effective control over the illicit
drug trade. The commission includes the former presidents or
prime ministers of five countries, a former secretary general of
the United Nations, human rights leaders, and business and
government leaders, including Richard Branson, George P.
Shultz and Paul A. Volcker.
The report describes the total failure of the present global
antidrug effort, and in particular America's "war on drugs,"
which was declared 40 years ago today. It notes that the global
consumption of opiates has increased 34.5 percent, cocaine 27
percent and cannabis 8.5 percent from 1998 to 2008. Its
primary recommendations are to substitute treatment for
imprisonment for people who use drugs but do no harm to
others, and to concentrate more coordinated international effort
on combating violent criminal organizations rather than
nonviolent, low-level offenders.
These recommendations are compatible with United States drug
policy from three decades ago. In a message to Congress in
1977, I said the country should decriminalize the possession of
less than an ounce of marijuana, with a full program of

47

treatment for addicts. I also cautioned against filling our prisons with young people who were no threat to society, and summarized by saying: "Penalties against possession of a drug should not be more damaging to an individual than the use of the drug itself."

These ideas were widely accepted at the time. But in the 1980s President Ronald Reagan and Congress began to shift from balanced drug policies, including the treatment and rehabilitation of addicts, toward futile efforts to control drug imports from foreign countries.

This approach entailed an enormous expenditure of resources and the dependence on police and military forces to reduce the foreign cultivation of marijuana, coca and opium poppy and the production of cocaine and heroin. One result has been a terrible escalation in drug-related violence, corruption and gross violations of human rights in a growing number of Latin American countries.

The commission's facts and arguments are persuasive. It recommends that governments be encouraged to experiment "with models of legal regulation of drugs ... that are designed to undermine the power of organized crime and safeguard the health and security of their citizens." For effective examples, they can look to policies that have shown promising results in Europe, Australia and other places.

But they probably won't turn to the United States for advice. Drug policies here are more punitive and counterproductive than in other democracies, and have brought about an explosion in prison populations. At the end of 1980, just before I left office, 500,000 people were incarcerated in America; at the end of 2009 the number was nearly 2.3 million. There are 743 people in prison for every 100,000 Americans, a higher portion than in any other country and seven times as great as in Europe. Some 7.2 million people are either in prison or on probation or parole — more than 3 percent of all American adults!

Some of this increase has been caused by mandatory minimum sentencing and "three strikes you're out" laws. But about three-quarters of new admissions to state prisons are for nonviolent crimes. And the single greatest cause of prison population growth has been the war on drugs, with the number of people incarcerated for nonviolent drug offenses increasing more than twelvefold since 1980.

Not only has this excessive punishment destroyed the lives of millions of young people and their families (disproportionately minorities), but it is wreaking havoc on state and local budgets. Former California Gov. Arnold Schwarzenegger pointed out that, in 1980, 10 percent of his state's budget went to higher education and 3 percent to prisons; in 2010, almost 11 percent went to prisons and only 7.5 percent to higher education. Maybe the increased tax burden on wealthy citizens necessary to pay for the war on drugs will help to bring about a reform of America's drug policies. At least the recommendations of the Global Commission will give some cover to political leaders who wish to do what is right.

A few years ago I worked side by side for four months with a group of prison inmates, who were learning the building trade, to renovate some public buildings in my hometown of Plains, Ga. They were intelligent and dedicated young men, each preparing for a productive life after the completion of his sentence. More than half of them were in prison for drug-related crimes, and would have been better off in college or trade school.

To help such men remain valuable members of society, and to make drug policies more humane and more effective, the American government should support and enact the reforms laid out by the Global Commission on Drug Policy.

Jimmy Carter, the 39th president, is the founder of the Carter Center and the winner of the 2002 Nobel Peace Prize

Jimmy Carter: Call Off the Global Drug War
October 2011

On June 16, 1971 with the words "If we cannot destroy the drug menace in America, then it will surely in time destroy us," Richard Nixon ushered in the 'war on drugs'. Nixon may have been well intentioned, but four decades later, the destruction to our country has many citizens believing the war on drugs is fueling the destruction instead of resolving it as Nixon had promised. Supporting this belief is the United Nation's Global Commission on Drug Policy. The panel's report, publicly released on June 2, 2011, calls for global experimentation "with models of legal regulation of drugs…that are designed to undermine the power of organized crime and safeguard the health and security of [our global] citizens (Carter, 2011, p. 2)." However, the U.S. Drug Czar's office has represented the Commission's report in the media as "misguided" (Lemaitre, 2011). In response, on June 16th, 2011, the 40th anniversary of the 'war on drugs,' former President Jimmy Carter and Reverend Jesse Jackson both published passionate op-ed pieces in major national newspapers calling for immediate drug policy reform. This essay is an analytical analysis of *The New York Times* op-ed written by Carter.

Written in a simple and unpretentious manner that includes passionate statements and bold word choices, the former President carefully considered the connotations of the words he uses to acknowledge those most harmed by the 'war' and the words used to admonish the American government for failing to act on its citizen's behalf. Carter's message boldly addresses many of our society's ills and effectively demonstrates how they are connected to the war on drugs. For example he considers: "explosive" and "excessive" prison populations, "disproportionate" and oppressive treatment of *millions* of minorities, the "destruction" of human lives, and "increased" violence associated with "the illicit drug trade (Carter, 2011, p. 1)."

Further, he shows an appreciation for the social circumstances that have brought us to the point that we must end the war on drugs.

Call Off the Global Drug War

Jimmy Carter opens his June 6th op-ed with gusto entering a discussion with the American people on "an extraordinary new initiative announced earlier this month" by the Global Commission on Drug Policy. The title of the op-ed *"Call Off the Global Drug War"* is Carter's call to action. Throughout the op-ed, Carter provides a common sense analysis on the 'war' directly related to the commission's report. To start, he offers a concise analysis of the report stating, "Its primary recommendations are to substitute treatment for imprisonment for people who use drugs but do no harm to others, and to concentrate more coordinated international effort on combating violent criminal organizations rather than nonviolent, low-level offenders (Carter, 2011, p. 1)." Carter's summary provides an umbrella that encompasses the core concerns the commission's recommendations are designed to address. The panel's recommendations include break the taboo: pursue an open debate; replace the criminalization and punishment of people who use drugs with the offer of health and treatment services to those who need them; challenge, rather than reinforce, common misconceptions about drug markets, drug use and drug dependence; and more (Global Commission on Drug Policy, 2011, p. 10-17). Carter's statement condenses the eleven panel recommendations into a brief statement that embraces their objectives.

Further establishing ethos, Carter immediately lauds the Commission's "courageous and profoundly important recommendations" as testament their report is credible. In his second sentence, Carter gives a nod of recognition to the credibility and ethos of the commission's members. The commission includes the former presidents or prime ministers of five countries, a former secretary general of the

United Nations, human rights leaders, and business and
government leaders, including Richard Branson, George P.
Shultz and Paul A. Volcker (Carter, 2011, p. 1). By listing the
positions of members whose names are not immediately
recognizable to a majority of Americans and listing well-
known businessman, Richard Branson, Carter speaks to a
broad audience; however, by mentioning Volker and Schultz,
Carter also speaks directly to a privileged audience of
relatively few in comparison. He does this to assure the
people who recognize the prominent economists that this
panel is 'bi-partisan' and both are well-qualified panelists.
These few sentences establish a strong ethos base and
credibility for the panel's recommendations, which may at
first surprise many Americans.

Throughout the op-ed there are a number of
examples of Carter moving fluidly between these two very
different audiences, the general public and the privileged in
our society, each with incredible stakes in seeing this 'war'
end, whether they realize it or not. His goal is to help them
recognize the urgent need for immediate action. In the
following sentence, he successfully addresses both audiences
and identifies a reason for action: "Not only has this
excessive punishment [increased prison populations]
destroyed the lives of millions of young people and their
families (disproportionately minorities), but it is wreaking
havoc on state and local budgets (Carter, 2011, p. 2)." In
speaking about "the lives of millions" he has spoken to the
many, by discussing "state and local budgets" he has reduced
his audience to those in more privileged positions.
Specifically to the most privileged citizens, he later states,
"Maybe the increased tax burden on wealthy citizens
necessary to pay for the war on drugs will help bring about a
reform of America's drug policies (Carter, 2011, p. 3)." The
dialogue chosen is epideictic (Selzer, p. 284), in that citizens
are being asked to reconsider personal views and beliefs
regarding drug policy and more specifically, how current drug
policy affects millions of our fellow citizens. In a dialogue

designed to address the common good for all, Carter does not mention the "about $1 trillion dollars" the U.S. has spent thus far on this "new Jim Crow offensive" (Jackson, 2011, p. 1). Instead, the former President helps readers understand that a major reform of drug policy is in the interest of *all* U.S. citizens.

Carter's discourse also has strong elements of forensic rhetoric (Selzer, p. 283) and memoria (Selzer, p. 284) connecting the reader historically to "three decades ago" (Carter, 2011, p. 1). Repeatedly throughout the piece, he makes historical reference to the 1980's when "President Ronald Reagan and Congress began to shift from balanced drug policies, including the treatment and rehabilitation of addicts, toward futile efforts to control drug imports from foreign countries (Carter, 2011, p. 2)." Building his own ethos he establishes that when he was President, just before Reagan, he "cautioned against filling our prisons with young people who were no threat to society (Carter, 2011, p. 2)." He again connects this back to Reagan's presidency, by pointing out that "the number of people incarcerated for nonviolent drug offenses" has increased "more than twelvefold since 1980 (Carter, 2011, p. 2)." This has occurred because "Drug Policies here are more punitive and counterproductive than in other democracies and have brought about an explosion in prison populations (Carter, 2011, p. 2)." By comparing current crime, incarceration, and drug usage rates against those of the 1980's he makes a deliberative argument. Carter methodically stacks up point after point in favor of *Call*[ing] *Off the Global Drug War.* Further he appeals to the readers' ethos while reinforcing his own.

Carter uses our nation's shocking incarceration statistics to effectively bolster his stance. As mentioned earlier, Carter highlights the effects of incarceration that show he was indeed correct in 1977 when he also stated, "Penalties against possession of a drug should not be more damaging to an individual than the use of the drug itself (Carter, 2011, p.

1)." He shows readers just how dire a concern incarceration is in our society by stating: "At the end of 1980, just before I left office, 500,000 people were incarcerated in America; at the end of 2009 the number was nearly 2.3 million (Carter, 2011, p. 2)." If these statistics don't shock the reader, he breaks it down further to account for "743 people in prison for every 100,000 Americans" and even further to "some 7.2 million people are either in prison or on probation or parole—more than 3 percent of all American adults (Carter, 2011, p. 2)!" Ending with an exclamation point and a graphic demonstration of how the 'war' marginalizes millions of our citizens. Although it goes unmentioned, by declaring incarceration statistics an indicator of failure instead of success he is supporting the Commission's recommendation to "establish better metrics, indicators, and goals to measure progress (Global Commission on Drug Policy, 2011, p. 13)." Strongly insinuated is Carter's support of the commission's finding that "the expenditure of public resources should therefore be focused on activities that can be shown to have a positive impact" on our global society. Further increasing our prison populations in an attempt to stop drug usage is not among the 'activities' that have 'a positive impact' on our society as Carter's narrative indicates (Global Commission on Drug Policy, 2011, p. 13).

Perhaps, the final two paragraphs of Carter's op-ed provide the strongest emotional appeal for readers and a true sense of his ethos and character. Inserted in the description of his lived experience working alongside inmates are comments that are my interpretation of how his specific words empower his closing message:

> A few years ago I worked side by side (as equals) for four months with a group of prison inmates (time enough to get to know these human beings), who were learning the building trade, to renovate some public buildings in my hometown of Plains, Ga. (Carter welcomed these men into his

community). They were intelligent and
dedicated young men, (positive representation
of a negative stereotype), each preparing for a
productive life (future generations) after the
completion of his sentence. More than half
of them (the majority of prisoners) were in
prison for drug-related crimes, (represents
shocking factual statistics), and would have
been better off in college or trade school
(better education; better environment;
improved lives for the men and their
families—and our society).

To help such men (3% of our population)
remain (not become, but remain) valuable
(contributing) members of society, and to
make drug policies more humane (current
policies are inhumane) and more effective
(current policies are ineffective), the American
government (our leaders) should support and
enact (we must take action!) the reforms laid
out by the Global Commission on Drug
Policy (panelists who have provided credible
and relevant information on making
significant change in global drug policy).
(Carter, 2011, p. 3—with inserts by Nelson)
This short narrative succeeds in providing a voice to those
marginalized in the 'war on drugs' and supports the pathos,
logos, and ethos of Carter's message.

Conclusion
Whether or not you agree with Carter's politics, as a former
U.S. President, Nobel Peace Prize recipient, and globally
acknowledged philanthropist, who remains actively involved
in Habitat Humanity, Jimmy Carter has earned credibility as a
leader engaged in global and domestic issues. In this op-ed,
he uses that credibility and that of the commission's panel,

effectively constructing ethos. His response also establishes pathos, in that it "persuades through the character and trustworthiness of the...writer (Selzer, p. 287)." His impassioned plea is built upon a strong belief that the report issued by the Commission contains "courageous and profoundly important recommendations" that are "persuasive" in nature and that they should be "supported and enacted" by the American government (Carter, 2011, p. 2-3).

Carter's message is timely for medical cannabis advocates. In the U.S. seventeen of our fifty states and the District of Columbia have passed legislation to decriminalize cannabis for medical use, yet, they are unable to obtain federal support even though they 'do no harm' to others. Both left and right agree that the 'war' has failed but no one wants to enter a debate and plan a strategy to resolve this enormous, multifaceted crisis. Carter suggests the commission's report "will give some cover to political leaders who wish to do what is right (Carter, 2011, p. 3)." In this sense, he calls out those who do not wish to do the 'right thing' and remain in a war against our own citizens, which contributes to the reestablishment of "Jim Crow Laws" (Alexander, 2010, p. 2; Jackson, 2011, p. 1). Ron Paul and Barney Frank have worked together to submit legislation that is being hailed as a *bipartisan* attempt to begin a debate on our 'war on drugs;' unfortunately, Lamar Smith and other law makers have publicly stated they will refuse H.B. 2306. It is an easy leap to believe congressional leaders like Smith will seek to squelch the debate, which is essential to our nation's ability to develop and implement improved drug policy.

President Nixon was correct when he said, "If we cannot destroy the drug menace in America, then it will surely in time destroy us." He certainly did not comprehend the destruction prohibition would take upon our society but he did understand illegal drugs are a societal issue that must be addressed. Legalization is a frightening concept for American's, even those who understand that prohibition feeds the illegal drug market and thus much of the violence within our society. Perhaps, as Carter, Jackson, and members of the U.N. Global Commission on Drug Policy believe legalization may "bring more effective control over the illicit drug trade" (Carter, 2011, p. 1). As they all elucidate we must at least begin the debate.

An Analysis of a Medical Cannabis Movement Logo
September 2011

It's funny sometimes when I'm in the midst of writing something I realize I have no idea what the hell it is I am writing about—but I keep going, and somehow I end up with something, not necessarily something special, but something. This paper was much this way, I just keep putting bit and pieces together and then I had something...and then it went through a major revision (killing more than a few of my brain cells) and had something I liked but thought I had no purpose for. But, the thing is, I have referenced this paper more often than perhaps others that are "in my arena" (leadership driven papers), because it became special to me. As I've come to live my life among cannabis soldiers, those who've cleared a path for the journey I'm on...and the cannabis warriors who suffer still and so many others who pass in pain, I'd like to consider this paper a small homage to those who help many...those willing to risk everything...those who helped me learn to care for myself and those who help others every single day: Cannabis Patients. Every single time I spy a green cross or a red cross with a leaf or when I walk into a medical cannabis dispensary I say a little prayer for all who've fought and those who continue to fight the war on drugs. Thank you!

I was lost in downtown Denver searching desperately for the hotel where I was registered to stay. As I attempted to make an illegal U-turn, I saw an apparently thriving new business (the parking lot was nearly full) in a converted 1950's style gas station. On this sunny spring day, the sun was shining brightly upon a brilliant white building with a large red cross painted across the middle of the building, but setting it far apart from the iconic Red Cross emblem was a giant green cannabis leaf right in the middle of the cross. Any passerby could tell immediately that this was one of Colorado's many medical cannabis dispensaries without even catching the name. Not all dispensaries are this flamboyant in their presentation; many show no outward signs of the business that lies within. Nevertheless, similar to how the golden arches represent McDonald's franchises around the globe, most dispensaries use a signifier (i.e. logo) that identifies their business to new customers. Again and again on websites, blogs, advertisements, and even as a backdrop to CNN and Fox News clips, the presentation of a red cross with a cannabis leaf at the heart of the cross is one of many symbols that have come to represent the medical cannabis movement. This brief essay will be an analytical critique of this particular logo as a visual argument for the legalization of the use of cannabis for medical purposes. The design of the logo is deliberate; the unauthorized use of an iconic symbol is an argument against the status quo of the war on drugs and criminalization of cannabis in favor of an ethic of care which includes every human's right to cultivate and administer their own medicine when able.

 (Unknown, 2011)

In contrast to the cannabis leaf which represents a counterculture with limited power; the International Committee of the Red Cross (ICRC), who adopted the Red Cross emblem in 1863 during their first international conference, represents a social institution of considerable global power. The goals of the conference committee who designed the emblem were to find a "distinctive" symbol "backed by the law to indicate respect for army medical services, volunteers with first aid societies, and the victims of armed conflicts (International Committee of the Red Cross, 2011)." The design of a bright red cross met the primary objective of being "simple, identifiable from a distance, known to everyone and identical for friend or foe

(International Committee of the Red Cross, 2011)." Since 1863 the Red Cross Emblem has certainly come to be universally recognized.

The American Red Cross and other Red Cross chapters throughout the world have "authorized permission" to utilize the Red Cross emblem through treaties with the Geneva Conventions that "ensure universal respect for the protective nature of the Red Cross symbol (American Red Cross, 2011)." The medical cannabis movement and its advocates have received no such authorization to utilize this symbol; instead it has simply been re-appropriated due to its recognition as a symbol representing medical need. Perhaps, for this reason, it has not been possible to identify the designer of the medical cannabis emblem or determine its origin. The unauthorized use of this iconic symbol; however, does support the belief that those in the medical cannabis community are seditious, as does the unauthorized use of other symbols such as the caduceus.

Cannabis, even that used specifically by patients under a doctor's care and recommendation in states that have "decriminalized" its use, remains illegal within the United States on the federal level. For this reason, medical cannabis advocates openly oppose the 'war on drugs'; considering it a war against America's own citizens (Alexander). By using a symbol identified with protection of war victims, advocates have re-appropriated the iconic image to support their own cause: reducing suffering among victims of the 'war on drugs'. The ICRC "plays a humanitarian role" worldwide and "continuously works to persuade States to expand the legal protection of war victims, to limit suffering (International Committee of the Red Cross, 2011)."

The significance of the Red Cross within the medical cannabis logo is fundamental to the message communicated through this visual medium. Cannabis advocates are associating themselves with the ideal of limiting suffering instead of promoting "the high", the most prevalent association with cannabis use. Connected directly to the notion of limiting suffering is the concept of compassion and the need to be compassionate toward our fellow citizens. An ethic of care as ascribed by Martha Nussbaum acknowledges we "share possibilities" with these patients, in that we may find ourselves in similar circumstances. Those who do not "recognize him-or herself as sharing a common humanity with the sufferer will react to the suffering with an arrogant hardness, rather than with compassion (Nussbaum, 2001, p. 237)." Advocates are able to imagine this "common humanity"; therefore, most see this issue as more than one of morality; instead they view it as a public health issue.

Even before the 'war on drugs' began over four decades ago, cannabis use was controversial. The contentiousness that surrounds cannabis is embedded in a much lengthier historical narrative that constructs U.S. Drug Policy. However, cannabis became a well-known and easily accessible "recreational" drug in the 1960's during the counterculture movement. It was during this period that the cannabis or "marijuana" leaf became a prominent symbol of resistance in our society and around the world. Since the 1960's, cannabis has been described as part of political opposition, hippie culture, and in relation to certain preferences in music (jazz, reggae, and later rock n' roll). Sociologist Edward Suchman argues cannabis consumption is "more likely to occur among those…whose behavior, attitudes or values, and self-image, were indicative of opposition to the traditional order (p. 146)." Cultures consist of "patterns, explicit and implicit, of and for behavior acquired and transmitted by symbols (Couto, Munley, & O'Neill, 2010, p. 499)." In other words, cannabis is a popular drug among those who consider themselves creative, subversive, or rebellious in nature; thus it is fitting that those who support the use of cannabis as medication are open to re-appropriating an iconic emblem to support their cause.

In determining the cultural value of a symbol it is important to hear from those whose movement it represents. Recently, I raised this issue with local NORML (National

Organization for the Reform of Cannabis Laws) members during a monthly meeting in Carrolton, Texas to see what significance the insignia of a cannabis leaf had for them. As you can imagine I got a wide array of answers. Interestingly, aside from the many responses regarding legalization—which is a given among cannabis legalization advocates—many argued it was a sign of freedom, although the legal use of cannabis is not a freedom they currently have in the Texas or the United States. Others reinforced the definition I provided earlier of "resistance," "revolution," and even "anarchy." In short, for advocates it represents an argument for legalization and is a sign that brings together like-minded persons. For opponents of cannabis legalization, I asked several local Chamber of Commerce members who admitted their disfavor of cannabis use their opinion on the meaning of a cannabis leaf as a symbol. They responded with labels such as "rebellious," "lawlessness," and "drug user" (Nelson, 2011). Both groups provided similar answers given their position on the subject and supported the cannabis leaf as a cultural symbol with a wide variety of meanings, often for the same individual.

During these conversations, I found one other type of response quite prevalent among those within cannabis culture: the cannabis leaf also signifies *access*. For example, one college student stated a cannabis leaf signifies "the kid with it on his shirt in the library reading Murkowski is totally going to hook me up and make my Wednesday better (Nelson, 2011)." Although others described access in less unlawful terms, the cannabis leaf signifies that a conversation about cannabis and its use can occur 'safely' with a party displaying such an emblem. It is a symbol of the cannabis community. Now, whether that same conversation ends with access to cannabis is uncertain, but it is a held belief among cannabis users (medical and recreational) as a potential means to access. Arguably, the cannabis leaf from the medical cannabis emblem also signifies access. For a culture that is "coming out of the closet," so to speak, the ability to recognize a kindred soul and engage in a conversation without judgment is critical to patient access.

This particular symbol is only one of many visual images that have been designed to represent the medical cannabis industry and its advocates. As mentioned earlier, a wide variety of images containing a cannabis leaf and a caduceus, another iconic symbol for medical assistance are also used frequently online, on television, and on products. In *Representation: Cultural Representations and Signifying Practices* Stuart Hall states, "Any sound, word, image or object which functions as a sign, and is organized with other signs into a system which is capable of carrying and expressing meaning is 'a language (Hall, 2010, p. 19)." The design of the logo expresses an argument against the status quo of the drug war and criminalization of cannabis in favor of an ethic of care, as espoused by Nussbaum, Gilligan and Rorty, among other care theorists. In fact, Gilligan explicates that "one who labels moral statements as expressions of approval or disapproval, and takes the matter to be finished with that, misses the very heart of morality. He misses both feeling and content (Gilligan, 1987, p. 19)." Perhaps the Red Cross, even more than the caduceus, is befitting the medical cannabis movement because of its connection to the need to limit suffering, whether friend or foe. Certainly, the sight of a red cross with a cannabis leaf speaks volumes to most citizens whether or not they support the medical cannabis movement.

Before I left Denver I decided to enter this establishment, mostly out of curiosity; I had never seen a medical cannabis dispensary. On my way in the front door I encountered three elderly White women hugging a large Black man wearing a Raiders jersey—an unlikely scene on most street corners. As they thanked him for his assistance, they turned to me and one stated, "You are in the right place, if you need help this man is one of best in the business. He has helped me feel better than I have in years." Witnessing their exchange brought a smile to my face, because they seemed an unlikely pairing; one that argues for and supports "decriminalization" and access for patients who chose to use cannabis for medical purposes.

Creativity is...
October 2012

Creativity is perhaps my favorite subject. I've always found why people do what they do curious—humans behave in the strangest ways. But, they also behave very creatively—and it's not just artists I am speaking about, but in all aspects of life, all people are creative. Andrea Scarpino was a blessing to work with during this term. I do believe she was more concerned about my health than I was...she cared and the subject matter she shared added great value to my life, gave me insight into myself, and stretched me in new directions! (Thank you, Andrea—I think of you often reading poetry, and breathe a sigh of relief that there are good people and good poets left in this world).

The truly creative mind in any field is no more than this: A human creature born abnormally ...by some strange, unknown, inward urgency they are not really alive unless they are creating.

Pearl Buck
Winner of a Nobel Prize in Literature in 1938

Creativity, like other complexities, is a system of textured, layered constructs. As Rob Pope defines creativity, "it is extra/ordinary, original and fitting, full-filling, in(ter)ventive, co-operative, un/conscious, fe<>male, re...creation (Pope, 2005, p. 3)", every spectrum in-between these poles, and *so much more*. Mihaly Csikszentmihalyi presents that creativity springs from a "complex personality" and "none of its components alone can explain it (Csikszentmihalyi, 1996, p. 56-57)." Because of this complexity, Robert Sternberg rightly states, "Creativity as a problem of study is large, unwieldy, and hard to grasp (Sternberg, 2004, p. 1)." For these reasons, a reliable definition has been elusive to scholars. Creativity is different things to different people and, further complicating the matter, how each individual engages with creativity or the creative process is unique. Yet, creativity is observable: we know it when we see it. Within the medical cannabis community, creativity is an observable component of each new business and owners walk a fine line of quasi-legality in an industry that many still consider spurious. This essay will explore how the elements of creativity including innovation, problem-posing and problem-solving, and risk-taking manifest through the complex creative traits of medical cannabis business owners.

Over the last several months, I have been speaking with leaders in the medical cannabis community: business owners, non-profit executives, and leadership in the advocacy community. These individuals are a very diverse group of people with three main things in common. First, all are currently involved in criminal activity. Their enterprises are only quasi-legal, in that they are state sanctioned, but owners are culpable of purchasing, using, cultivating, or distributing a substance that remains illegal under U.S. federal law. These creative individuals "seek to conquer taboos and social prejudices" associated with cannabis use in an attempt to "emancipate" this industry and our society (Gamman & Raein, 2010, p. 173). Second, the individuals leading the way in this new marketplace show an amazing amount of creativity. Both criminal and creative, medical cannabis business owners are "exploit[ing] creativity to drive profit (Gamman & Raein, p. 156)." Lorraine Gamman and Maziar Raein explicate, "The ability to scan, spot, and exploit a situation" especially one involving profit "is a characteristic that is consistent among some criminals, but it is also a characteristic that is shared by many creatives (Gamman & Raein, p. 159)." Third, along with this drive for profit business owners and advocates share one other trait consistently: compassion. Although most will admit to making a tidy profit, they are truly empathetic toward others, especially those within the medical cannabis community. Gamman and Raein draw from Daniel Goleman's notion that "the human capacity for empathy, particularly feelings of group or social allegiance (Goleman in Gamman & Raein, p. 166) are a driving factor for many creatives. This explains why some medical cannabis business owners exhibit concern for community values rather than the profit they generate. It also explains the large number of volunteers that donate their time and energy to medical cannabis businesses. Creative criminals are flocking to medical cannabis states and opening businesses that allow them to pursue their desires and dreams at a profit while compassionately helping others.

From a product standpoint, studies on 'big C creativity" are usually focused on usefulness and novelty (Sawyer, 2006, p. 27); however, as Keith James and Aisha Taylor state in their essay *Positive Creativity and Negative Creativity (and Unintended Consequences)*, "[u]sefulness is subjective: what is useful to me could be either useless or harmful to you (James & Taylor, 2010, p. 33)." Creative products must also be "appropriate" or "recognized as socially valuable in some way to some community (Sawyer, 2006, p. 27)." Products and services useful to medical cannabis patients, including cannabis and devices necessary to consume cannabis, remain illegal in thirty-four states and federally in all fifty states; therefore, their appropriateness for public consumption is a relatively new notion. As an example of creativity in this marketplace, medical cannabis patients can utilize cannabis with virtually none of the harmful effects associated with smoking. Creative business owners asked patients what they needed and developed alternative delivery methods based on their responses. Sublingual tablets (sometimes flavored with *Kool-Aid*) and "medibles" or "edibles" (cannabis-infused edible products such as cookies or salad dressings) have also become hugely popular among patients in states with favorable medical cannabis legislation. Further, some owners are retooling ideas; smokeless "cigarettes" with hashish oil cartridges in lieu of nicotine cartridges; a vapor delivery system that is safer for patients than smoking. These alternative delivery methods are often invented on shoe-string budgets, from garages or basements because these business owners understand that for medical patients inhaling smoke is not the healthiest option for delivery and few initially have the financial means to set up business outside of their own home. Innovation in this arena can be attributed to the ability to creatively pose and solve problems that few outside of this industry are even considering.

Newly recognized access to this field has provided an opportunity for individuals to "come out of the closet," so to speak, and engage with others, who share the willingness to explore cannabis related problems from a variety of creative angles. The importance of engaging with others, listening to patient needs, and exchanging ideas with other business owners has been instrumental to innovation in the medical cannabis industry. Community driven problem-posing and problem-solving have both exponentially increased the knowledge about their chosen field, which frequently leads to the development of new products. Sternberg states, "Wise judgments require knowledge regarding topics about which one had to make judgments (Sternberg, 2010, p. 320, spelling revised)." Very few of these business owners have the type of "formal" knowledge learned through "school and books," instead they overwhelmingly possess the "informal" knowledge associated that "is picked up through experience (Sternberg, 2010, p. 320)." In fact, the only advocate I met to date with "formal" knowledge is completing his doctoral dissertation on symptom relief in HIV/AIDS patients as it relates to medicating with various strains of cannabis. His desire to do so stems from his passion to help others through creative problem-solving and his breadth of knowledge in biology, cannabis cultivation, and usage, much of which was gained "informally" as a recreational cannabis user, and is the base of the knowledge he is building on through more formal means. (Note: I have since met several academic cannabis advocates).

Another primary key to creativity is the willingness to take risks. There are few greater risks than imprisonment and possible forfeiture of your business and/or home for maintaining a business that is in violation of federal law.

With "decriminalization" of cannabis for medical use in sixteen states, an opportunity for innovation and change presented itself and resourceful creatives were willing to risk everything for the ability to make a profit doing something they are passionate about, even if it is only legal on the state level. Many of these business owners gained their knowledge of cannabis in the illicit marketplace, allowing former black market users and growers the opportunity to create a new business or expand an existing one when allowed the opportunity by their state and have been hugely successful from a customer satisfaction and a financial standpoint.

The rapid growth and diversity in cannabis products in states that have "decriminalized" medical cannabis, is a testament to these business owners creativity. But it is important to note, the risk to their business from federal authorities is sizeable. Gamman and Raein elucidate, "Creatives will solve problems in order to gain access to a state of mind that will deliver their desires and/or an income (Gamman & Raein, p. 164)." They further acknowledge that creative people "may enjoy revealing or interrogating power structures at work in different ways, which takes both ingenuity and often, courage (Gamman & Raein, 2010, p. 171-172)." Business leaders in the medical cannabis community embrace this "state of mind" and their desires for access to cannabis for medicinal purposes came with an income, as well as an opportunity to confront the power structures that curtail federal "legalization" of this industry. The passion these business owners bring to their product resembles both that of an advocate and of a "connoisseur" (Sawyer, 2006, p. 127); much as others are connoisseurs of wine, these individuals are connoisseurs of cannabis. They "know the most about their domain," have been "socialized into the domain," and "they play a disproportionately important role" to their audience (consumers) in that "less experienced people trust their opinions" and depend upon them for access to a quasi-legal medication (Sawyer, 2006, p. 127). Many medical cannabis patients, even those who have used cannabis in the past, often have little knowledge of how it should be used as medication or how many ways it can be consumed; therefore, education is a critical service provided by business owners for patients.

At a medical cannabis exposition I recently attended in Albuquerque, New Mexico, I asked business owners if cannabis had any effect on their creativity. The question was presented with no expectations, just genuine curiosity. As you can imagine I received a wide array of answers and entered a number of very interesting conversations. One trend that emerged rather quickly is that many said when they felt "creatively blocked" or were "wrestling with an idea" they would put the issue aside and smoke cannabis; "shortly afterwards," in one owner's words, "everything comes together making order out of chaos (B. Atwood, personal communication, July 29, 2011)." Supporting the notion of "an increase in creativity while under the influence of cannabis," in a recent study on the effects of cannabis on divergent thought processes, a majority of participants described cannabis usage as bringing about "an expansion of unusual and original thoughts (Bourassi & Vaugeouis)." Within these examples are descriptors of creativity and most fall within the definition of divergent thought processes. Divergent thinking makes possible the ability of "seeing the known in a new light, producing multiple answers, shifting perspectives, giving surprising answers, and opening up risky possibilities (Cropley, Cropley, Kaufman, & Runco, 2010, p. 6)." Cannabis use increases this possibility in some people (Bourassi & Vaugeouis). The use of these 'divergent processes' are easily recognized in the medical cannabis industry and have significantly influenced its rapid growth. In fact, many business owners directly connect cannabis usage with the creative ideas that sparked their product innovation. The business owner that produces the smokeless cigarettes with hashish cartridges mentioned earlier stated he had been considering this issue for months before he invented the product he currently manufactures. He declared that after several failed attempts he was about to give up, when one night after smoking cannabis he understood exactly where the errors lied in his design. In only two short hours, he had revamped his previous design plan and had a product that is now available in over two hundred dispensaries in each of the sixteen states that have "decriminalized" its use (M. Brown, personal communication, April 21, 2011).

As stated during the introduction, each belief we hold to be true about creativity has an opposite meaning that may also be true of creativity (extra/ordinary, etc...). In short, we know it when we see it, but it is hard to describe. This is because creativity can happen at either end of the spectrum or somewhere in between. As Csikszentmihalyi elucidates, in *The Creative Personality,* creativity "involves the ability to move from one extreme to the other as the occasion requires...creative persons definitely know both extremes and experience both with equal intensity and without inner conflict (Csikszentmihalyi, 1996, p. 57)." Creatives in the medical cannabis community easily maneuver extremes between the "traditional and conservative" and the "rebellious and iconoclastic (Csikszentmihalyi, 1996, p. 71)." Many, for instance, have helped develop state and local law or practices that support local laws and they carefully comply with state requirements, but they also blatantly break federal law without inner conflict. During discussions, not one advocate expressed inner conflict about remaining outside the law. Each articulated a desire to be a law-abiding citizen (and the majority assert they are otherwise law-abiding citizens), but the distinction made is they are often adamantly committed to breaking the law until this particular substance is legalized for medical use. In comparing creative artists to creative criminals Gamman and Raein explicate:

> The artist is as resourceful and amoral in his or her pursuit of the project as the criminal. The likeness of the artist to the criminal was celebrated by Degas and is a familiar trope in art writing. "A painting calls for as much

cunning, roguishness and wickedness as the
committing of a crime, "Degas commented,
and he advised the neophyte artist to be
"devious." (Gamman & Raein, 2010, p. 159)
Certainly, medical cannabis business owners draw upon the
same risky strategies associated with crime, because they're
participating in a quasi-legal enterprise. There really is no
doubt these business owners are risk-takers. With the
medical cannabis population expanding rapidly in the U.S.
and statistics showing that in 2009 over 500,000 ("Medical
Cannabis Usage," 2009) patients were being prescribed
cannabis and an estimated 6-12% of our population was
using cannabis on a regular basis, it's likely that many more
creative criminals will enter this industry with novel new
ideas.

Creativity is tied to culture as a social construct. The
medical cannabis community is a safe space for creative
criminals to engage in creative activities; in fact, it is
encouraged. Whether it is the cannabis that induces a state of
open-mindedness or it is simply a trait easily observed among
those in the medical cannabis community creativity is
embraced within this subculture. Innovation, problem-
posing and problem-solving, and risk-taking are only a few of
the creative traits manifested through the actions of medical
cannabis business owners. While it is true that creativity and
creative processes are "neither good nor evil" (Cropley, et al.,
2010, p. 6), the medical cannabis industry and its leaders
represent an unusual relationship between criminal and
creative tendencies in our society. Perhaps some citizens
consider their businesses and their product evil or bad, but
others including medical cannabis patients would surely
disagree. These business owners are advocates who are truly
passionate in regards to cannabis legalization and its use as
medication. Although many medical studies support their
beliefs business owners in this field remain outside federal
law; thus, they will continue to be creative criminals in our
society. Perhaps, as Hilton (2010) points "When there are no

bounds to creativity, creative processes may equally identify and apply opportunities for good and evil, although the concept of good and evil is a human construct relating to helping or harming (p. 134)." Many consider the medical cannabis industry harmful; however, the patients I've spoken with assure me they find great relief in medical cannabis use; therefore, the construction of whether medical cannabis is harmful or helpful is greatly dependent upon, whom one is conversing.

Regina Nelson

Medical Cannabis Leadership Through the Lens of Conventional Leadership Theories
November 2011

You'd have thought we'd have explored this topic sooner since it's my major: Ethical and Creative Leadership; but, I struggled with this class—the first Leadership course in this program. Why? Don't know. I was excited to work with Dr. Richard Couto (I'd quoted him often during my master's studies) and Cohort 10's Owen and Rebecca joined me on this journey, along with Sherri, a returning student with very interesting insights. It was Rebecca, who though opposite me in so many ways, become like a sister prodding me along the way after my near-death experience. (In fact, it's Rebecca that I called from the hospital, well before my family—I was that concerned about my Ph.D. work…and that my Cohort, my scholarly family, know I needed their help. And, they all responded with support!). But even without my health issues, I would have struggled through this course—again, not sure why (still self-reflecting)… I learned a great deal working with Dr. Couto and wish I had pulled more of his words of wisdom or stories into this paper, perhaps then I would be more satisfied with it. It's one of the papers that I say, "It is what it is." But upon reflection, it is also the beginning of my understanding that there are no virtually no organizations advocating for medical cannabis patients from a standpoint of shared values and goals—those that exist are lobbyist, almost completely unconcerned about the patient. And, simultaneously as a patient, I was coming to understand that "access to" medical cannabis has a wide variety of meanings—in practice, access to cannabis medicine can be virtually non-existent even under policies these organizations lobby for. Again, no one is lobbying with the needs of cannabis patients fully in mind, the political agendas of the cannabis organizations are most concern with 1) raising funds 2) taxing and regulating cannabis 3) using patient stories to push taxation and decriminalization versus supporting real, true legalization. It was during this semester as I was beginning to interact with other cannabis patients that I began to understand these things, because I was experiencing them. I had access to cannabis I could not afford, in quantities so severely limited the needs of those most seriously ill could not be addressed, and few options beyond "smokeable flower" products. I couldn't find answers to my questions within the medical cannabis program I was a part of or from the lobbyists that run the organizations I mention (I spoke with them all at some point this term); instead I had to seek assistance from patients that I'd meet (often at the very dispensaries that could not help me).

It was also at this time I began to recognize that the leadership capacity of this movement has been overlooked—it lies not among the few notable faces and names, but among thousands of patients who quietly share their stories with others, so they may understand this plant and its healing capabilities. It is from these leaders I learned the most during this term, it shames me that I didn't discuss them here, but it is what it is...so, instead I will make a public commitment to the cannabis patient leaders: Since I've been unable to find an organization led this way, it has become my goal—shared with my partner, Mark Pedersen, to ensure our organization, Cannabis Patient Network Institute (www.CPNInstitute.Org) helps build and develop cannabis leaders, not cannabis power-wielders.

This essay will explore a variety of leadership models that look beyond traits or characteristics of individual leaders to contemplate leadership from a paradigm of collaborative process involving many. Specifically, this essay will consider leadership as demonstrated through non-profit public-interest advocacy organizations supporting the use of medical cannabis. Americans for Safe Access (ASA), Marijuana Policy Project (MPP), and the National Organization for the Reform of Marijuana Laws (NORML) are the largest member-based marijuana advocacy organizations in the U.S.; their membership consists of recreational cannabis users, as well as medical cannabis patients and caregivers, including some medical professionals. These organizations promote the therapeutic use of cannabis, scientific and social research, and safe legal access to cannabis with an ideological position that supports the medical use of cannabis as a civil liberty and right of any American citizen with a physician's recommendation to do so. Each organization has assisted in the design and implementation of state and local policies and regulations and combined they represent a significant lobbying force on Capitol Hill. Focused on the ratification of federal policy that supports the needs of medical cannabis patients, an arguably marginalized population, these nationally-recognized organizations have a strong base, a national network of citizen-advocates, who voluntarily provide leadership on state and local levels. This paper will not consider the leadership capabilities of a specific individual leader; instead, it will examine how leadership is demonstrated through these organizations. [Note: Or so I thought at the time…I've gotten to know the leaders of these organizations and their agendas much more clearly since this time—but have chosen not to rewrite this, but to just let it stand].

This is a critical time for the medical cannabis movement because for the first time since cannabis was prohibited in 1937, there is pending federal legislation designed to end the prohibition on cannabis (H.R 1983; H.R 1984; H.R 1985; and H.R 2306). This legislation came about in large part due to advocacy efforts; therefore, leadership in these organizations play an essential role in obtaining support for this legislation from both the electorate and public officials. Specifically, H.R. 2306, the "Ending Federal Cannabis Prohibition Act of 2011," is a legislative measure seeking to remove cannabis from the Schedule of Controlled Substances and eliminate the prohibition on the import and export of cannabis products within US borders among states with favorable cannabis legislation (S. 2306, 2011). None of these bills legalizes cannabis per se, but the passing of H.R. 2306 would allow states to medicalize, decriminalize, or legalize cannabis for adult recreational use should they choose to do so.

The goal of these organizations is to act upon the shared values and beliefs that unite medical cannabis advocates in a manner that significantly modifies current U.S.

Drug Policy as it relates to cannabis use. However, leadership in these organizations has many obstacles to overcome, including a dominant culture that represents cannabis as an immoral substance and a gateway to harder drugs and ultimately addiction though these accusations are false. Additionally, a stigma is attached to cannabis users through the promulgation of stereotypical representations that portray users as stoners—lazy, dim-witted characters without ambition. Although many studies support the use of cannabis as medication, research has yet to be conducted on the ways our society views cannabis users, as leadership or as marginalized citizens.

It has been over thirty-five years since James Macgregor Burns introduced *Leadership*, a seminal text that has become a fundamental resource for leadership scholars. In this text, Burns describes leadership as, "no mere game among elitists and no mere populist response but as a structure of action that engages persons, to varying degrees, throughout the levels and among the interstices of society. Only the inert, the alienated, and the powerless are unengaged (1978, p. 3)." This is a solid explanation of leadership, but as Burns recognizes, in times of crisis, as we are currently experiencing, the marginalized in our society are left out of the leadership equation. Although citizens are begging for leadership, too often they seek a new breed of hero, an individual who can help traverse the social and political landscape: a leader. But, in this scenario, the marginalized in our society remain outside of leadership. For this discussion it is important that we define leadership in inclusive terms.

Scholars have attempted to define leadership in more comprehensive terms; yet, the domain of leadership studies remains without a recognized, unambiguous definition of leadership. Therefore, for the sake of clarity in this essay, Dr. Richard Couto's more inclusive definition of leadership will be utilized: "leadership is taking initiative on behalf of shared values and common benefit (R. Couto, October 20, 2011)." This definition was chosen because it is wide-ranging enough to include all of our society, signifying all human beings demonstrate leadership. This essay will explore a variety of leadership models, including both conventional and post-conventional models and look beyond leadership as traits or characteristics that individual leaders demonstrate to contemplate leadership from a paradigm which considers leadership as a collaborative process that involves many.

Conventional leadership philosophies have built a solid foundation for leadership studies. Many of these notions help leadership scholars bridge the gap between conventional theories, such as Burns, and post-conventional leadership themes on which the transition to future leadership studies rely. One thesis that has been instrumental in guiding post-conventional scholars is Burns concept of "transforming leadership." Burns elucidates, "[t]he moral legitimacy of transformational leadership…is grounded in conscious choice among real alternatives (1978, p. 36)." In this sense, leadership is a process of morality, in which both leaders and followers must determine their "true" needs (Burns, 1978, p. 36) and attempt to find real choices to the problems they face in satisfying these needs. Leadership is not detached from social and political surroundings; instead leadership seeks to change social or political contexts in order to meet the true needs of society. This type of leadership occurs when "one or more persons *engage* with others in such a way" that they "raise one another to higher levels of motivation and morality (Burns, 1978, p. 20)."

When one considers Burn's theory of transforming leadership in relation to the medical cannabis movement one must consider ideology but be willing to deliberate beyond ideology to recognize *purpose* as a driving force. Leadership within a politicized movement such as this must be dedicated to explicit goals and focused on leading political actions that pursue these goals. The purpose of the movement must "embody and personify collective goals (Burns, 1978, p. 248)," so that the needs of leadership and followership are both equitably represented. The dominant ideology of any movement is a dialectic function of leadership.

One message fervently communicated by medical cannabis leadership concerns safe and legal access for patients and caregivers. Leadership is involved in creating a vision and supporting a framework that encompasses the true needs of patients based on safe and legal access to cannabis as medication. Much of the national debate around medical cannabis remains focused on the legality, ethics, and morality of cannabis use. However, leadership within advocacy organizations such as ASA, MPP, and NORML bring "the patient's voice to the table" (Americans for Safe Access) causing the national debate to shift, speaking to their collective purpose. In this example, medical cannabis leadership is actively taking initiative on behalf of shared values and common benefit as ascribed earlier by Couto.

The test of ideological leadership, such as leadership within the medical cannabis movement, "is the realization of purpose measured by popular needs manifested in social and human values (Burns, 1978, p. 251)." Movements such as this are united by a moral purpose, and strengthened by opposing ideological conflict. Burn's captures the qualities of such a relationship in the following passage:

> The striking aspect of this model is the full congruence of the key elements of ideology: *cognition, conflict, consciousness, value,* and *purpose.* What leaders and followers see in their environment and in one another; the conflict with opposing ideologies that draws them together; their social and historical consciousness; the values that build moral significance for them; the social and political purposes that emerge from such ideology—all of them mutually fortify one another. A movement of followers possessing these qualities obviously provides an enormously

powerful base for leadership that expresses
and embodies it. (Burns, 1978, p. 250)

In the medical cannabis community leaders and
followers unite as like-minded individuals who share strong
beliefs about the utilization of cannabis as medication and
moralizing civil liberties and freedom. They merge around
conflict, against a dominant ideology that opposes the use of
cannabis for both medical and recreational/adult use
purposes; and, they share a social and historical consciousness
regarding individual freedoms and rights that have moral
significance for them. The commonalities between leadership
and followership drive this movement forward. For nearly
forty years, leadership within the cannabis movement has
been tested by "achievement of purpose" or "real and
intended social change (Burns, 1978, p. 251)." It has only
been the past decade that this movement has seen significant
legislative change. Since California first decriminalized
medical cannabis in 1996, sixteen states and the District of
Columbia have enacted medical cannabis legislation, most in
just the last few years. These accomplishments attest to the
leadership strength they possess.

Robert Greenleaf's theory of servant leadership also adds
value to the analysis and discussion of leadership within the
medical cannabis movement. Greenleaf's notion of servant
leadership requires leadership to create "high-trust cultures"
that embrace "an empowerment philosophy that turns bosses
into servants and coaches, and structures and systems into
nurturing institutionalized servant processes" (Greenleaf,
2002, p. 2). At the core of servant leadership are Greenleaf's
"Four Dimensions of Moral Authority" (2002, p. 6-10). I
posit these four dimensions can be used as a lens to consider
leadership within the medical cannabis movement. Greenleaf
(2002) presents the first dimension as, "*The essence of moral
authority or conscience is sacrifice*—the subordinating of one's self
or one's ego to a higher purpose, cause, or principle (p. 6)."
Leadership within this movement vocalizes their moral beliefs
and opinions publically, giving voice to their cause and to

many silent cannabis patients; doing so subjects them to public scrutiny and stereotypical representations that establish them in the minds of the dominant culture as either stoners, radicals or both. Films, television, news media, and even public service announcements diminish the message of advocates as the dominant culture reinforces these stereotypes through their narrative. Second, *"Conscience inspires us to become part of a cause worthy of our commitment* (Greenleaf, 2002, p. 7)." Greenleaf (2002) observes servant leaders do not ask "What is it I want?" but "What is wanted of me?" Leadership within the medical cannabis movement has found meaning in the suffering of their fellow citizens; shifting the national debate to the concerns of patients: access, civil rights, and attempting to debunk stereotypical representations.

Third, *"Conscience teaches us that ends and means are inseparable* (Greenleaf, 2002, p. 8)." Medical cannabis leadership is dedicated to reaching their end result: favorable federal legislation that supports the state's right to design cannabis legislation. But, their language and actions demonstrate they do so by respectable means: public education that debunks myths and false claims about cannabis consumption and cannabis users, assisting in public policy reform through lobbying efforts and the co-develop of public policy, drawing media attention to their efforts, and organizing peaceful demonstrations. And, finally, *"Conscience also transforms passion into compassion* (Greenleaf, 2002, p. 9)." Many recreational cannabis users initially entered the medical cannabis movement because of their passion for the product. Yet, in spite of this, as they listened to patients and learned about their true needs, creative business owners have led the way in developing alternative delivery methods that allow patients to utilize cannabis without the need to smoke (Nelson, 2011; M. Brown, April 21, 2011). This is but one example of how some in leadership have turned passion into compassion. In adopting these "Four Dimensions of Moral Authority" into their leadership philosophy medical cannabis advocacy organizations sustain cultures that foster servant processes.

A key to leadership in a movement such as this is to know what is transpiring at any given time in their community. Greenleaf (2002) suggests, "Servant-leaders are functionally superior because they are closer to the ground—they hear things, see things, know things, and their intuitive insight is exceptional (p. 56)." Cultivating a thorough understanding of the complex realities "on the ground" is key to catalyzing empowerment and collective action. Advocacy organizations lobby for sound public policy that considers the voices and experiences of patients and caregivers. They must also fully comprehend and navigate the political world our public leadership inhabits on behalf of those marginalized by the current laws. The ability to take on multiple roles, such as these, is not a capability of any one individual, but of many throughout each organization. In this same vein, focusing on one leader in any one organization does not provide a full accounting of leadership capabilities in this domain. Leadership appears to flow up and down throughout these organizations allowing individuals to "build wholeness through adventurous creative achievement" (Greenleaf, 2002, p. 26), by working together to right what they believe to be a considerable wrong in our society.

Juana Marie Bordas' leadership theory as described in *Inclusive Leadership* elucidates the importance of person as related to community and culture. Bordas (2010) explains, "Leaders in communities of color are respected not for how much they have, but for their generosity, which includes: listening to others, spending time with people, taking a personal interest in them, and sharing ideas, stories, and life experiences (p. 799)." This same tenet is observable in the medical cannabis community. Opening one's self up to others and being open to the experiences of others is extremely valuable in the eyes of followers who seek leadership. Bordas provides a description of what leadership can look like when leaders engage others and develop a participatory environment in which they can excel: Leaders can tap into of the spirit of collective cultures by consciously building a sense of community, seeking common purpose, and embracing values that stress working together and mutual benefit. Leaders can model inclusive- and collective-oriented leadership by sharing their time and talents, developing a reputation as someone who helps others succeed, and allowing others to take credit (Bordas, 2010, p. 798). A spirit of servitude, as espoused by Greenleaf, holds cultures together "because the self emerges from the collective, *giving and sharing are a way to nourish and regenerate oneself*" (Bordas, 2010, p. 799) and others. Relationships are always about give and take; therefore, responsibilities must be shared; "[c]yclical reciprocity means people are continually giving to one another and people can rest assured that their sharing will come back (Bordas, 2010, p. 799)." Although reciprocity is important in all relationships, it is particularly vital to those in a leader-led relationship because this type of sharing establishes rapport and trust between persons.

The social constructs of leadership and power are closely entwined. Burns (1978) argues that in order to obtain power, one must have both motive and resources (p. 12). Not only does leadership require power, it is also in and of its self, "a special form of power (Burns, 1978, p. 12)." Burns advises that the source of power in leadership lies "in immense reserves of the wants and needs of the wielders and objects of power (1978, p. 12)." In this sense, "power is a relationship among persons" and as such "part of a system of social causation (p. 12-13)." Foucault indicated that individuals are never outside of power (Foucault in Pearce, 2010, p. 526); therefore, effective leadership assures the power they wield is productive and shared, not "coercive, violent, or silencing (Pearce, 2010, p. 525)." In the essay, *Leadership: Gender Excluded Yet Embraced*, Laurien Alexandre (2007) explains, "Those who wield power over others are not leaders—they are power-wielders. Leaders, on the other hand, hold power differently. They share power and they empower their followers (p. 100)." The primary variable in any relationship of power is purpose. According to Carol Pearson, leadership is "all about understanding people and bringing out what is best in them (Pearson, 2010, p. 640)." This requires a shared purpose and a shared sense of values. Leadership within this movement predominantly consists of volunteer members: local and state leadership volunteer time and resources because of a sense of shared values and purpose with the national organization. For this reason, relational power between leadership and followership is critical to the success of the movement.

To reach their goals advocacy organizations must mobilize power. Burns (1978) proposes that in mobilizing power, "[t]he essential strategy of leadership... is to recognize the arrays of motives and goals in potential followers, to appeal to those motives by words and action, and to strengthen those motives and goals in order to increase the power of leadership, thereby changing the environment within which both followers and leaders act (p. 40)." Leading with common purpose advocate-volunteers are encouraged to become partners in leadership and as such are empowered to influence desired effects. Leadership is able to "discern signs of dissatisfaction, deprivation, and strain; they take the initiative in making connections with their followers; they plumb the character and intensity of their potential for mobilization; they articulate grievances and wants; and they act for followers in their dealings with other clusters of followers (Burns, 1978, p. 38)." As an example of how well these particular advocacy organizations have mobilized their troops medical cannabis advocates have consistently kept this issue as the top question asked of President Obama online through the White House website (www.whitehouse.gov). Further, leadership in MPP and NORML recently formed partnerships with organizations such as the National Association for the Advancement of Colored People (NAACP) and Americans Civil Liberties Union (ACLU), bringing together groups with common goals, like lowering incarceration rates among minorities who are disproportionately affected by the criminalization of cannabis (Membis, 2010). These strategic national relationships were facilitated in large part by "on the ground" leadership—volunteers from local chapters, who took the initiative to form partnerships on the local level (St. Pierre, April 21, 2011). Building these alliances from the bottom up demonstrates that power flows in an exchange that encourages members to have power over themselves and contribute to leadership from any level in the organization. Calling upon Nancy Hartsock and standpoint theory, Susan Pearce (2010) asserts, "power needs to be completely redefined as energy, strength and effective interaction, and that it involves mobilizing resources for oneself and others (p. 525)." This definition of power distribution correlates with Couto's definition of leadership as "taking initiative on behalf of shared values and common benefit" and as shown is reflected in medical cannabis leadership.

Power is not just an issue that affects marginalized populaces; power affects all human beings. Pearce (2010) maintains, "we need to sort out the various dimensions of power and view power, empowerment, and powerlessness as dynamics within social relations—between people—rather than as characteristics owned by one group versus another (p. 529). Although, we are able to view power constructs from a variety of lenses using notions from feminist theory and other epistemologies, Pearce acquiesces that "the process of challenging and changing power imbalances in both the political and civil sphere remains slow and unfinished" (Pearce, 2010, p. 529). A recent Gallup poll indicates as many as 70% of Americans "favor making it legal for doctors to prescribe cannabis in order to reduce pain and suffering" (Mendes, 2010); however, this dramatic shift in public opinion is not reflected in national public leadership. Scholars agree that research focusing on power relations should begin with the lives of the marginalized, like medical cannabis patients. Marginalized groups are socially situated in ways that make it possible for them to be aware of social and political inequalities than it is for the privileged; thus, this is a ripe area for future research. At this time, if it were not for the leadership in advocacy organizations the voices of these oppressed citizens would remain in virtual silence.

Nathan Harter's theory on the "Social Origins of Authority," lends a great deal to the construct of *authority* as it relates to leadership. Harter (2010) contends there are three key components to political rule "persuasion, coercion, and authority (p. 60)." Persuasion is a matter of appealing to "the hearts and minds of the populace about the merits of a particular course of action" being debated publically, such as U.S. Drug Policy (Harter, 2010, p. 60). Advocacy organizations share their values about reducing suffering of fellow citizens publically in an attempt to persuade others to reconsider cannabis as medication for those who choose to use it under the direction of a physician like other pharmaceutical remedies. In contrast, coercion entails a "use of force to impose compliance (Harter, 2010, p. 60)." Currently, because cannabis is illegal, the federal government uses coercion to enforce Drug Policy violations, such as the possession, use, cultivation, or sale of cannabis, even when the medical use is state-sanctioned and patients comply with state laws (Americans for Safe Access). Finally, this scholar recognizes that authority should be deemed a "complementary concept" that is "separate and aside from coercion or persuasion (2010, p. 60)." Harter elucidates:

> Authority resides in the sense of legitimacy enjoyed by a ruler before the need for a decision even arises. And that sense of legitimacy originates in the people being ruled. A sense of legitimacy is not necessarily created in a formal enactment, whereby people ratify a compact or elect a particular ruler; it can be implicit in the habits of obedience one finds even among the disfranchised. (Harter, 2010, p. 60)

In this sense, authority lies in current U.S. Drug Policy, as it regards the use of cannabis for any purpose, even as physician recommended medication. Because cannabis is an illegal substance, many citizens support retaining the status quo without understanding the true needs of patients who benefit by using cannabis as medication or that all humans have an endocannabinoid system. Complicating the understanding of cannabis as medication is a dominant discourse that discounts scientific research that supports its potential to help patients and that represents medical cannabis users as stoners and criminals (Nelson, 2011). Leadership within advocacy organizations challenges this authority by proposing alternative frameworks that support the medicalization of cannabis and offers protection including decriminalization or legalization for patients and caregivers.

Providing another interesting perspective on leadership that we can use to analyze the medical cannabis movement is John Gaventa and Jethro Pettit's (2010) power cube, which consists of three dimensions: spaces (closed, invited, claimed/created); forms of power (invisible, hidden, and visible); and levels of power (local, national, and global). Specifically, advocacy leadership challenges the power of closed places where elected political officials make decisions that affect their membership on local and national levels. These organizations affirm their place in claimed/created spaces where "leadership occurs not just in formal governmental places but also in these places of resistance and popular development (Gaventa & Pettit, 2010, p. 516)." Medical cannabis organizations empower their members through education and training to address the issues they are passionate about and encouraging their membership to embrace leadership roles in a visible manner in the local, state, and national communities.

Over the last decade, advocacy organizations have released nearly two dozen public service announcements (PSA) designed to convey the narrative of the typical medical cannabis patient to the public in order to overcome stereotypical representations that appear in media and which remain part of the dominant culture (Nelson, 2011). These PSAs contain a dialogue of compassion as contained in the narrative of care ethics as espoused by Carol Gilligan, Martha Nussbaum, and other care theorists (Nelson, 2011). Their objective is to move the hidden and invisible power structures they confront into a visible arena enabling discussion that has until recently been closed. The demand of popular participation, like that called for by Gaventa & Pettit, is a key component of social or political movements. This type of participation is "primarily about challenging power" (Gaventa & Pettit, 2010, p. 514) and medical cannabis advocates are challenging the dominant views on U.S. Drug Policy. The participation of marginalized citizens in medical cannabis leadership is "a process of gaining voice through *organized* groups and social movements, which have the awareness and capacity therefore to articulate and negotiate their demands (Steifel & Wolfe, 1994 in Gaventa & Pettit, 2010, p. 514)." Through leadership medical cannabis organizations take the initiative on behalf of shared values and common benefit for patients who are otherwise unable to share their narrative embracing Couto's definition of leadership.

In the essay, *A New Paradigm for a New Leadership*, Margaret Wheatley (2007) indicates that the questions surrounding leadership studies have changed considerably since Burns published *Leadership* in the late 1970's (p. 105). Conventional leadership theories provided a lens for the analysis for the dominant world view as it was; specifically, the individual as leader is a principal theme in not only Burns work, but of other scholars of this era of leadership studies. And, as Burns (1978) himself explicates, "For the study of leadership the crucial distinction is between the quest for individual recognition and self-advancement...and the quest for the kind of status and power that can be used to advance collective purposes that transcend the needs and ambitions of the individual (p. 106)." By considering *person* as both an individual and a group member it is possible to consider their contribution to group dynamics from a systems theory perspective.

If we view an advocacy organization from a systems perspective as Wheatley endorses each individual "has a unique contribution to make to the whole" (2007, p. 113) and "shared significance" (2007, p. 109) and "interdependence" (2007, p. 110-112) are viewed as key components to leadership. Leadership and followership within the medical cannabis movement are interdependent based largely on their mutually beneficial relationship; each individual is striving toward the same purpose but could never have the impact as an individual as does a collective group. By joining with others who share their values as well as their vision and goals they have become part of a system of leadership. As a part of a leadership system, "[p]eople who are deeply connected to a cause don't need directives, rewards, or leaders to tell them what to do" (Wheatley, 2007, p. 112) because they are empowered to take initiative. Greenleaf discusses this paradigm change in leadership, explaining:

> [E]verything is rumbling because the old rules of traditional, hierarchical, high-external-control, top-down management are being dismantled: they simply aren't working any longer. They are being replaced by a new form of "control" that the chaos theory proponents call the "strange attractor"—a sense of vision that people are drawn to, and united in, that enables them to be driven by motivation *inside* them toward achieving a common purpose. (Greenleaf, 2002, p. 3)

Citizens within the medical cannabis movement are drawn to a collective purpose. They challenge traditional government authority that stands as an obstacle to their shared beliefs and purpose.

Ronald Heifetz's notion of "leadership without and beyond one's authority" (Heifetz, 2007, p. 35) also speaks to

leadership as a system instead of an individual effort.
Building upon Burn's theories on leadership and the concept
of adaption in evolutionary biology, Heifetz (2007) suggests,
"A successful adaption enables a living system to take the
best from its history, into the future" and enables "us to view
authority and various forms of power as a set of tools and
constraints, rather than as an ends (p. 34)." In other words,
leadership is a means and an ends that groups use to
challenge social or political problems that lack clear solutions.
Certainly, current U.S. Drug Policy is one solution, even if
most argue that it is need of repair, few can envision a perfect
solution. These types of complex challenges compel
leadership to respond with "*adaptive work*, or actions that
generate progress in meeting adaptive challenges so an
organization or society can thrive (Heifetz, 2007, p. 37)."

In particular Heifetz stresses our society's need to
develop "an active citizenry in which people are willing to
take responsibility for their communities in the original spirit
of democracy (p. 41)." The advocacy organizations that
support medical cannabis legislation converge on this
objective, empowering members to exercise leadership
themselves instead of looking to authority for answers. In a
similar vein to how the Civil Rights Movement mobilized
citizens to take responsibility for the challenges in their
communities (Heifetz, 2007, p. 41), medical cannabis
advocates also aspire to engage citizens in resolving the
problems that face their communities. Preferring the term
adaptive to transforming in relation to leadership, Heifetz
(2007) declares, "Indeed, one doesn't transform a community;
at best I think one engages the community in an ongoing
process of adaptive work that probably will never end
because the environment or endogenous realities within the
community itself will continue throwing at it new and
difficulty challenges (p. 43)." Current and future medical
cannabis organizations are required to adapt to our current
social and political climate and because "most significant and
sustainable change builds largely on the past" they must

continue their adaptive work in order to support the shared beliefs and collective purpose of the movement.

After considering these varied theories and concepts of leadership, one can see there are many questions about leadership within the medical cannabis movement that remain unanswered. Future research should consider leadership in this domain from a systems perspective to more accurately determine how leadership flows through these organizations and how the organizations and their membership adapt as policy changes occur—or when they fail to transpire. Additionally, from my limited experience interacting with medical cannabis leadership I posit that leadership is perhaps demonstrated on the local and state levels more effectively than on the national level—certainly, this hypothesis would make for interesting future research. This analysis demonstrates how conventional and post-conventional leadership models that are inclusive of marginalized populations, like medical cannabis patients, provide a framework for future research and strongly suggests that this subject matter calls for more intense study. However, what can be determined is that leadership within this movement embraces Couto's description of leadership as "taking initiative on behalf of shared values and common benefit." The narrative and actions of leadership attest to this notion, as do demonstrations of legislative success in sixteen states. Leadership within this movement has helped shift public opinion significantly but there is much work left to be done to change the stereotypical representations of cannabis users that permeate our society. Yet, engaged in an ideologically driven movement guided by shared beliefs in the rights and Civil Liberties of marginalized citizens leadership within this movement provides voice for those most affected by the criminality of cannabis use: medical cannabis patients.

Chapter Three
January 2012 – May 2012

I survived my second semester and even completed most coursework on time with the help of "The Cohort 10" who cared for me, but most particularly Rebecca who cajoled me into action each week. As I pulled it together and tried to gather the strength to start a third term, my daughter, BreAnna and her family, which included Skylar and Shane, a hard-headed two-year old and an oxygen-toting six-month old, came from Michigan to camp in my living room for more than a month. All of us were ill—stomach flus and viral infections—hospital stays and doctor visits—it was insanity in less than 900 square feet! So when my third semester started I was really weak, extremely thin, anemic, in constant stomach pain, and on top of everything else, I had an intense eye infection that just made it painful for my Cohort friends to even look at me, but I persevered. Residency #3 was a vacation from my own home at that point.

I returned home from residency and reclaimed my space within a week and resumed recovery…and my studies. As a cannabis patient in New Mexico my studies began to take interesting turns as my studied knowledge became embodied knowledge. I was not physically able to return to work though I resumed applying for teaching positions and my unemployment was cut back to $125 a week (not even enough to make rent), so I began baking edibles (medicated cookies, granola, and popcorn) for patients I had gotten to know well—soon to be termed "My Old Man's Club"—not all were men and not all were old—but most were men just older than me (late 50's and 60's). It wasn't a legal cannabis business, but it kept me afloat (barely) and relieved most of these guys of their back pain and other ailments; it was really just one patient helping another, and another, and another—but in the end, it was several of these guys who saved me.

Especially Tim and Gerald, who would often sit in my tiny living room (or better yet, in my garden), and play their guitar and violin for only me...the sounds healed my soul and soon Tim talked me into venturing out into the community for dance lessons. Who knew East Coast Swing would be something this Okie with two left feet would be pretty good at? (And, it helped me wrangle a few dinner dates, including a few with a Yale educated Radiologist who enjoyed debating methodologies—oh how doctors actually love the double-blind clinical based trials that I love to hate).

My life revolved solely around studies, baking, taking care of myself, and a weekly dance lesson at the community center—each day was a challenge but I was garnering strength.

An Autoethnographic Study:
One Cannabis Patient's Story
April 2012

This was yet another course's final project that I wrote and scrapped, rewrote and scrapped, and then wrote the paper I had to write. It was harder to share my story than I would have thought—it was like pulling teeth (and that was just in overcoming my own obstacles). Dr. Lois Melina kept encouraging me to share from personal experience; it took several attempts before I pulled it off! (Lois, thank you for continuing to push me). In the end, this was a freeing project—another positive step along this ambiguous path. I had no idea where it would lead ...but it freed me to go so much further than I could have anticipated at the time.

I have been offered the opportunity to publish this article (with revisions) to Penumbra, *the Union Institute & University Peer-Reviewed Press—publication due Spring 2015. Given the fact that it's been nearly a year and half since I took a medical leave from my studies, this news is encouraging me to get back to it and finish this Ph.D.! However, please note that when the* Penumbra *article is complete the "My Story" portion will be edited significantly—in the more than two years since both my knowledge and the cannabis therapies that I use have changed significantly. I decided to include this version here both to save time getting this book to print, as well as having multiple versions of "My Story" available—this has been a learning experience and if you have the opportunity to read the* Penumbra *version online I know you will see significant growth, as well as learn more about the health changes I've experienced. I'm thrilled to be a peer-reviewed author—twice! And, especially honored to be offered this opportunity by my own peers at* Penumbra, *I have reviewed several articles and have to say I am so fortunate to be among the best minds in the world!*

For many years, much of my adult life actually, I have been a closeted cannabis user. Hidden in a safe in the back of my bedroom closet I've nearly always kept a small stash of marijuana (the terms marijuana and cannabis will be used interchangeably throughout this paper) and a pipe. At the end of many a long work day, my six children safely tucked into bed, work complete, house clean, and studying for college or graduate classes finished for the night, cannabis was my respite. Cannabis was more than a wine alternative, as I have heard it described; for me, it is also a medication: a mild anti-depressant that works effectively for me, more so than pharmaceuticals I have been legally prescribed, and found not only unhelpful, but also full of undesired side-effects. Additionally, the "high" releases stress and anxiety, engulfing me in a "sense of well-being," allowing me to truly relax and sleep. Yet, this side-effect unlike the side-effects of alcohol or many prescription medications also allowed me to remain in control and respond should my children need me. A small dose of cannabis prepared for another day in my life, as mother, wife, employee, student, friend, family and community member.

There were many reasons I spent years hiding in my closet, literally concealing my use of cannabis from others, but the primary reason was that I was afraid—very afraid—of stigmatization. I feared being labeled a 'stoner' and that this type of recognition would interfere with my family and career through either legal or extra-legal forms of control—imprisonment or stigmatization. Now as a medical cannabis patient, conducting research in this domain, I am confronted by this same stigmatization on a regular basis and believe that my story is not so different from many others. My story of becoming a medical cannabis patient may pale in comparison to the stories of other patients who are struggling against truly debilitating and terminal illnesses, but I believe that my story is just as important, because it is familiar and even normal among the cannabis patients I've met.

Cannabis's association with criminality and deviance persists in the dominant public narrative. In reality, other than the crime of using and accessing cannabis itself, the majority of adult marijuana users deny they engage in criminal behavior or use other illicit drugs (Hathaway, Comeau, &

Erickson, 2011, p. 463). Nonetheless, medical cannabis patients, like other cannabis users, must "contend with prejudicial labels and reefer madness sentiments that culturally endure (Hathaway et al., 2011, p. 463)." Like me, most medical cannabis patients are aware their behavior and beliefs related to cannabis use lie outside the dominant public discourse; however, the new-found status as 'State recognized' medical cannabis patients disrupts this narrative. For these reasons, it is important to an understanding of how the growing population of medical cannabis patients may be stigmatized or unduly harmed socially by the association and use of cannabis as medication.

The purpose of this paper is to explore the concerns of medical cannabis patients related to stigmatization incurred through exposure to the dominant narrative, which is misinformed about the experience of cannabis patients and the performative act of using cannabis as medication. Specifically, this essay will be an autoethnographic exploration from the standpoint of a female medical cannabis patient. It will consider the narrative and performative acts associated with medical cannabis use in relation to the dominant public narrative that lumps all cannabis users into a singular category of *stoner*. This particular narrative suggests all cannabis users, including medical cannabis users like me, are amotivated, unintelligent individuals living a counter-culture existence. This dominant stereotype, and others like it, is far from the truth. I will argue that the emergence of medical cannabis patients in sixteen States disrupts this narrative. Cannabis patients are rescripting the performative act of using cannabis by attaching new meanings to cannabis use that no longer support the dominant stereotypes in our society and this rescripting requires that all citizens, even those morally opposed to cannabis use, reconsider what it means to be a medical cannabis patient.

AUTOETHNOGRAPHY

Autoethnography is a way to share my own story, "with the

assertion that the personal narrative instructs, disrupts, incites to action, and calls into question politics, culture, and identity (Marshall & Rossman, 2011, p. 270)." My intention is to share my own narrative as a cannabis patient in a way that educates others, specifically non-cannabis patients, about what it means to be a medical cannabis patient and to demonstrate how the performance of cannabis use disrupts dominant cultural narratives about this practice. My hope is that through this autoethnographic tale others will come to understand the necessity of reassessing cannabis use and begin to view it as a significant political and cultural concern that influences the identities of cannabis patients. Cannabis patients disturb, disrupt, and challenge traditional notions embedded in the dominant discourse regarding cannabis use, and my own story, like that of other medical cannabis patients, is a good place to start in dispelling false beliefs.

Shamir et al contend, "Telling the biography is an important leadership behavior (Shamir, Dayan-Horesh, & Adler, 2005, p. 13)." Nowhere is this more important than within the medical cannabis community. Until I began exploring becoming a medical cannabis patient I had little interaction with other medical cannabis patients. As I have come to observe since entering this community, the willingness to share one's personal story with others is a necessity to gain respect and build rapport with other patients. Although patient's seldom "medicate" together, patients need to understand the experience of others so they can evaluate and validate their own experience. Further, others outside this community must understand why patients choose cannabis as medication and how they perform the act of "using" cannabis, so that they can evaluate their beliefs about this controversial medication. As I prepare to accept a board position with a Patients Alliance, Shamir et al remind me of the significance of sharing my story with others, as other leaders within this community have shared with me.

Like many other cannabis patients who have self-medicated in solitude for years, I have decided to step out of the closet, so to speak, expose myself to the dominant culture as a cannabis user, and embrace this medication. At first, this giant step in changing my "public" or social identity was daunting. I am fortunate enough to have the support of my family and friends, even my conservative, Republican father and step-mother have been accepting of my medical cannabis patient status, although they admit they are 'fearful' of others knowing. These fears, as they've expressed them to me, primarily concern "loss of status (Goffman, 1959)." My parents fear that others will see me as a less competent, less intelligent woman simply because I have taken control of my healthcare and insisted on an alternative treatment. My children, on the other hand, have been very supportive expressing few fears or concerns. Perhaps because their generation has a more "normalized" (Goffman, 1959) view of cannabis use than my parent's generation they more easily accepted my choice to become a cannabis patient.

When I first began to explore the medical cannabis community, I was unsure how to interact with others because I have never interacted as part of "stoner culture" and seldom did my use occur with others. I simply did not know what to expect beyond my limited experience of buying cannabis illegally through a friend whose brother is a self-proclaimed "hippie." Stereotypical representations of cannabis use seemed to suggest my experience of solitude use is abnormal, but I have found it is not; in fact, my observations and encounters with other patients suggest that solitary use, or use with only a spouse or significant other, is normal for medicating patients. Despite the fact that my own concerns initially reflected dominant cultural expectations, each person I've come into contact with in the cannabis community has been accepting of me, so accepting that it has made it easier for me to enter discussions with those who reiterate the dominant narrative. Further, very few of the patients I have encountered as a patient, or during research observations, perform as if they are "stoners" either, each appear to be confident and most extremely knowledgeable and articulate about how cannabis as medication assists them as patients.

Seemingly, medical cannabis patients are likely to be located, "with lesser or greater degrees of social visibility, all over the map" of actors and institutions (Hathaway et al., 2011; Pederson, 2009; Smucker Barnwell et al., 2006). Demographics in the sixteen "medical cannabis" States suggest that most patients are male and over the age of 40, (www.norml.org) but within New Mexico's medical cannabis community, one can observe patients that fit all demographics, young/old, male/female with varying ethnicity and social class. This new sense of community that I am experiencing compels me to share my story so that others, those still hiding in their closets, may consider de-closeting themselves and join the community.

STIGMA

Thinking of one's self as a "normal" person "means incorporating standards from wider society and meeting others' expectations about what we ought to be. The concept of stigma is therein a device that ensures the reliability of the interaction order by punishing people who do not conform to moral standards (Hathaway et al., 2011, p. 455)." Certainly, in the opinion of many, including our national leaders, being a cannabis patient does not conform to moral standards or accepted expectations in Western medicine—if it did, perhaps federally "decriminalizing" or ensuring patients have the "right" to use cannabis as medication would be afforded to our citizenry.

Hathaway, et al, use Sociologist Erving Goffman's work as a frame from which to view the theoretical distinction between 'normalization' and 'normification' to interpret "extra-legal forms of stigma" experienced by regular adult recreational cannabis users in Toronto (Hathaway et al., 2011). Although the Hathaway et al study does include a few medical cannabis patients they were not sought out for participation, nor were they the primary population of interest. Instead because the researchers sought after "regular" (i.e. daily) adult cannabis users, their study came to contain several medical cannabis patients. This study is one of very few that provides an insight into the social stigma attached to cannabis users and substantiates what medical cannabis patients have mentioned during my observations and discussions with other patients. Goffman suggests personal identity "resides within the cracks (Goffman in Hathaway et al., 2011, p. 455; Goffman, 1959);" therefore, one's ability to perform in a given situation as normal or ordinary is not the same as normalizing the stigmatized behavior. For Goffman, "full normalization…requires that others be accepting of the stigmatized individual and the treatment of such persons as if they have no stigma (Goffman in Hathaway et al., 2011, p. 465; Goffman 1959)." Therefore, until medical cannabis patients are no longer subjected to stigma based on their relationship with cannabis as medication, they remain stigmatized, and thus marginalized, by dominant cultural narratives.

When probed on the "disadvantages of using cannabis,' participants in the Hathaway study frequently spoke of stigma as an 'informal' source of control (Goffman in Hathaway et al., 2011, p. 456). Turner elucidates, "…all human act is impregnated with meaning, and meaning is hard to measure, though it can often be grasped, even if only fleetingly and ambiguously. Meaning arises when we try to put what culture and language have crystallized from the past together with what we feel, wish, and think about our present point in life (Turner, 1986, p. 33)." The act of using cannabis, even when medicating, is strongly stigmatized behavior in our society, even though the health benefits, at least for me and many other patients I've met, far outweigh the risks of smoking cannabis. Almost seventy (70) percent of respondents said they hid their use from someone (typically family or co-workers). They did so to avoid conflict, as well as remain discrete, around their usage, but a third of participants also reported "past encounters with non-users resulting in some status loss or social disapproval

(Hathaway et al., 2011, p. 456)." The researchers found that "while 'reefer madness' attitudes were typically rejected, in favour of more nuanced understandings of the practice, other mainstream sentiments were tacitly accepted or echoed" in participant responses (Hathaway et al., 2011, p. 457). In short, cannabis users avoid encountering cultural stereotypes and stigmatization by avoiding use or discussion of use with those they believed would condemn their actions and them personally. This was certainly the stance I took for many years to avoid being stigmatized. For medical cannabis patients, the act of using cannabis is comforting, but their past experiences—as cannabis users or not—shows that the stereotype of 'stoner' in not just solidified in the dominant narrative, but it is also embedded within the narratives of patients. In fact, this is an area ripe for future study.

Gee states, "When any human being acts and interacts in a given context, others recognize that person as acting and interacting as a certain "kind of person" or even as several different 'kinds' at once (Gee, 2001, p. 99)." In this sense, medical cannabis patients often are labeled as a 'stoner' in the context of using cannabis regardless of its medical efficacy or the other "kinds" of roles the patient performs in life: parent, child, sibling, friend, employee, co-worker, etc. In sharing how we medicate or use cannabis, I am not surprised by the number of rituals that patients have established around using cannabis, but I am finding few of these experiences resemble "pot-smoking" as it is portrayed in the dominant narrative, by groups of 'stoner' friends sharing a joint or bong and engaging in silly antics.

Does changing the performative act of cannabis use from smoking to an alternative delivery method have an effect on the dominant cultural narratives that regard cannabis patients as stoners? Is a 72-year old great-grandmother who uses a cannabis tincture in her tea still considered a stoner in our society? As a 48-year old grandmother, Ph.D. student, Business Consultant, and community leader will others still view me as a stoner because

I am a medical cannabis patient and advocate. This is a question I had to consider before choosing to conduct research in this arena. Because my "core identity" (Gee, 2001, p. 99) is other than "cannabis user" I have had little trouble concealing this small part of my identity for many years. It was not until I came a member of a medical cannabis community and began to interact with like-minded, understanding others with whom I felt a sense of "belonging" (McMillan & Chavis, 1986) that I realized just how important cannabis as medication has become to me. McMillan et al state, "Sense of community is a feeling that members have of belonging, a feeling that members matter to one another and to the group, and a shared faith that member' needs will be met through their commitment to be together (McMillian 1976 in McMillan & Chavis, 1986, p. 9)." In a sense it is this "shared faith" that encourages me to share my story with others—because the answer to the earlier question is, yes; yes, many people outside this community still consider me a stoner because I am a medical cannabis patient.

Hathaway, et al elucidates, "The use of cannabis…no longer designates a sub-group with a distinct ideology or pattern of behavior" (Hammersley 2005, Hathaway, 2004 in Hathaway et al., 2011, p. 454), but instead, "its use is but one aspect of a person's daily life, rather than the focus of his or her biography (Hathaway et al., 2011, p. 454)." As cannabis has become more normalized in mainstream culture "there are signs of a convergence between how users view themselves and how they are identified by others (Hammersley in Hathaway et al., 2011, p. 454). Cannabis use by patients need not be one's "master status" (Gee, 2001, p. 99), as my own story demonstrates, but all medical cannabis patients are aware that its use, "evokes a deeply-rooted sense of cultural anxiety for many," including many young mothers, who fear knowledge of their use will cause others to consider cannabis usage as their 'core identity' (Becker, 1963 in Hathaway et al., 2011, p. 454).

The fact that my children are all adults, and supportive of me becoming a cannabis patient, was central to my decision to speak publically about my past and current cannabis use and cannabis patient status. When I was raising my family in Oklahoma and Texas, I spent many years fearing that my children might be removed from our home if my cannabis use was discovered. Although I am no longer plagued by this particular fear, I have spoken with many patients—particularly mothers—who are still quite fearful that their use of cannabis as medication will result in a similar fate. Patients only have a small modicum of legal protection given that cannabis remains illegal on the federal level—and patients in states without medical cannabis legislation have no protection at all. Certainly, this remains a valid fear for patients who are parents of minor children.

MY STORY

California became the first state to decriminalize cannabis for medicinal use in 1996, since then fifteen additional states and the District of Columbia have followed suit and nearly a dozen others are considering similar legislation. Yet, to date scholarly research has failed to consider 'who' an adult medical cannabis patient is and fewer consider either the social identity or the narrative of the medical cannabis patient. In fact, there is surprisingly little research regarding the use of medical cannabis by patients or the social stigma experienced by medical cannabis patients. The majority of research on cannabis or cannabis use primarily focuses on its use among adolescents and youthful members of our society. Because media representations also focus heavily on cannabis usage in these age groups (under the age of 25), few understand or recognize responsible adult usage of cannabis, much less its use as medication. For this reason, to explore the effects of our dominant narrative on patients and how the performative acts of using cannabis as a patient are disrupting this narrative, I begin this exploration using my own experience as a medical cannabis patient.

Although I admit being a closet cannabis user for years, my relationship with cannabis changed dramatically just over two years ago. At the time I was not using cannabis "recreationally" or to "self-medicate" as I described earlier, I wasn't using it at all. For several years I had been struggling with chronic pain associated with fibromyalgia and osteoarthritis, as well as several other health issues that compound the pain I experience each day, when I also began to experience a great amount gastric distress, believed to be associated with the prescriptions I was on to manage the symptoms of these two illnesses. With the help of my physician, I managed to wean myself off all prescription drugs—thirteen different prescriptions in all. In a wholly natural state of being, I found myself in only slightly less gastric distress, still dealing with constant nausea and frequently vomiting; in addition, I still needed to relieve the pain in my hips, shoulders, arms, and legs that I contend with on a daily basis. Now mind you, I am not a wimp when it comes to pain, I have experienced several natural childbirths and have recovered from several serious surgeries during my life. In all cases, I avoided pain medication when at all possible simply because I do not like the side-effects and my personal tolerance for pain is rather high.

Opiates and narcotics leave me feeling as if I have no control of self—I am spacey, disassociated, and not able to think effectively at all, more often than not I end up in bed knocked out, unable to perform my life because pain medication makes it impossible for me to act. The long-term physical side-effects of prescribed pain-relief medications were far worse than the loss of control. In fact, my physician believes the gastric pain I continue to suffer from on a daily basis is 'permanent damage' related to the prescription treatments I endured seeking relief from pain. If the average life span for a woman in America is age 82 (www.census.gov) that means I can expect to spend the next 34 years battling unrelenting nausea and probable vomiting on a daily basis. Given this expectation, cannabis, which provides almost immediate relief from these symptoms, is a great option for me—and certainly, the fact it does not have toxic or physically harmful side-effects (Grinspoon & Bakalar, 1997; Holland, 2010) is an advantage.

In addition, to the suffering I have already mentioned, during this time I was also beginning to experience para-menopausal symptoms, including hot flashes and insomnia. In short, for well over a year I couldn't eat (I lost 30 lbs. off an already thin frame) and I couldn't sleep (I was lucky to sleep intermittently for a total of two or three hours sleep every 24-36 hours). Instead, I spent nearly every night roaming the halls of my home in pain, praying for sleep and relief, and wishing the nausea would subside long enough I could at least eat a couple of crackers (little nutritional value but it was all I could keep down, sometimes days at a time). I was miserable and quite honestly I was sick and tired of being sick and tired.

It was late one pain-filled night when I began to reminisce about how much better cannabis made me feel when I began to wonder, would it work? Would cannabis work as medicine for me? It seemed reasonable to believe it would help the nausea and vomiting, but could it also help with the constant pain in my joints and limbs? I began to investigate online—academic and medical research, books, and patient and caregiver blogs, anything I could get my hands on. It did not take long for me to determine I should give it a try, but there was one huge obstacle to this plan: I was living in Texas, and I am confident that long before a medical cannabis initiative passes Texas' State Legislature or a proposition is passed by the voting public in this conservative State our federal government may finally address this issue and provide cannabis with a national solution. Perhaps, I am mistaken in this view, but in meeting with congressional leaders in Texas, my hopes that medical cannabis legislation could be enacted were sorely dashed—repeatedly and without remorse.

Regardless, the use of cannabis as medication was

against both state and federal law, plus I had no access—no trusted friend I could purchase cannabis from—I was perplexed but determined. A few months later, I moved to New Mexico, near my oldest daughter and three of my six grandchildren. Just weeks after moving here, I had emergency surgery that doctors suspected would remedy the gastric issues I had been suffering from for more than two years. Although, overall my health improved following the surgery, daily nausea and stomach pain persists and makes it quite difficult for me to gain back the weight I lost. In early 2012, with my physician's approval, but not her recommendation (she is prohibited from recommending cannabis to patients by the healthcare organization for which she is employed—a rather common occurrence), I took my medical records to a "pot-doctor" seeking a recommendation for a 'state license.' Later that day, I mailed the completed application and coveted "recommendation" and five weeks later, I became a state licensed medical cannabis patient under the "Lynn and Erin Compassionate Care Act" in New Mexico for the approved condition of "intractable nausea and vomiting" (New Mexico Department of Health Cannabis Program).

Becoming a medical cannabis patient has significantly changed my life and in a very short amount of time. When I first considered applying for my "patient license" (Medical Cannabis Card) I had a couple of important, personal reasons for doing so. First, I was suffering, unable to live a "normal" life. I knew from prior experience with cannabis that the "high" alone would provide a sense of well-being, but I was not sure how well cannabis would control my medical symptoms: persistent nausea, vomiting, and pain throughout my body. Based on the harmful side-effects I was experiencing through conventional medical treatment, I believed that trying cannabis, as medication couldn't hurt. I wasn't sure it would help, but from my experience using cannabis I was confident it wouldn't hurt.

Second, I wanted access to "experts" those with

experience in this field: medical cannabis providers, dispensary personnel ("bud-tenders"), and other patients. Without a patient license, in a state that recognizes the necessity of medical cannabis programs through public policy, access to these resources is simply unavailable. These experts are as necessary to a patient like me, as any physician, pharmacist, or support group member are to any other chronically or seriously ill patient, perhaps even more so because so few exist and most conventional medical providers have little knowledge to share about this particular medical choice. Further, as mentioned in relation to my own physician, many medical providers are either unable or unwilling to provide a recommendation for a patient's medical cannabis license. In fact, in Albuquerque, where I am a patient, the two largest healthcare organizations that provide care for a majority of our city and counties residents, forbid medical providers from providing cannabis program recommendations. Additionally, even medical professionals who may be willing to provide a recommendation do not because they are either uneducated about cannabis as medication or they are morally opposed.

In my opinion, this disconnect between traditional medical providers and cannabis patients is vast and it causes further suffering for many patients who must navigate these obstacles, including gather extensive medical records to "prove" their health condition qualifies them as a medical cannabis patient. This is made even more difficult for those who are unable to afford a "pot-doctor" recommendation when their own physician is unable to assist them. Like me, most patients only approach their physician about a cannabis recommendation after all other options have been exhausted and the patient has educated him or herself, usually via the internet. It is for this reason, my experience and success as a cannabis patient can be largely attributed to cannabis experts. Their openness and willingness to share their stories with me, so that I could gain knowledge and learn how to properly medicate myself with this controversial medication has been indispensable. For, even with my doctor's support in my decision to become a patient, she had little personal or professional knowledge about its use, so even had she been able to provide a recommendation her advice was to see a medical provider who was more knowledgeable about this particularly medical therapy.

As I consider "why" I chose to become a cannabis patient, my reasons center on self, family, and society. As someone tired of suffering I came to a place where it was important to put *self* first, to care *about* myself and to care *for* myself—to take control of my medical needs and experiment with a safer option (Tronto, 1989). When one discusses the "ethic of care" most often it is in relation to *others* we care about, but as Tronto discusses caring "for" and caring "about" one can see that this theory also applies to self. As espoused by Tronto, *caring about* refers "to less concrete objects: it is characterized by a more general form of commitment;" while *caring for* implies "a specific, particular object that is the focus of caring (Tronto, 1989, p. 103)." In this sense, I care about medical cannabis legislation on a federal level, because I care for myself, and am concerned about my own health issues. As a cannabis patient, I also care for other patients, those who also find relief using cannabis, and those who may find this medication a viable option in the future, including my own children and grandchildren. If in sharing my own story, I can encourage other patients to do the same, perhaps our collective voices will be heard and future generations will not be required to fight this same battle. Perhaps, future generations will not feel the impact of stigmatization for choosing cannabis-based medications, in 'caring for' myself, I also "care for" others.

From the standpoint of family, my health issues negatively impacted my relationships with my children, grandchildren, and parents. Having always been active and responsive to my ever-expanding family, I found myself isolated and depressed as I fought I regain some measure of health. In becoming a cannabis patient and experiencing relief from the symptoms that separated me from my family, I have begun living my life again; my relationships with my family have improved exponentially as my health has recovered. I am ready and able to get out of bed each morning, I can play in the park with my grandchildren with minimal pain, I can take evening walks with my parents when they visit, and I can enjoy each day, because I am no longer focused on managing my pain and nausea. I have control of my life again. In addition, because I have managed to gain back 10 of the 30+ pounds I lost, I now have more energy and stamina than I had just a few months ago. The change in my health significantly improved the relationships I have with my family.

Additionally, as a mother and grandmother, I *care for* my family, and this caring is partially manifested in my desire to support the medical cannabis movement and help change the way cannabis patients are viewed in our society. As a scholar, clinical research regarding the body's own endocannabinoid system that supports the use of cannabis to manage the symptoms of patients, or perhaps even provide effective treatment for some serious illnesses was critical to my decision to become a medical cannabis patient. Although, cannabis currently remains an illicit drug in our country, its value, as medication cannot be easily dismissed. Studies show cannabis to be helpful in relieving symptoms associated with a variety of serious and chronic illnesses such as cancer (Baker, Pryce, Giovannoni, & Thompson, 2003), Multiple Sclerosis (MS) (Baker et al., 2003; (Pryce & Baker, 2005), Post-Traumatic Stress Disorder (PTSD) (Ganon-Elazar & Akiraz, 2012), depression (Blass, 2008); neuropathic pain issues (Ellis, 2008), as well as many others. It is not far-fetched to estimate that a majority of U.S. citizens do not understand cannabis' use as medication or its effectiveness in so many medical situations. Even as an educated woman and cannabis patient, I have trouble understanding how cannabis works for so many serious health conditions, which is why it is important to interact with experts, who help increase my knowledge and understanding. However, instead of considering the issue as one of public health, which supports the rights of patients who medicate with cannabis and embraces an ethic of care, the dominant narrative simply reiterates a discourse which explicitly asserts, "all illicit drugs are bad" without considering the efficacy of this particular plant's medicinal value. For this reason, it is important that cannabis patients share their stories. As a parent and grandparent, I do not want those I love the most to experience the marginalization I currently experience as a patient who uses cannabis-based medication.

As a cannabis patient I am aware that authoritative and powerful others categorize and stigmatize cannabis use, nowhere is this more obvious that within the dominant discourse that surrounds the use of cannabis as medication. The stigmatizing power of this societal discourse is consequential to the social narratives and identities of patients like me. Although medical cannabis patient is not my "master identity (Gee, 2001, p. 99)," I do identify as a medical cannabis patient and am attuned to society's narratives regarding patients. I have often heard patients mythologized in the dominant discourse as "just people who want to get high." This dominant perception makes each patient at least a bit self-conscious about the use of cannabis as medication and frequently causes patients to conceal use from others, although the degrees to which we experience this marginalization varies significantly, based on each patient's personal experiences and their perceptions of how others view them as cannabis patients.

Although recent polls state that 50% of Americans support legalizing cannabis and over 70% support legalizing cannabis for medicinal purposes (Newport, 2011; Mendes, 2010), the distance between the narratives of patients, like me, and those who oppose medicinal cannabis are vast and the dominant societal narrative remains steadfastly opposed. The amount of cannabis "used," the "quality" of the product, as well as how it is consumed, often is at the center of public discussions on cannabis as medication. Consistently media and public leadership has maintained that if patients are allowed to use cannabis as medication little good can come from "smoked" or "illicit" drugs. Perhaps, just the thought of patients "getting high" is unacceptable to many, and it is the most controversial aspect of this medication. Yet, like many other patients, I embrace the "sense of well-being" cannabis often provides.

I've heard many medical cannabis supporters jest that if cannabis were put in pill form fewer people would react adversely to it as medication. Studies find, however, that when compared to Marinol, a synthetic THC pharmaceutical product in pill form, patients find smoked cannabis a better alternative for nausea, vomiting, and pain control (Musty & Rossi, 2001). Additionally, patients, like myself, who experience pain on a continuous basis often "find the high pleasurable," because this particular side-effect provides a "sense of relief" that pharmaceutical pain relievers do not. When a person struggles each day with pain or nausea they are exhausted simply from trying to "be," for me, cannabis allows me to let go of the pain and truly just "be." In my personal opinion, this type of relief is as necessary as relief from the actual pain or nausea. Perhaps, efforts to package cannabis in forces like capsules or transdermal patches will help its overall acceptance back into Western medicine. However, as a patient, I want access to whole plant options as well, like I do now—and I want to choices to include both non-active and psychoactive options, because I do not want to fully lose the sense of relief cannabis provides. Further, I believe this is a fairly common perspective among cannabis patients, but research in this area would help determine how significant this belief is among patients.

My performative act of using cannabis has also changed a great deal simply due to the newfound access I have as a patient. As the medical cannabis industry grows, patients like me have been afforded options that include non-psychoactive forms for cannabis to treat illnesses and pain-related symptoms. In fact, "juicing" cannabis has become quite popular among patients with Lupus, Rheumatoid Arthritis, and other painful, chronic health conditions (Dr. William Courtney, 2012). Patients also are gaining access to "alternative delivery systems" such as vaporizers, edible products, oils, tinctures, and salves. Many of these alternatives, oils and salves more specifically, can be produced through an infusion process that does not heat the cannabis, which means the psychoactive properties of the THC are not activated, thus the patient does not experience psychoactive side-effects. Assuming roles that are usually performed by pharmacists or even pharmaceutical researchers, patients are finding ways to measure dosages via edible products and consume cannabis in ways far more ingenious than smoking. Just last week a hospice nurse shared with me that she makes suppositories for cannabis patients in her care, because most would be unable to swallow an edible product and none, of course, should be smoking. But, a cannabis suppository? Surely, that is a novel idea born from care and compassion.

Since becoming a patient I have learned through experimentation that vaporizing instead of smoking cannabis is not only a healthier alternative, but for me, it also provides additional relief through pain control. Vaporizing heats the cannabis to the point that the plant evaporates instead of combusting as it does when smoked and patients inhale a mist or vapor instead of smoke. A recent study showed cannabis smoking has *far fewer* negative effects than tobacco smoking (Pletcher et al., 2012); and vaporizing is safer alternative for seriously ill patients. Through vaporizing, I experience a greater 'body-effect' from the medication. In other words, when I vaporize the aches, pains I experience deep within my joints are relieved more effectively, and for longer than if I smoke the cannabis. Just a few months ago I did not understand that a change in the delivery method would change the way the medication works for me. This new information is empowering, even if it is a bit confusing.

When I became a patient I began keeping a journal of the various strain of cannabis I tried and the pros and cons each offered in way of symptom relief—some are more effective at treating nausea, others appetite, and still others, pain or insomnia. Most days, vaporizing twice during the day with a high *sativa* strain, once in the morning and once in the evening, helps me manage my pain successfully for the entire day. I vaporize once more late in the evening, an hour or two before bed, with a high *indica* strain which induces far more relaxation, but which is more difficult to function on during the day when I am required to work—it simply makes me sleepy. There is not the space to explore types or strains of cannabis-based medications in this paper, but local experts in the medical cannabis community are happy to help new patients like me learn how this medication can work best for symptom management.

As pleased as I am with the relief I experience using a vaporizer, some days I experience increased pain or nausea which I've found can be more readily controlled by smoking cannabis. For smoking, I prefer a glass pipe, but any smoking method works equally well. Typically, two or three inhalations of cannabis will intervene and remedy the increased nausea or pain; infrequently I need just a bit more. All in all, I use less than one (1) joint or one (1) gram of cannabis a day through vaporizing and smoking, frequently half that amount. Rarely, except late in the evening when I increase my medication and change strains to facilitate sleep, do I ever feel high, but the sense of well-being I experience always presents itself and provides me with relief. My mind remains clear, I am able to respond proactively to daily interactions and tasks, as well as go about my day in a normal fashion.

I have arrived at this steady daily dosage by adding other cannabis products to my healthcare supply. In experimenting with alternative delivery methods, I have found that a small edible product, like a cookie or a cracker, an hour before I am ready to go to bed helps me sleep like a baby. I believe that the ability to sleep well each night has probably had the most significant impact on my overall health. Once I was again well-rested on a regular basis and not roaming my halls in search of sleep, not only was I better able to cope with my health issues, my quality of life improved enormously. Constant exhaustion and lack of sleep negatively impact one's ability to heal, to process thoughts, engage with others, or live a normal life.

The equivalent of one (1) teaspoon (tsp) of canna-oil, half a small cookie, or a handful of medicated granola or popcorn helps me fall asleep and allows me to sleep well throughout the night, plus I wake up feeling refreshed and ready for a new day. Nearly two dozen pharmaceutical sleep-aids failed to provide a similar result and each had unique side-effects that often made it hard for me to function well even after a night's sleep.

The final products that I have added to my daily healthcare routine are salves or topical products. The pain in my joints and limbs is deep and often the muscles in the surrounding area become knotted exacerbating the pain I experience. Over the years, I've tried nearly every over-the-counter muscle pain relief topical remedy with little success. About a month ago, I was given a sample of a cannabis salve that has multiple purposes (moisturizer, antibacterial, etc.) that I use as a topical pain reliever. When I used the salve for the first time my right neck and shoulder were excruciatingly painful and I could not raise my arm above my head. Honestly, I had little hope that a topical remedy would do much for my neck or shoulder, which were both throbbing as I rubbed on the salve. Much to my surprise, thirty-minutes later my neck and shoulder felt much better, I was not out of pain, but the pain had been reduced from a 7 to a 2, on a typical 1-10 scale physicians use to gage a patient's pain control need. In using this product for two weeks, I cannot imagine my life without it. Each morning and as needed throughout the day, I use a homemade cannabis salve on the areas of my body where I experience the most pain. What

I've found is that my pain used to rise to a 7 or 8 each day, now I rarely exceed a 5. As I continue to learn about these products and experiment with them I am hopeful the pain level will continue to diminish.

Shamir et al elucidate, "Narratives are not records of facts, of how things actually are, but of a meaning-making system that makes sense out of the chaotic mass of perceptions and experiences of a life (Josselson, 1993 in Shamir et al 17). My story may not be factual, but it is true based on my own perceptions as a past cannabis user and a current medical cannabis patient. As a closeted cannabis user I ignored and concealed my use because I was fearful of social and professional stigmatization. Now as a medical cannabis patient and advocate I must highlight "certain parts" of my history that I have until recently kept hidden away (Shamir et al, 17). This shift in how I present myself to others is both frightening and freeing. It is frightening because I must engage with others by sharing an innermost secret, but it is freeing because I share that secret with others—and within this community I am fully accepted. It is not unusual for state recognized patients, to be fearful about sharing information about their cannabis use. Hathaway found that "open use and openness about one's use is guarded to avoid the threat of sanctions from authorities, or loss of status, or offending non-users who may disapprove (Hathaway, 2011, p. 453)." After concealing their cannabis use, sometimes for many years, some patients have become accustomed to hiding this part of their identity from others, certainly I engaged in this type of concealment for many years. Patients are frightened of changing this behavior and acknowledging their use of cannabis, for they fear stigmatization and scorn from others. Although patients do not all experience stigmatization the same, each has stories of differing degrees of stigmatization that they have experienced, but each has experienced stigmatization and copes with it in their own way. Future research that demonstrates the effects of stigmatization and explores how patients cope with it are warranted.

Although I do not always find acceptance as a cannabis patient outside of medical cannabis community, I have come to realize that in facing the stigmatizing narrative of others, I become stronger and more resolute about sharing my story. Shamir et al acknowledge that, "we know or discover ourselves, and reveal ourselves to others, by the stories we tell about ourselves (Lieblich et al, 1998: 70 in Shamir et al 17)." In sharing my story, I have developed a stronger identification with this movement and a sense of community with fellow patients, which increases my resolve to share my story, to find ways to help others share their stories, and to help other patient embrace rather than conceal their cannabis patient status for it is at least a small part of their identity, perhaps like me, more than they realize.

Note: I'd like to say again how freeing this piece was for me to write and most importantly share! The feedback from my peers, family, friends, and instructor was invaluable! Like all of us, I have many stories and many more to share but rarely do I share the personal, the very personal—this has been enlightening, increased my self-awareness, and helped me understand the significance of not just hearing an impacting story, but in sharing one. Now as more and more cannabis patients share their stories with me I realize the capacity for leadership within this movement and within our society—it is enormous! But, we must let the people speak, and we must listen so that we may understand. Thank you for listening to my ramblings, they pale in comparison to so many stories I've heard, but they're significant to me. Please share your story, no matter what it may be with others, for it will be significant to someone else!

And, if you have time visit the Cannabis Patient Network YouTube Channel and view some of the videos CPNI Co-Founder, Mark Pedersen has collected over the years—A

National Archive of Patient Stories—the first stories I heard from others online, a reason I knew the path I was on was important!

Perceptions of the Dominant Public Discourse as Experienced By Female Medical Cannabis Patients
May 2012

This paper represents my first research project as a Ph.D. student. The women who participated have become my friends and their words express the concern, fear, and understanding that many women experience as cannabis patients; certainly their stories often mirrored my own. In the years since I've spoken with hundreds more women—these days many, many mothers—and still the stories remind me there is much more research to be done here and many more stories to share!

Dr. Jennifer Raymond became my hero during this term, helping me make order out of the chaos that was rumbling around my mind. She was able to take my third term rants and ramblings and help me turn them into tidy little questions that directed my path. It's really too bad she can't do that for me on a daily basis, and with my private life—she's quick and concise, I am not...at least not the concise part.

Abstract:

The purpose of this paper is to consider the concerns of medical cannabis patients related to stigmatization involving the use of medical cannabis in the hope of gaining a better understanding of how stigmatization may affect individual patients. Specifically, this project uses a phenomenological approach and qualitative methods to make problematic the standpoint of female medical cannabis patients, seeking to understand why women choose to be recognized as medical cannabis patients (what are their reasons for obtaining a medical cannabis license/card) and the associated fears of stigmatization that accompany this decision, as shown through their personal narratives. The most prominent themes to emerge centered on *Self*: personal health and necessary resources to use cannabis as medication; *Career*: fear of status or job loss; *Family*: familial acceptance and/or stigmatization; and *Society*: addressing the dominant perception that the use of cannabis is incompatible with the roles and responsibilities of female patients.

Although California became the first state to decriminalize cannabis or marijuana (terms used interchangeably throughout this report) for medicinal use in 1996, fifteen additional states and the District of Columbia have followed suit over the last decade—and nearly a dozen other states are currently considering "compassionate care" or "medical cannabis" legislation. Yet, few studies consider 'who' a medical cannabis patient is and fewer still have considered the social identity or narrative of the medical cannabis patient or the stigma with which they must contend. Although some medical cannabis patients may not see the use of cannabis as particularly significant to their social identity, their awareness that authoritative others categorize and stigmatize cannabis use is consequential to their social narrative and identity.

Unlike the 'war on drugs' stance the federal government maintains, many states are normalizing cannabis for medical use through "compassionate care" legislation, such as New Mexico's *Lynn and Erin Compassionate Use Act*. Public policies such as this one encourage citizens—fellow human beings—to regard medical cannabis patients as an integral part of the larger community, individuals who must be protected, not prosecuted or otherwise excluded from the community due to their use of cannabis as medication. In much the same way "care theories" espoused by Carol Gilligan, Joan Tronto, Marsha Nussbaum, and other prominent theorists suggest that "compassion" is the key for societal issues to be viewed from a "care perspective" rather than strictly a "justice perspective" (Gilligan, 1987, p. 49). This means that when we consider the use of cannabis we must consider it as valid medication, not just an illicit drug; we are required to view the issue with compassion and consider the needs of patients, not simply the laws that govern our justice system. Gilligan elucidates, when considering a care perspective, the conflict between self and others recedes and places "the self as moral agent" able to perceive and respond "to the perception of need" (Gilligan, 35). However, the challenge of transferring power to people who are living in a vulnerable condition, like medical cannabis patients, can only be possible if society perceives them as competent instead of deviant. The dominant cultural discourse, stigmatizes patients and blocks federal consideration for the medical utilization of cannabis, obstructs the transfer of power to medical cannabis patients by labeling them deviant, and must be examined in relation to how this narrative stigmatizes patients.

Stereotypes persist around the dominant narrative that associates cannabis use with criminality and deviance. In reality, other than the crime of using and accessing cannabis itself, the majority of adult cannabis users deny they engage in criminal behavior or use other illicit drugs (Hathaway, Comeau, & Erickson, 2011, p. 463; www.norml.org) Nonetheless, cannabis patients, like other cannabis users, "contend with prejudicial labels and reefer madness sentiments that culturally endure (Hathaway et al., 2011, p. 463)." Medical cannabis patients are not only aware their behavior and beliefs related to cannabis use lie outside the dominant societal discourse, but the dominant societal discourse also is deeply embedded in their own narratives, even those that are disrupting the dominant conversation about cannabis use. This study argues that cannabis patients disrupt this narrative when they share their stories and begins by considering why women chose to become State-recognized cannabis patients. Although many patients conceal their status as a cannabis patient to avoid stigmatization, others appear to be open to sharing their alternative story in an attempt to change these stereotypes and remove the stigma associated with cannabis's use as medication.

Studies have shown adult cannabis "users self-regulate and censure from a multi-layered perspective, employing frames of reference from sub-culture and lifestyle and mainstream constructions of" cannabis use (Hathaway et al., 2011, p. 463). Further, dominant cultural "practices of moral regulation are related to both the transformation and intransigence of stigma in the everyday experience of cannabis users (Hathaway et al., 2011, p. 463)." Certainly the illicit status of cannabis, which remains illegal on the federal level and in many states, influences non-user perceptions about those who use cannabis as medication.

It is unlikely 'medicalization' of cannabis will transform the social stigma associated with its use in the short-term. Until a citizen has a need to consider medical cannabis as a treatment for oneself or a loved one, one may have little to no knowledge or understanding about the medical efficacy of marijuana, much less how it should be used by the patient. Although cannabis currently remains an illicit drug, its value, as medication cannot be so easily dismissed. Studies have shown cannabis to be helpful in relieving symptoms associated with a variety of serious and chronic illnesses such as cancer (Baker, Pryce, Giovannoni, & Thompson, 2003), MS (Baker et al., 2003; Pryce & Baker, 2005), PTSD (cite), depression (Blass, 2008); neuropathic pain issues (Ellis, 2008), as well as many others. It is not far-fetched to estimate that a majority of U.S. citizens do not understand cannabis' use as medication or its effectiveness in so many medical situations. Instead of considering the issue as one of public health, which supports the rights of patients who medicate with cannabis and embraces an ethic of care, some simply reiterate the dominant national discourse which explicitly asserts, "all illicit drugs are bad" without considering the efficacy of this particular plant's medicinal value or the fact that every human being has an endocannabinoid system which reacts favorably to the use of cannabis. For this reason, it is important to gain an understanding of how the growing population of medical cannabis patients may be stigmatized or unduly harmed socially by their association and use of cannabis as medication.

The majority of research on cannabis use focuses on its use and abuse among adolescents and youth in our society. Because media representations foster these same stereotypes, few understand or recognize adult usage or more specifically responsible adult usage, much less cannabis's application as medication. For this discussion it is important to remember that not everyone misuses drugs like cannabis, in fact, cannabis use may be one of the best examples of a drug that can be easily distinguished by users as falling between use and misuse based on their pattern of usage and perceptions of 'normal' (non-abusive use) within their community (Hathaway, 2004; Hathaway et al., 2011; Pederson, 2009). Regardless, at this particular time in our history, cannabis cannot be considered simply an illicit drug of choice; it must be reconsidered as medication—and medication that is not any more abused than other medications (either over-the-counter or pharmaceutical) in our society.

Certainly, medical cannabis patients consider their use of cannabis normal and non-abusive; further, as a growing population of cannabis users are recognized as patients within the state they reside, it behooves us to take a look at this population. After all these are the citizens disrupting the argument between those 'for' and those 'against' the "legalization" of cannabis for responsible adult "recreational" usage and make us reconsider cannabis as "medication" instead of "weed" and users as "patients" instead of "pot-heads;" certainly their stories are important to this discussion.

As a starting place to understanding how medical cannabis patients understand and identify themselves, we must consider 'who *are* medical cannabis patients'. In my observation and not differently from the few studies on adult cannabis users, medical cannabis patients are likely to be located, "with lesser or greater degrees of social visibility, all over the map" of actors and institutions (Hathaway et al., 2011; Pederson, 2009; Smucker Barnwell et al., 2006). State demographics suggest that most are male and over the age of 40, (www.norml.org; ASA, MPP) but within New Mexico's medical cannabis community, one can observe patients that fit all demographics, young/old, male/female with varying ethnicity and social class.

Just recently I assisted with a traveling medical cannabis clinic. In observing the patients that attended this particular clinic one would have a hard time distinguishing them from patients in any other doctor's office. Most were over the age of 50, with a significant portion over the age of 60; at least half were women, and the ethnicity of the patients varied widely (Caucasian, Black, Hispanic, and Native American similar to the demographics of the state). Several brought young children with them to their appointment and other older patients sat with children or grandchildren who provided assistance and moral support. Not one conformed to dominant stereotypes of a cannabis user—all were seemingly non-deviant, ordinary citizens. However, in conversation all expressed some concern about stigmatization from others—those outside the medical cannabis community, who may marginalize them based on their choice to medicate with cannabis. For this reason, many chose to hide their patient status from others, even while affording themselves the 'quasi-legal' protection this status holds for patients. This study will explore what motivates individuals to become a medical cannabis patient and the stigmatization they encounter because they're cannabis patients.

Objectives

- This study explores the standpoint of female medical cannabis patients seeking to understand why women choose to be recognized as medical cannabis patients by the state (what are their reasons for obtaining a medical cannabis license/card).

- This study examines whether these same patients are open about their use of cannabis as medication or if they conceal their use from some or all others in their life due to fear of stigmatization, and if so, why.

Literature Review

Hathaway, et al (2011) build upon Sociologist Erving Goffman's theoretical distinction between 'normalization' and 'normification' to interpret "extra-legal forms of stigma" experienced by 'regular' (daily) adult recreational cannabis users in Toronto. Although this study included a few medical cannabis patients, the patients were not recruited as the primary population of interest, instead because the researchers sought after "regular" (daily) adult cannabis users, their study came to contain several medical cannabis patients. Regardless, study is one of very few that provides an insight into the social stigma attached to cannabis users and substantiates what many medical cannabis patients mention during my observations and discussions. The authors' state, "Being a 'normal person', when thinking of ourselves, means incorporating standards from wider society and meeting others' expectations about what we ought to be. The concept of stigma is therein a device that ensures the reliability of the interaction order by punishing people who do not confirm to moral standards" (Hathaway et al., 2011, p. 455). The dominant narrative, provided through media and public leadership, frequently infers that medical cannabis patients, because they are cannabis users, do not conform to our society's moral standards. Further, the medication they use is an illegal drug, practice of its use is outside normal Western medical practices, and how it is used differs greatly from other medications.

Goffman suggests personal identity "resides within the cracks" (Goffman in Hathaway et al., 2011, p. 455); therefore, one's ability to perform in a given situation as normal or ordinary is not the same as normalizing the stigmatized behavior. For cannabis patients, being seen as normal only within the medical cannabis community is not acceptable, they would like to be viewed 'normal' in the way that Goffman describes "full normalization," requiring "that others be accepting of the stigmatized individual and the treatment of such persons as if they have no stigma" (Goffman in Hathaway et al., 2011, p. 465). If we are to develop ways to address the social stigma experienced by medical cannabis patients we must first understand the roots of the stigma producing discourse, as well we must have an understanding of how the patients' narrative offers an alternative way to consider cannabis use, and therefore, patients. Inquiring about the stigma experienced by cannabis patients is a start on a path of understanding how the meaning dominant cultural stereotypes and stigma shape their lived experience.

When probed about the 'disadvantages of using cannabis' participants in the Hathaway et al study frequently spoke of stigma as an 'informal' source of control (Goffman in Hathaway et al., 2011, p. 456). Almost seventy (70) percent of respondents said they hid their use from someone, typically family, co-workers, or unknown suspected non-users; most did so to avoid "conflict or loss of status," as well as remain "discrete" about their usage, but a third of these participants also reported "past encounters with non-users resulting in some status loss or social disapproval" (Hathaway et al., 2011, p. 456). The researchers found that, "while 'reefer madness' attitudes were typically rejected, in favour of more nuanced understandings of the practice, other mainstream sentiments were tacitly accepted or echoed," in participant responses (Hathaway et al., 2011, p. 457). In short, like the cannabis users participating in this study, cannabis patients avoid encountering cultural stereotypes and stigmatization by evading the use of cannabis or discussion of use with those they believe will condemn their actions or them personally. A better understanding of 'concealment' including from 'who' patients hide, 'why' they conceal their patient status or use, and 'what' stigmatization they most fear may help us understand how stigmatization marginalizes cannabis patients.

Studies suggest patients offer excuses to satisfy the dominant narrative that presumes the use of cannabis—even for medical reasons—is incompatible with conventional responsibilities and roles (family and work). The conflict between cannabis use and role expectations is especially apparent in the narratives of parents. Parents who engage in cannabis use, even as patients, may "reflect paternalistic and moral obligations that are assumed in mainstream perceptions of the practice" (Hathaway et al., 2011, p. 461). In fact, "cultural assumptions about gender roles were strongly evident in narratives of mothers in particular" (Hathaway et al., 2011, p. 461). Studies indicate that for adult cannabis users "being single with no children" may be "associated with increased cannabis use" and "while there were no gender-based differences in prevalence during the adolescence years, when the respondents were approaching 30 years of age, men had twice the rate of current cannabis use" suggesting that women, especially young mothers, choose not to consume cannabis during their 'parenting years' or moderate and conceal their use in order to avoid stigmatization (Pederson, 2009, p. 146). Interestingly, both the Hathaway et al and Pederson studies found parents who smoke cannabis recreationally still feel obliged to respond punitively to similar behavior in their children, family members, or community members in order to maintain a particular social identity without a loss of status (Hathaway et al., 2011; Pederson, 2009). These findings suggest that in asking medical cannabis patients if they conceal their use from others and why they do so, if in fact they do, may provide insight into the consequences of stigma produced by dominant cultural narratives as they are experienced by cannabis patients.

Sociolinguist James Paul Gee states, "When any human being acts and interacts in a given context, others recognize that person as acting and interacting as a certain "kind of person" or even as several different "kinds" at once" (Gee, 2001, p. 99). In this sense, though medical cannabis patients may not consider themselves 'stoners' they are often labeled as so by others in the context of using cannabis regardless of its medical efficacy. The performative act of using cannabis itself is central to arguments "for" and "against" cannabis as medication and this "personal narration" occurs in the everyday life of cannabis patients (Ochberg, p. 114). So the question has become, how will cannabis patients be viewed in our dominant culture given that many medicate with cannabis by alternate means than smoking? For instance, is a 72-year old great-grandmother who uses a cannabis tincture in her tea considered a stoner in our society? How about a 45-year old professional who medicates with cannabis oil on her salad during her lunch break each day? Are patients who resemble these examples still considered deviant in our society? Certainly a majority of cannabis patients who medicate express some concern that others know whether or not they *use* cannabis as medication. In fact, many may in fact choose to conceal their usage in order to avoid being labeled as a deviant person—a cannabis user. However, if a patient's "core identity" (Gee, 2001, p. 99) is other than "cannabis user," and for a majority of patients this is the case, one may have little trouble concealing this small part of her identity.

Hathaway, et al elucidates, "The use of cannabis...no longer designates a sub-group with a distinct ideology or pattern of behavior (Hammersley 2005; Hathaway, 1997 in Hathaway et al., 2011), but instead "its use is but one aspect of a person's daily life, rather than the focus of his or her biography (Hathaway et al., 2011, p. 454)." As cannabis has become more 'normalized' in mainstream culture "there are signs of a convergence between how users view themselves and how they are identified by others" (Hammersley in Hathaway et al., 2011, p. 454). Cannabis use by patients need not be one's "master status" as shown in the example of the great-grandmother but all medical cannabis patients are aware that using cannabis, even for medicinal purposes, "evokes a deeply-rooted sense of cultural anxiety for many," who fear knowledge of their use will cause others to consider cannabis usage as their 'core identity' (Becker, 1963 in Hathaway et al., 2011, p. 454). Further, until it is recognized that a large number of patients share similar stories and fears, patients will continue to be marginalized for choosing cannabis as medication against dominant cultural expectations.

In contrast to our society's expectation that one be *productive* is the myth that cannabis users are amotivational. Smucker, et al address the dominant cultural narrative that describes cannabis users as "listless and incapable," demonstrating low motivation, an apathetic approach to life, and poor academic or work performance (Smucker Barnwell et al., 2006, p. 1). These researchers found that "the daily use of cannabis does not impair motivation" and that productivity is "less of a concern" for adult users "than the internal conflict that cannabis presents to their own professional identity and status (Smucker Barnwell et al., 2006, p. 1)." For this reason, many medical cannabis patients conceal their status as a cannabis patient from their employers, fearing loss of job and social status.

Currently, no state has implemented legislation to protect medical cannabis patients during pre-employment or post-employment drug testing, which places many patients in an arguably marginalized position. Even patients with long, steady employment histories and positive employment reviews fear being perceived as listless, incapable, or apathetic by others, especially those who control their employment status. Certainly, many people demonstrate low motivation even though they do not use cannabis or other drugs. However, as the authors suggest, "In the public eye, the minority of heavy cannabis users who show low motivation represents the majority (Smucker Barnwell et al., 2006, p. 2)."

Interestingly, Smucker et al found that when contrasted with non-cannabis users, "cannabis users were significantly older and earned more money in their work" than non-users. In other words, demographics show cannabis users are mature employees whose success in monetary terms, a dominant cultural indicator of success, suggests amotivation or low productivity is not problematic. This knowledge corresponds with my experience with medical cannabis patients, many of whom are employed or retired and would not be considered amotivational by an impartial observer. This "internal conflict," that some medical cannabis patients may find inconsistent with "their own professional identity and status" (Smucker Barnwell et al., 2006, p. 1), should be explored in future research.

Methods

For this study, a phenomenological approach that provides "meaning and structure of the lived experience" (Remler & Van Ryzin, 2011, p. 61) is an appropriate method for interpreting the phenomenon of stigma in relation to the medical cannabis patient's experience. Phenomenological research allows a researcher "to understand several individuals' common or shared experiences of a phenomenon...in order to develop a deeper understanding about the features of the phenomenon" (Creswell, 2007, p. 60). The goal is to more fully understand the research participant's experience—"how they perceive it, describe it, feel about it, judge it, remember it, make sense of it, and talk about it with others (Patton, 2002, 104 in (Marshall & Rossman, 2011, p. 19). For this class project, I will conduct interviews with two (2) patients, asking open-ended questions regarding their motivation to become and their experiences as a cannabis patient in the State of New Mexico. In order to "bracket out" (Creswell, 2007, p. 61) my own knowledge and experiences regarding this subject matter, I documented my personal experience as a cannabis patient prior to engaging with participants in an interview setting. Both interviews were conducted in a private location to assure participants' confidentiality was maintained. Interviews were recorded and then deleted immediately following transcription. No personal data was included on the transcript of the interview and no personal data linked the participant to her interview.

Since my future research will focus on women in

leadership, within the medical cannabis social movement, a feminist epistemology has been applied as a framework to this project. Creswell states, "Feminist research approaches center and make problematic women's diverse situations and the institutions that frame those situations (Creswell, 2007, p. 25)." This study will center on and make problematic the experience of female medical cannabis patients, in order to find meaning in, and a better understanding of, the stereotypes and stigmatization female cannabis patients' experience. The goal of feminist research theories are to "establish collaborative and nonexploitative relationships, to place the researcher within the study so as to avoid objectification, and to conduct research that is transformative (Creswell, 2007, p. 26, 247)." Gender is not the sole or even most essential category that identifies a person; however, as a female cannabis patient, this scholar believes that female patients have a unique perspective on stigma and stereotypes that permeate our society and that these perspectives should be explored. As the researcher, building a rapport with participants and being willing to share my own story will help avoid objectification and help me to look beyond my own perceptions and understand "the meaning that the participants hold about the problem or issue" (Creswell, 2007, p. 39). Data analysis explores "significant statements" (Creswell, 2007, p. 60) that provide an understanding of how the participants experienced becoming a medical cannabis patient and any stigmatization based on this status.

Data collection consisted of one-on-one interviews with volunteer participants identified as state recognized medical cannabis patients. Because the target population of interest is hidden within society it made sense for this project to use a "convenience sample" (Remler & Van Ryzin, 2011, p. 141). Participants are patients who "volunteered" to be sampled at a local medical cannabis clinic and dispensary, Zia Health and Wellness. Permission from Zia Health and Wellness' owner was acquired prior to sampling. The owner gladly assisted by providing access to the facility and patients, and a private office was designated for the researcher's use, helping preserve participant confidentiality. Sampling this population assured that only state 'licensed' medical cannabis patients were approached and that the patients who chose to participate did so of free will. The sample was "random" in that I recruited only female patients who entered the clinic on the day I was visiting.

Recruitment was not problematic, in all five women were sourced as potential participants. Interviews were conducted with two respondents. Due to the time constraints for conducting interviews and concluding this project in a timely manner (before this paper is due), two participants were selected based solely on our ability to meet at a convenient time within the following week. The women participating in this project have lengthy histories of medical conditions, which to a great degree; I have agreed to keep confidential. In order to qualify as "licensed" medical cannabis patients in the State of New Mexico both suffer from one or more of sixteen (16) serious or chronic health conditions that cannabis has been recognized as being "beneficial...for alleviating symptoms caused by debilitating medical conditions and their medical treatments (www.nmhealth.org)." Although their health conditions are not identical, both participants suffer from chronic pain and each experiences depression. As a researcher, I share a history of chronic pain and depression with these participants, as well as the status as a cannabis patient. Because of these commonalities I was able to establish a rapport quickly with each participant and have in-depth discussions around the identified questions.

Internal Review Board (IRB) consent to participate in research was thoroughly reviewed with each participant prior to their interview ensuring that they fully understood their rights as participants in academic research. Further, participants were not asked to sign the consent to participate until the interview was complete, so that they were fully aware of the interview content, and in agreement that the information they shared with me could be used for this class project. In accordance with an IRB request to explain to participants that I was *not* inquiring about any usage or experience with cannabis *prior to* them becoming medical cannabis patients, during the interview both *insisted* in briefly describing their prior experience with cannabis. Although both admitted to some prior experience with cannabis their experiences, like my own, differed significantly: one had minimal exposure in her teen years but no experience in the two decades since, another admitted to occasional, but certainly not heavy, use that continued into her adult years. Regardless, both thought information regarding their prior use, even use that was limited to a few teenaged experiences, was pertinent to understanding why they chose to become a medical cannabis patient ("My experience told me this was not a harmful drug/Because I had used it before, I knew that it would at least help my depression and mood").

Most medical cannabis patients, like these participants and myself, have some personal experience using cannabis, either as a teenager or even occasional to moderate use as an adult; however, neither of these participants were using cannabis to medicate immediately prior to becoming a patient. Because these women were not using cannabis prior to becoming cannabis patients, they were able to clearly articulate how they believe the medication is helping improve their personal health condition, based on changes in their health since they've become patients. At the conclusion of both interviews, each participant consented to participate in this project, allowing the data from our interview to be included in this body of work.

Each interview followed a standardized interviewing format utilizing guided, open-ended interview questions that allowed participants the room and flexibility to expand on their answers or engage in a deeper discussion about the topic if engrossed.

The primary questions were:

- What was the significance for you in becoming a state recognized medical cannabis patient?
- Do you share your status as a medical cannabis patient with others? If so, what concerns do you have about sharing your status as a medical cannabis patient with others.
- Has becoming a medical cannabis patient changed how you use cannabis or how you conceal your use from others?

As anticipated, these questions allowed for an open discussion between the participants and me, so that together we were able to explore the patient's experience, fears, concerns, and expectations regarding becoming a medical cannabis patient and their fears regarding the stigmas or stereotypes attached to the "role" of medical cannabis patient by dominant societal narratives. To help ensure validity, that participants were fully understood, and that any meaning I interpreted was in fact a correct analysis, this researcher followed-up with each participant less than five (5) days after our interview. Patients viewed a transcript of our interview for correctness, clarifying questions were asked, and participants were asked if they had any additional thoughts to contribute to the project. This data was combined with the transcripts to ensure clarity and understanding during data analysis.

The qualitative data from both interviews was analyzed for "categories and themes" (Marshall & Rossman, 2011, p. 212) that were "clustered" or "subclustered" (Marshall & Rossman, 2011, p. 213) within the participant's narrative. During data collection and analysis, it became increasingly evident that although this was a very small sampling, "salient themes, recurring ideas or language, and patterns of belief" (Marshall & Rossman, 2011, p. 214) would connect between these participants experiences; as well they would connect with my own. For this reason, I devoted a section of my "field notes" to "self-reflections" (Marshall & Rossman, 2011, p. 97) and sought to separate my own thoughts and opinions from those expressed by each participant. Additionally, in order to clearly understand each participant's true meaning, I assured my interviewing model was not strict or inflexible, so that participants could assist in analyzing and interpreting the data (Marshall & Rossman, 2011, p. 162). Frequently during interviews participants were asked, "What specifically did you mean when you said _____?" This tactic helped me separate out my own thoughts and beliefs from those of the patient; as well it helped me focus specifically on the participants' perspectives during the coding process. Using this technique, each participant provided an analysis of their own statements during the interview and follow-up.

For as many similarities as these participants share— both are in their late 30's, mothers of two sons, professionals with long careers in one field, and similar health related issues, it is important to note, they also had differences that are significant to this study. To start, the amount of time these women have been a state recognized cannabis patient varied significantly. One has been a patient for nearly two years; the other became a patient only two months ago. Although both are passionate about their personal experience using cannabis as medication, because of this difference in experience one was far more knowledgeable about its use as medication and had experienced stigmatization more often simply based on her length of experience as a patient. Both participants were also unemployed at the time of their interview "taking time off to recuperate" from their acknowledged health issues. At the time of the interview, the Registered Nurse was returning to work within a few days, after accepting a job offer and passing a pre-employment drug test that required she abstain from using cannabis, even as medication, during her six-month job search. Based on this changing career status and chosen profession, plus, differing levels of family acceptance, these two participants varied significantly in the amount of social stigma they have experienced as patients. Despite these differences, during the coding process, trends began to emerge as the narratives of the patients were compared and contrasted. The most prominent themes to emerge centered on Self, Career, Family, and Society.

Findings & Discussion

SELF

Both participants' narratives demonstrate an awareness in patients of the stigma attached to responsible cannabis usage, even if such usage is primarily for medical purposes ("a history of people not approving of its [cannabis] use,"). This disapproval dominants our cultural narratives and is concerning to these medical cannabis patients. Each participant wanted to address a particularly distressing and stigmatizing narrative, "all patients are just people who want to get high," by countering that cannabis is their "best option" for pain control, to "feel better," and to "function on a day-to-day basis more normally." In short, both patients chose to become a medical cannabis patient because they believed it was "an option"; albeit one at the end of a long line of traditional medical options that had proved "disastrous/caused more suffering because of the side-effects/were just ineffective in treating my pain." What each found is that in choosing to become a cannabis patient, at least for them, was "the best option" available at this time given their previous experience with Western medical treatments. Both were tired of suffering and had finally come to a place that it was important to put *self* first, "to care about myself and to care for myself—to take control of my medical needs and experiment with a safer option."

As mentioned earlier, I specifically asking both patients *not to discuss prior cannabis use*, and clarifying that I was only inquiring about their experience as state recognized patients. Yet, both insisted upon explaining their prior relationship with or experience using cannabis, at some point in the interview. This indicates that this information was important to their decision to become a medical cannabis patient, whether they recognized it or not. Through my observations, the population of medical cannabis patients appear to fall into three categories of experience regarding previous cannabis use; those who have had no prior experience using cannabis are among the minority of patients, but few fall into the category of heavy or chronic users prior to becoming a patient either, though dominant narratives suggest otherwise. Most cannabis patients are like these participants and myself, they have *some* personal experience using cannabis, either as a teenager or even occasional to moderate use as an adult, that caused them to consider cannabis a safer alternative than the traditional medical treatments they were receiving. Over 25 million adults used cannabis last year in the U.S. and over 44% of all America adults have tried cannabis at some point in their life (www.norml.org); it is not surprising to find many patients have some experience with cannabis.

For many patients, previous experience with cannabis prompted them to consider cannabis as a legitimate medical alternative or at least "a harmless alternative that might or might not work." Even just a small amount of use as a teen may influence an adult to consider cannabis "a safer medical alternative" when faced with a serious health condition later in life. In fact, these participants expressed just this sentiment when they insisted on discussing their prior experience using cannabis. However, neither of the participants were using cannabis immediately prior to becoming a patient, perhaps because of this, they were both able to clearly explain how they believe the medication is helping improve their personal health. One journals her "experiences with this medicine," so she can better understand how it affects her particular health-related problems. In other words, these patients did not take medicating with cannabis lightly or consider it recreational by any means, instead they consider it "the best option" at relieving pain and suffering given that they reside "in a state that supports the use of cannabis as medication" and they've taken their treatment seriously.

Chronic and severe health issues were the driving force for both participants to become medical cannabis patients; however, both expressed additional reasons for applying for a state license (a medical cannabis patient card). Neither participant was particularly concerned about "penalty by law," in fact, only one mentioned it, albeit briefly, during the interview. Instead their desire to become a patient was centered on having access to the *resources* needed to educate themselves about cannabis as medication. The ability to interact with "experts" in this domain through "dispensaries" (New Mexico state law does not support a dispensary model but does allow for 'limited pick up locations' that both patients referenced, as well as the "bud-tenders" they employ), medical providers ("pot-doctors"), and other patients was fundamental to each participant's decision to apply for a state license. In fact, the greatest changes in their use, besides beginning 'medical' use, revolve around the patient's ability to "educate myself" about "healthier alternatives to smoking" and "the different types/strains of cannabis and what help they provide." One participant shares that, "becoming a medical cannabis patient enabled me to make better choices and improve my medication delivery system," which resulted in the patient "being able to live my life again."

From claims of improved health that include "better control of pain, improved symptoms of depression and mood," and "an overall sense of well-being," both patients expressed that when compared with previous pharmaceutical attempts to control these same health issues, cannabis has so far been "more successful" and even, "lifesaving" for them personally. Both participants commented about harmful side-effects they experienced using traditional Western pharmaceutical remedies, and both expressed some concern that they were becoming "addicted" to or that prescription medications "were interfering with" their ability to live a normal life, prior to entering the medical cannabis program as a patient. In describing this experience one participant said, "As the narcotics prescribed began to become stronger and stronger I realized that not only was I having severe side-effects from these medicines that at times were almost worse than the pain but I was having issues with becoming addicted to these substances." These concerns were accompanied by feelings of helplessness and powerlessness that was remedied by "taking control of my medical care" and "educating myself about this [cannabis] medical option." What motivated these participants to "take control" of their health cares options and choose cannabis? "Sheer frustration with always being sick and tired of always being sick and tired—I simply couldn't take it anymore, I was nearly suicidal between the pain, the depression, and the pharmaceuticals, something had to change!"

CAREER

As stated earlier, these two participants differed greatly in their experiences dealing with stigmatization based on their status as medical cannabis patients. This gap in experienced marginalization can be attributed in large part to differences in career fields and family acceptance levels. For a Registered Nurse to "continue a career in medicine—a career I really love," she considers it "vital" that she conceal her use from others especially, "co-workers and hospital administration," in order to avoid stigmatization, loss of status, and/or loss of employment. Expressing her fear of stigmatization she states, "I do not tell people I work with that I am a medical cannabis patient—they would do a random drug test on me and I would be fired and not be able to get a job in this town again." Her main concerns include that "co-workers" will "assume my judgment is impaired, even if I have not been using cannabis," or that "I would be considered more lazy than others." She believes, "...especially in my last position, in the supervisory position I had, the knowledge I am a medical cannabis patient would have hindered my ability to do my job because of the stigmas associated with cannabis use. So, I don't tell anyone I work with I am a patient. I am still very much a 'closeted' patient because it is just too big a career risk."

On the other hand, the participant states that she and her co-workers ("the doctors and nurses") have had conversations as "experienced professionals that are out there seeing what it can do for patients…how much better patients can control their symptoms with cannabis at times." She maintains these conversations "never get personal," because the only time she shared the "news of receiving my patient card" with a "trusted" colleague, she was admonished by her "friend." She was told, "He had lost faith in me and my ability to return to school to be a Nurse Practitioner," because "now all you'll do is sit around and smoke pot all day." This participant felt an immediate *loss of status* and *marginalization* from this interaction—with someone she "knew understood this medicine can be good for patients like me—who'd even suggested I try to get my card." Experiences like this oppress cannabis patients and cause them to fear and hide from marginalization. In a workplace known for both pre-employment and random drug-testing and medical cannabis assuring a failed test result, and an environment in which this patient knows "not one willing to admit [their patient status] in the workplace," she is very frightened and arguably marginalized. Patients who are medical professionals seem to have little job security and assume much risk for "challenging the medical establishment by choosing a non-toxic and safer alternative to prescription drugs." As mentioned earlier, further research into this area is warranted and should be explored in the future—especially as it relates to medical professionals having a solid understanding of the endocannabinoid system and how this knowledge affects stigmatizing behaviors in the workplace.

Although the other participant initially denied concern about others knowing she is a medical cannabis patient, when asked, "When you return to work do you believe you will have concerns about co-workers or customers knowing you are a medical cannabis patient?" The participant stated that she hoped to find work within the medical cannabis community when she is "physically, mentally, and emotionally able to sustain employment," because she "cannot imagine the energy it would take to conceal her use." However, she acknowledges it is "highly likely" that she would conceal her patient status, at least "when confronted with non-patients who are uncomfortable or nervous" and "people who do not understand this is medicine." Her preference when confronted with non-cannabis patients would be to, "kindly ask not to be judged by my medical condition or by my option to use marijuana as a treatment option." However, from my own patient perspective, I wonder, how effective this particular response will be with others. My own experience has shown that most conceal their cannabis use at least until they are able to acquire "enough education to be productive in explaining its effectiveness," but even after learning how it helps them, few share their stories with others in a way that is effectively disrupting the dominant cultural narratives that insist medical usage is just a gateway for "legalization of cannabis." For the few who become outspoken advocates in their communities, many others remain in concealment, "respecting non-patients" but feeling the need to "swallow {their} own voice from time to time" when confronted by dominant cultural narratives that seek to marginalize them. Concealing a role like medical cannabis patient requires energy and causes anxiety; added stress ill patients needlessly suffer from; however, it may also be the same marginalization and oppression that later urges a patient to public advocacy. Further, exploration in this area is also warranted.

FAMILY

In addition to career-oriented stigmatization, participants experienced stigmatization within their family systems though to largely varying degrees. One participant found "nervousness" combined with "support," when she told her family she was "curious about this program and this medication." Living with her parents while she recuperates, she feels "obligated but also relieved" to abide by their "rules" that govern her usage. For example, she states, "they don't want me smoking out in front of the house, or in the house—or things like that—all totally fair things. I also keep my medicine in the garage; they prefer I don't bring it in the house." The participant's parents willingness to support her "trying this medicine" has paid off; "they have both commented that the difference they see since I started this program two months ago is amazing." However, the concerns expressed by her parents suggest that they are also aware that the use of cannabis, even as medication, can lead to stigmatization and marginalization in our society. If their daughter's use is "out of sight" where others do not see her perform the act of using marijuana, they believe she will be "safer," using what remains an illegal drug in the eyes of the federal government. Certainly, the informal rules that they've laid down to govern her use were set with the best of intentions—protecting their child from society's harmful stigmatization, but in doing so one can see that the actions came from managing fears associated with illicit drug use that are deeply embedded in the dominant societal narrative.

The second participant relays the following story describing her arguably more marginalized experience:
I have had a long personal relationship with marijuana. As child I was raised with family who self-medicated with marijuana for PTSD and pain issues. I was taught marijuana was an herb…that it should be respected—it has the potential to be a great medication for many. I was told there was no real justification for it being illegal except for history—a history of people not approving of its use. As a nurse and now as a patient, this is the best herb and product that I can use to function on a day-to-day basis as a mother, as an employee, as a human being. It is personal because I have a history and was aware of its medical use through my two Uncles when I was a child—but it wasn't until a couple

of years ago that I experienced the need to use it as
medication. When I told my family I had received my card, I
thought they would be happy because I had been suffering
since I was a child with this pain from a C1 fracture when I
was 8. They weren't happy though. It was okay for my
Uncles to use marijuana as medication—or so I've always
been told and witnessed—but it was not all right for me. My
grandmother told me that as a Hispanic female and mother
this was just wrong and my family agrees, even those who use
marijuana themselves. I have been cut-off from them since,
simply because I chose the same medication as my Uncles.
How hypocritical is that? Why should I suffer as a woman
when the men in my family use this medicine successfully to
relieve their suffering?
Certainly, these two participants experienced very different
reactions from their families. Regardless of the stigma that
each participant is willing to accept from others, both fear
that same stigma upon their child, "coming from my use as a
patient being seen as deviant by close-minded people."

Based on their experiences, participants also
recognize that the expectations for mothers and perhaps
females in general differ when it comes to being a medical
cannabis patient. Although only one participant thus far has
experienced stigmatization from family members, based on
her feminine role as mother, the other participant has yet to
tell family, other than her parents whom she lives with, and
neither has discussed their status as a medical cannabis
patient with their children. Hathaway et al found that the role
of parent often creates "conflict between cannabis and role
expectations" for parents who are cannabis users, even those
whose use is strictly medicinal in nature (Hathaway et al.,
2011, p. 454). Although both of the participants are medical
cannabis patients disrupting the mainstream perceptions of
the practice of using cannabis, their parenting views, "reflect
paternalistic and moral obligations that are assumed in
mainstream perceptions of the practice" (Hathaway,
normalization, 461).

In one case, the participant's sons are young, under the age of 10. In this participant's opinion, she has time to educate them before discussing her own choice with them. She hopes that, "by the time I need to share all the details with my sons people will understand that it's about medicine, not about getting high…right now I don't know what I would say to them about this drug. I want them to know it is safe, and I want to dispel any myths they hear about how bad it is—but I also don't want to encourage them to use it until they are responsible adults."

The other participant is anticipating having a conversation with her sons soon, perhaps in the next few months. With teenaged sons, one in college and the other not far behind, this participant states she, "has nothing to hide," but acknowledges the need for her to, "feel comfortable and knowledgeable enough," to have the conversation with her sons. Her sons live in another state so this conversation will wait until they see each other again; it is not one she wants to have via telephone. She believes that "they will see a great improvement in my health and well-being, which will matter more to them than the medicine I use to treat my symptoms." As parents, both participants are concerned that their children understand the difference between medical and recreational use of cannabis. Neither necessarily opposes "legalization" that would allow for lawful 'recreational' use, but they express the same concerns "any normal parent" has about their children using illicit drugs. Research that explores the messaging from parents, who are cannabis patients, to their children about the use of cannabis as medication would increase our knowledge of both the parent and the child's perceptions of cannabis use and dominant cultural stereotypes.

SOCIETY
(Community)

As demonstrated medical cannabis patients' awareness that authoritative and powerful others categorize and stigmatize cannabis use is consequential to their social narrative and identity. Both participants shared their awareness that the use of cannabis, even as medication, can lead to stigmatization and marginalization in our society ("…it just isn't okay to be a patient/I don't want to be seen as a pot smoker"). Although 'medical cannabis patient' may not be either participant's "master identity" (Goffman, 1959), both identify as a medical cannabis patient and are attuned to society's narratives regarding their status. Both recognize that patients are mythologized in the dominant discourse as "just people who want to get high" ("I've heard some people say that all patients are just people who want to get high/he thinks the people who get the card don't really need the card, they just want to smoke pot"). This dominant perception makes them both self-conscious about their use and causes both to conceal their use from others, although the degrees to which they experience this marginalization vary significantly. Future studies that incorporate a larger population sample will more accurately demonstrate the consequences of stigmatization in cannabis patients.

Although recent polls state that 50% of Americans support legalizing cannabis and over 70% support legalizing cannabis for medicinal purposes (Mendes, 2010; Newport, 2011) the distance between the narratives of patients and those who oppose medicinal cannabis are vast and the dominant societal narrative remains steadfastly opposed. However, the amount of cannabis used, the "quality" of the cannabis, as well as how it is consumed, often is at the center of public discussions on cannabis as medication. Consistently media and public leadership has maintained that if patients are allowed to use cannabis as medication little good can come from "smoked" or "illicit" drugs. Cannabis medical providers and caregivers agree, but instead of continuing the illicit status of cannabis, they seek alternative delivery methods to medicate with cannabis. Perhaps, just the thought of patients "getting high" is unacceptable to many, and it is the most controversial aspect of this medication.

Yet, like many other patients, me included, participants embrace the "sense of well-being" cannabis provides. Many medical cannabis supporters jest that if cannabis could be put in a pill fewer people would react adversely to it as medication. Studies find, however, that when compared to Marinol, a synthetic THC pharmaceutical product in pill form, patients find smoked cannabis a better alternative for nausea, vomiting, and pain control (Aggrawal, 153 & Iverson, 59-61). Additionally, patients who experience pain on a continuous basis often "find the high pleasurable," because this particular side-effect provides a "sense of relief" and "relaxation" that pharmaceutical pain relievers typically do not.

As the medical cannabis industry grows, patients are being afforded options that include non-psychoactive forms for cannabis to treat illnesses and pain-related symptoms. In fact, "juicing" cannabis has become quite popular among patients with Lupus, Rheumatoid Arthritis, and other painful, chronic health conditions and because the THC (the main psychoactive component in cannabis) is not heated during production, raw cannabis medication is not psychoactive. Patients also are gaining access to "alternative delivery systems" such as vaporizers, edible products, oils, tinctures, and salves that offer both non-psychoactive and psychoactive options for patients. Both of these participants expressed an interest in alternative delivery methods but steadfastly maintained that given an option between psychoactive and non-psychoactive products, they would prefer the psychoactive products much of the time simply because of the "sense of well-being and relaxation" they experience. Certainly, a sense of well-being is important to a seriously ill patient.

Conclusion
Although this study was very small in nature it yielded a great deal of interesting data. As mentioned, because there is little scholarly research and few scholars pursing research in this

domain, many questions remained unanswered and many research projects are ripe for discovery. However, after analyzing the data, this researcher could see that the participants, further validating the small amount of research in this field, touched upon many of the themes discussed in the literature review. For instance, participant narratives demonstrate an awareness of the stigma attached to cannabis usage, even if such usage is primarily intended for medical purposes. This disapproval is deeply ingrained in our society's dominant narrative regarding cannabis use. There seems to be no room for medicalized use of marijuana in this narrative even though the medical efficacy is supported by numerous medical trials, and as shown is stigmatizing to medical cannabis patients. As more patients lend their stories to this movement, the dominant narrative will be required to adjust and allow voice for these citizens, whose narratives disrupt it.

Additionally, study participants spoke about stigma as an "informal source of control" (Goffman in Hathaway et al., 2011, p. 456) as described in the Hathaway (2011) article, around the categories of self, career, family, and society. Like the Hathaway study's respondents, this study's participants admittedly hide their use from someone, in these cases family, co-workers, and those they believe "might not understand." Participants do so to avoid conflict and stigmatization. As we can see in the two different descriptions of the participant's family support systems, both reported encounters that resulted in "some status loss or social disapproval" (Hathaway et al., 2011, p. 456). However, one participant was arguably more marginalized through her familial experiences than the other. From my own experience and having listened to the stories of dozens of medical cannabis patients, acceptance from family is important to patients. I, myself, was fearful of sharing my patient status with some family members, and like these participants, I also avoided conflict and stigmatization by evading discussions about cannabis as medication until I was knowledgeable enough to counter the dominant narrative with my own story and credible facts. My experience differs from that of both of these participants, but certainly we share commonalities in our experiences—and regardless of our experiences, our fears of stigmatization are real. To some degree, we have each experienced stigmatization because of our medical cannabis patient status and each of us wonders when the dominant discourse will consider our needs as patients within its narrative. Concealing a role like medical cannabis patient requires energy and cause anxiety, added stress ill patients needlessly suffer from considering they are already being marginalized simply because of their status as a cannabis patient.

Chronic and severe health issues were the driving force for both participants to become medical cannabis patients; however, additional reasons for applying for a state license centered around *resources* necessary for cannabis patients. Participants described the resources needed to educate themselves about cannabis as medication and at the top of the list was the ability to interact with "experts" in this domain through "dispensaries," clinics, medical providers, and other patients. In fact, as noted, the greatest changes in their use revolve around the patient's ability to educate themselves about using cannabis as medicine for their specific health issues.

Study participants also expressed anger that their primary medical provider was "unable" or "unwilling" to recommend cannabis as a legitimate medical option. The following statement by one participant speaks to this frustration:

> When you have tried everything there is to try, you know you feel like you've done everything you can and this medicine is the last resort, so be it. I think maybe it needs to be the first resort, not the last one. I feel mad—I mean I am grateful for the medicine—but I am also mad, just for the fact that none of my doctors shared knowledge about this medication with

me—and I have seen *a lot* of doctors. After
trying it, I am mad that it isn't an option to
use earlier in treatment and that all doctors
aren't trained to understand it or don't even
consider it an option, because had I used this
first I think I would not have suffered like I
have.

In our society, patients are expected to rely upon doctors to
treat their medical ails. The expectation is that Western
medical providers are the experts, the patients merely the
passive recipients of this expertise.

The "social control" (Conrad & Schneider, 1992, p. 7)
exerted in the medical profession over patients, and their
right to control their own medical choices, especially the use
of cannabis as medication, was clearly experienced by these
participants. As these participants demonstrate, more and
more patients are taking an active role control in their health
care and insisting on alternative options, including cannabis.
As one participant who works in the medical field points out,
medical professionals that admit to medical cannabis use or
work within the medical cannabis industry may have for all
intents and purposes committed "career suicide." Perhaps,
this is why so few medical cannabis patients are able to obtain
a recommendation for state licensing from their primary care
physician and must seek (and pay for) a "pot doctor" to
certify their state applications. This is an area ripe for future
study.

One participant's story of stigmatization in the
medical field for exploring a non-traditional medical path
personally relays deep-seated fears and concerns about her
medical cannabis patient status. Her description of "stopping
my medication [cannabis] for six months, until after accepting
this job offer" and passing a pre-employment drug test,
which caused her "great pain and discomfort," suggests that
more study of this particular phenomenon is also warranted.
Pending on Capitol Hill is a bill designed to resolve this
particular issue as well. However, until cannabis is

reclassified from a Schedule 1 Controlled Substance, which is viewed as having no medicinal purpose and disallows clinical research on subjects using a Schedule 1 substance, like cannabis or heroin, few patients will find relief from this particular stigmatizing requirement for employment, and even fewer are hopeful that political leadership will act upon this issue during the next congressional session.

Certainly, study participants experienced very different reactions from their families. In the one example, by working together and embracing an "ethic of care" as espoused by Carol Gilligan, Joan Tronto, and Martha Nussbaum that suggests that caring for one's fellow human beings, and particularly one's own family member, alternative health options, even one that is only "quasi-legal," can be embraced. As cannabis has taken on a new purpose, no longer used to "get high," but to "medicate," the dominant narrative that surrounds this matter must consider suffering seen as the kind of thing that could happen to anyone, including oneself (Gilligan). None of us knows when we may suffer equally to the other. Gilligan elucidates, when considering a care perspective, the conflict between self and others recedes and places "the self as moral agent" able to perceive and respond "to the perception of need (Gilligan, 35)." As demonstrated, even in families where one might anticipate support and understanding, such care is not always forthcoming simply because the dominant expectations of what is right or wrong are influenced by dominant discourses that are dismissive of an issue viewed solely as wrong because it is illegal. Yet, as other studies have shown, this study validates that the views of parents who engage in cannabis use, even those who are licensed cannabis patients, "reflect paternalistic and moral obligations that are assumed in mainstream perceptions of the practice (Hathaway, 2011)." Parents struggle with their children, rather than themselves, being the focus of the "social disapproval that contributes to maintaining a 'culture of control'" as espoused by Goffman (Hathaway, 2011, 453). However, the "presumption that the use of cannabis is incompatible with conventional responsibilities and roles" remains strong in the dominant narratives regarding cannabis use.

Another interesting area of inquiry involves the rhetoric and language used within this domain. For example, one participant referred to cannabis primarily as "medicine" ("I purchase my medicine once a month/ I am just really learning about this medicine/This is the first medicine that has really helped me/having this experience with this medicine has enhanced me spiritually") and occasionally "cannabis," only rarely as "cannabis," and never as "pot." As this participant had the least lifetime experience with cannabis and no recent experience prior to becoming a patient, she was the least knowledgeable about cannabis but the most exuberant, stating:

I want to share how wonderful this medicine is with others, but I still have a lot of knowledge to gain. As I have begun to meet other patients, I have found a real sense of belonging, of community…a willingness from others to help me learn, to help me understand myself better and this makes me want to share my experience with them—and, it makes me less scared to share it with others who believe I just want to get high. I know what is right for me…cannabis is right for me and for that I am grateful (long pause) I feel better, so much better— I want to share that with non-believers, I was skeptical but I believe now. I've been to medical support groups, never— *never*—have I found a better support system than the one I am finding in this community, among patients and professionals. I am grateful, so grateful.

The other participant, who had some experience as an adult responsibly using cannabis to "self-medicate for mild depression and everyday stress and anxiety…from time to time," most often used the term "marijuana," although she occasionally used "cannabis" the preferred terminology in the medical cannabis community, and several times used the term "pot," but more often than "pot" or "cannabis" she used the term "herb" demonstrating I believe her, "preference for a more holistic approach than pharmaceuticals." To date I have not seen an academic study pertaining to the dialogic shift occurring in the medical cannabis community suggesting that leadership is aware that language shifts culture and to shift this discussion we must begin to shift our language. There are of course many other nuances within the language chosen by the participants as they shared their stories with me. I have only touched the surface of how language is playing a part in this social movement and witnessed within the narratives of patients—certainly, increasing knowledge of this sort would help scholars better understand this social movement and perhaps, provide a way for others to understand the stigma cannabis patients must often endure.

Finally, there is much to be said by the participants insistence upon addressing one particular narrative, "some people say that all patients are just people who want to get high," for this is perhaps the most dominant message in our society regarding medical cannabis patients and their use of marijuana. This action by participants and their narratives as patients supports Hathaway's finding that, "The social status of marijuana and its users might alternatively be viewed on a normative continuum that has shown signs of shifting in the theorized direction of greater sociocultural acceptance (or indifference) of the practice, while retaining vestiges of social disapproval that contribute to maintaining a 'culture of control'" as espoused by Goffman (Hathaway, 2011, 453). As these participants demonstrate, cannabis patients are not using marijuana to get high, they are medicating with a whole plant medication, as an option to improve health conditions that Western medicine is unable to address in an equally successful way. Until the myths that are embedded in the dominant narrative are openly addressed by cannabis patients in public forums patients will continue to be marginalized simply for taking control of their healthcare issues and opting to medicate with an alternative medication that itself remains stigmatized as "weed."

In my opinion, the best chance at changing the

dominant narrative is for cannabis patients to share their voices with others. Stereotypes will not be broken unless other characterizations of cannabis use are shared publically, so that those outside this movement begin to understand the true needs of medical cannabis patients and begin to view their behavior as normal instead of deviant.

During this term, I participated in three courses—two of which you've now read the final paper for: The Performance of Leadership and Research Methodologies—the third course, Group Dynamics was led by Dr. Toni Gregory, my Associate Dean. Toni was an interesting woman to work with and a Ph.D. who'd been "given hell" on her path, so she seemed to enjoy giving others hell as well, or perhaps this is just my impression, given that she chose to give me hell at every turn. A class I had looked forward to became my nemesis, I fought this woman tooth and nail with text from each lesson, listened to my partner cry week after week, and thought perhaps I'd totally lost my mind thinking I wanted a Ph.D. if it meant I'd end up working with people as crazy as she appeared to be. But come to find out, this was just a lesson taught in a way I couldn't seem to comprehend at the time…a very unpleasant lesson.

By the end of the semester, Toni and I had come to some respectable terms between us—I have to say she seemed to respect and enjoy the drama—and while she was taking time to recover from surgery (to which she did not share details), I took a short road-trip to Tucson, AZ and attended the 7th Annual Medical Cannabis Therapeutics Conference hosted by Patients Out of Time. It was here, sitting on the steps outside the conference, listening to patients from all over the country discuss their needs and desires as cannabis patients, that some of the ambiguity began to clear and it became apparent that I was to help begin a patient organization focused on the holistic needs of patients—but I was still clueless as to what this would mean to my life or my studies.

I returned home from the conference, empowered from sharing my own story with others including many notable researchers and doctors I have been quoting in my studies, and typed out the first draft of my final term paper in less than 6 hours. A day or two of tweaking and off it went…when it returned, Dr. Gregory stated that although I had led the class throughout the term (led them in confronting her) and had produced excellent work in my final paper...she "could only give me an A-" for the course. This statement chapped my ass! I mean "give" me an A-; I'd worked my damn ass off for that A- (and I didn't expect to get a grade that high after all the drama). Grades are earned not given...language is important here.

Seven months and many revisions later, my final paper was published in *Integral Theory & Practice*, a journal led by Ken Wilber—an intellectual hero of Dr. Gregory's and now mine. As Ken Wilber read the article during the final conference call—during which I received his approval for publication—he stopped after reading the section on Cash Hyde, and choked up by the story, told me my work was "vitally important." Huge validation that I am on the right ambiguous path!! Plus, he's right—it's not so much about what I am doing—it's about sharing the knowledge I am gaining! This is vitally important! And, his words were the affirmation I had hoped to receive from Toni. The hard-won validation, just a year after my near-death experience, solidified my belief that I am on the right path, ambiguous as it may be—still don't know where it will lead, but down the path I continue to go, one foot in front of the other, despite the seeming lack of support from my Institution's administration.

Dr. Toni Gregory passed in May 2013 and despite the complexities in our relationship it's easy to see the void she left at Union Institute and University and it saddens me that we cannot work together to further Integral Theory as it relates to healthcare. May she rest in peace as I continue to contemplate what it means to lack Integral Diversity Maturity particularly in health care. She posed a question that I will find a scholarly response for...

Nelson, R. (2012) Framing Integral Leadership in the Medical Cannabis Community. *Journal of Integral Theory and Practice*, 2012, 7(4), pp. 81–95).

There is an increasing recognition for the need to develop integrative approaches to understanding and explaining organizational sustainability or change. Few have considered, however, the need to use an integral approach when developing community-based organizations, such as patient groups and non-profit service organizations like cannabis collectives, dispensaries, or other healthcare centers serving cannabis patients. My research interests concentrate on leadership within the medical marijuana (MMJ) community, and as I interact with patients, I have recognized that the capacity for leadership in this community is abundant. Overcoming stigmatization, however, is critical to patient emancipation. At this time, cannabis use falls into what anthropologist Victor Turner (1987) describes as a "liminal" phase. Patients find themselves "between and betwixt" living an experience in which they do not belong to the society they were previously a part of (i.e., one that stereotypes marijuana users as out-of-control, unable to focus, speak rationally, or any number of other pejorative conjectures) and one in which cannabis use has been accepted and normalized. Thinking of one's self as normal means "incorporating standards from wider society and meeting others' expectations about what we ought to be. The concept of stigma is therein a device that ensures the reliability of the interaction order by punishing people who do not conform to moral standards (Hathaway et al., 2011, p. 455)."

Some cannabis patients note a considerable cultural shift in opinion toward cannabis users, and polls suggest a growing majority of Americans support the medicalization of cannabis. In contrast, other patients fear being exposed as cannabis patients with internalized and institutionalized stigmatization notably affecting their quality of life. This article examines current attitudes regarding cannabis use, which appear to be related to the extent of one's understanding or ignorance of the evidence rather than the virtue of one's convictions about cannabis use. However, lingering stigmatization, dismissive of cannabis users, continues to affect cannabis patients, as well as leadership within this critical social movement.

ABSTRACT In a world of increasing complexity where existing models of leadership are becoming obsolete, an ongoing and current healthcare controversy provides us with a rich vein of study for integral models of leadership. This article draws on research from and about the medical cannabis community, revealing human universals of leadership, with pressing practical implications for community building, research methodology, medical interventions, and public policy. Specifically, this article examines the suitability of the AQAL model as a frame for constructing healthcare organizations promoting, centered on, and with leadership shared by patients themselves. Critical elements include support for the individual and the collective, as well as an avenue for knowledge exchange. Additionally, such organizations and groups have the potential to develop a sense of community, increase diversity maturity, and offer leadership opportunities.

Cannabis remains a Schedule I Controlled Substance under the American Controlled Substances Act (CSA), which classifies it as having no recognizable medicinal value and as a highly addictive substance.
Both of these descriptions are false. Research supports the notion that cannabis helps to regulate immunity, inflammation, analgesia, neurotoxicity, appetite, blood pressure, bone formation, body temperature, gastrointestinal functioning, and physical and psychological responses to

stress and trauma, among other potential affects (Baker et al., 2003; Courtney, 2012; Grinspoon & Bakalar, 1997; Holland, 2010). Additionally, social scientist Amanda Reiman (2009) promotes the notion of cannabis as an *exit drug* that helps patients with alcohol or prescription drug dependencies find relief from addiction; observation in the MMJ community supports the reduction of pharmaceutical treatments as a primary benefit for cannabis patients. In short, the evidence supports cannabis as being less addictive and relatively side-effect free in comparison to most prescription drugs (Grinspoon & Bakalar, 1997; Holland, 2010). These findings prompt us to reconsider cannabis and its potential medical benefits.

The reasons for research into the medicinal efficacy of cannabis are numerous, but include advances in understanding of the endocannabinoid system on which cannabis acts. In short, our neurological, immune, circulatory, digestive, endocrine, and musculoskeletal systems all contain endocannabinoid receptors and their ligands are cannabinoids (Holland, 2010). The Schedule 1 classification has discouraged cannabis research in the United States, much as international drug policies have repressed researchers worldwide. Despite these obstacles, scientists have identified five cannabinoids that the human body produces, and cannabis plants produces perhaps a 100, although we only have an elementary understanding of a few, like THC (delta-9-tetrahydrocannabinol) and CBD (cannabidiol). Recent research points to cannabis as an effective treatment for cancer due to "the cumulative effective of CBD and THC in blocking proliferation of brain-cancer cells... [and] breast-cancer metastasis" (Project CBD), suggesting that cannabis research is of utmost importance and serves the common good. If humans all have an endocannabinoid system, then collectively there is a stake in learning more about cannabinoids, the endocannabinoid system, and cannabis.

Numerous factors, including the medicalization of cannabis through medical marijuana or "compassionate care"

policies in 18 states and the District of Columbia, indicate
that there is a cultural readiness for an integral embrace of the
MMJ movement and cannabis patients in general. However,
as Ken Wilber (2004) elucidates, "No matter how high-
minded, idealistic, or altruistic a cause might appear—from
ecology to cultural diversity to world peace—the simple
mouthing of intense support for that cause is not enough to
determine why, in fact, that cause is being embraced" (p. 24).
The cannabis movement is an ideal example of this fact. It is
a movement driven by activists, most of who are patients and
experienced with the use and symptom relief of cannabis, but
the majority consensus among medical practitioners is that
advocacy is a poor substitute for the dispassionate analysis of
evidence-based medicine (EBM), and the media tends to
portray marijuana users as those who "just want to get high."
Cannabis patients have yet to be recognized as knowledge
bearers and leaders, who have much to contribute to this
debate. Hathaway and colleagues (2011) comment on the
social status of cannabis users: [Cannabis] users might
alternatively be viewed on a normative continuum that has
shown signs of shifting in the theorized direction of greater
sociocultural acceptance (or indifference) of the practice,
while retaining vestiges of social disapproval that contribute
to maintaining a "culture of control," as espoused by
Goffman. (p. 453). Certainly, stigmatization requires more
scholarly attention.

The AQAL Model

Leadership scholars like Mark Edwards (2005), Wendelin
Kupers, and Jürgen Weibler (2008) have demonstrated the
suitability of the Integral framework in the study of
organizations, particularly regarding organizational
sustainability or change. As noted above, few scholars discuss
the use of this framework in developing an organizational
model focused on cultivating leadership potential from within
a marginalized membership and for the organization to be
centered on the needs of the collective membership using an

Integral approach.

With this type structure as a goal, I was compelled to explore the Integral approach as an interdisciplinary model with practical application. Throughout his vast work on Integral Theory, Wilber (2000) describes his efforts as an endeavor to "honor and embrace every legitimate aspect of human consciousness" (p. 2). The AQAL model, the foundational structure of the Integral approach, has two axes: the horizontal axis denotes a continuum between interior and exterior realities; the vertical axis signifies a continuum between individual and collective realities. Together, the four quadrants are the fundamental domains in which change and development occur in individuals and collective groups. By definition, the AQAL model effectively supports an integral approach, as the interaction of its dimensions produce the fundamental domains through which all developmental change occurs. Further, the Integral approach maintains that understanding any social phenomenon requires that at least two fundamental dimensions of existence be considered. This section analyzes this frame from the perspective of MMJ leadership and observable issues that require our attention.

Starting in the Upper-Left (UL) quadrant, the AQAL model references the interior reality lived by a person. In relation to leadership, Torbert and associates (2004) find that efforts to transform an organization are dependent upon the level of consciousness of leadership. However, leadership development and practice are most effective when the individual interior dimensions are linked and supported by external action and tangibles (Kupers & Weibler, 2008, p. 449). In other words, when leadership development and practice are linked across dimensions, leadership is best positioned to take action based on shared values. When this type of integral frame is applied we begin to conceive of leadership not as a science or an art, but as a state of consciousness, much as leadership scholar Jonathan Reams posits. From this standpoint, we can "begin to grasp the phenomenon of leadership as the field of awareness rather than a personality trait or personal attribute" (Reams, 2005, p. 6). Integral leadership considers the needs of others, knowing that knowledge and change are co-created in learning situations. The MMJ community has no shortage of learning situations that stand in need of integral approaches and integral leadership.

The Upper-Right (UR) quadrant refers to reality as it is perceived externally. In particular, development in this quadrant concentrates on behavior, but as a bodily experience physical health is also located here. Stigmatization affects individuals with a variety of medical conditions (HIV/AIDS, hepatitis, post-traumatic stress disorder [PTSD], chronic pain conditions, cancer, among others); cannabis patients with these conditions are dually stigmatized as marijuana users. Stigma is internalized in the UL quadrant, but enacted through individual behaviors, like those associated with either concealment or revelation in this quadrant.

Encouraging marginalized citizens who habitually live their life in concealment to share their private voice publicly and engage in community is laudable, but integral leadership that approaches patient support with a patient-as-leadership philosophy and an AQAL frame offers patients the opportunity for *whole* wellness. In an organization, training and development opportunities as well as "coaching, planning, decision making and any skill that develops individual effective acting and practice in the environment of an organization" (Kupers & Weibler, 2008, p. 449) are included in this domain. Traditional medicine, as practiced in the United States, occupies this quadrant and arguably has a singular quadrant focus on "the physical organism using physical interventions: surgery, drugs, medication, and behavior modification" as it relates to individual and collective health concerns (Wilber, 2007, p. 92). For this reason, any organization that supports patient development and growth, especially among a marginalized and physically weak population, should consider the individual and collective patient needs from an integral perspective. Conducting integral research in this domain will also allow us to resolve the fragmentation of knowledge we have regarding the United States' rapidly growing population of cannabis patients.

The Lower-Right (LR) quadrant refers to the tangible or physical world, which is measurable and quantifiable and can be comprehended from outside. Kupers and Weibler (2008) elucidate: [L]eadership here is more likely to be associated with a transforming system. As such irreversible, progressive contexts and not repetitive ones within an emerging order characterize it; this implies that chaos and complexity are not problems to be solved, but the triggers of evolution, adaptation, and renewal. (p. 451) Many national organizations that advocate on behalf of cannabis patients, including the National Organization for the Reform of Marijuana Laws (NORML) and Marijuana Policy Project (MPP), are situated directly in this quadrant as they concentrate on issues of law and public policy related to patient access to medication, and ending criminal penalties related to cannabis use. Although they may well be aware of patient needs related to other dimensions, their approach has a nearly singular focus that exponentially limits their ability to address the whole patient through public policy initiatives. The argument can be made that it is as vital for organizations concentrating on public policy (vs. those directly involved in healthcare) to develop integral approaches. Integral public policy would better serve citizens and improve legislative outcomes. The case of AIDS patient Ryan White, which educated citizens and required medical practitioners receive education about HIV and AIDS, as well as the funding for research and community support structures for HIV patients, provides an example of our failure to learn from and hence repeat our past. There are certainly parallels between the stories of Ryan White and Cash Hyde, a young cannabis patient whose brave battle with brain cancer recently ended amid much political turmoil in his home state of Montana regarding MMJ policy (Cash Hyde Foundation). Chemotherapy, initiated at the age of one, made Hyde blind and too sick to eat. Yet only weeks after his father began administering cannabis oil to his son, Hyde was able to eat again and even regained his sight. Although Hyde did not survive his battle with brain cancer, he experienced two full remissions and lived years longer than medical professionals anticipated; moreover, his quality of life was exceptional given that he was indeed a cancer patient. At the age of four, he passed peacefully in the arms of his parents (Cash Hyde Foundation). Cases like Hyde's illustrate that it is time for scholars and policymakers to consider alternatives to the status quo; the Integral framework offers the possibility of broader, more comprehensive policies that provide support to patients.

Finally, the Lower-Left quadrant (LL) contains the subjective as expressed through the collective: groups, organizations, society, and our global community, as well as collectively expressed levels of consciousness. Paulson (as quoted in Kupers & Weibler, 2008) provides a solid description of this quadrant as a space of mutual recognition, as well as delineating the internal collective aspects of leadership conveyed in this dimension:

> The intersubjective world of shared history, myths, stories, values, norms are all part of this quadrant, so it encompasses cultural dimensions such as deal with group identity and meaning-making issues. Correspondingly, it is also the domain of unwritten beliefs, shared meanings, and worldviews. As such it includes taboos and informal norms that can be discerned from how people justify and explain what they think and do together in terms of leading and following. This area of culture calls for a focus on the deeper

significance of collective aspirations, valuing
and meaning making for example in rituals,
ceremonies and symbols, socio-cultural
purposes and visions. Approaching this realm
allows us to not only tap into what is held by
individuals, but also to access and create a
composite of what is held collectively. (p. 449)
Although little attention has been paid by scholars to the
cannabis community, perhaps only a bit more has been paid
to the significance of leadership as it relates to this quadrant.
Integral organizations understand that leadership "cannot
manipulate this sphere directly, because to a great extent it is
determined and controlled by members of the organization"
simply because it includes "corresponding levels of
consciousness expressed on the collective cultural level"
(Kupers & Weibler, 2008, p. 450). However, for these
reasons, shared or distributed leadership is developed from
this quadrant and of concern for any organization whose
purpose is to empower members.

The "all-quadrants" aspect of the AQAL model refers to "the
I, We, and It dimensions (or self, culture, and nature; art,
morals, and science; first-person, second-person, and third-
person) (Wilber, 2000, p. 138)." Thus, an integral
understanding of cannabis patients might include, for
instance, a phenomenological analysis on the subjective
meaning to individual patients (UL); observations of
individual behaviors (UR); promoting tools and processes to
be used at the collective level (LR); and the uncovering of the
social and cultural characteristics that affect patients (LL).
Using the AQAL model and interdisciplinary methodologies,
one can study the perspective of each quadrant from a series
of complex, interconnected relationships. The perspectives
gained when we focus on the cannabis community
demonstrate a clear need for further research in this subject
field.

Public Policy and the Need for Integral Leadership

Based on the cross-stigmatization associated with cannabis as an illegal drug, a "recreational" substance, and an alternative healthcare option, cannabis patients are often marginalized by their own physicians for considering cannabis as a treatment option. As a patient, I find it perplexing and unsettling that I frequently have a better understanding of the endocannabinoid system than the physicians managing my healthcare. If human beings have an endocannabinoid system, an important physiological system critical to homeostasis, known to react favorably to cannabinoids, *all* medical practitioners should be required to be aware of this system and have a comprehensive understanding of it. It is quite surprising that this particular argument is not central in the medical cannabis movement. Its absence indicates attitudes regarding cannabis use may be related to the extent of one's understanding or ignorance of the evidence rather than exclusively to one's moral beliefs. Research exploring stigma from an Integral frame will add value to the processes undergirding patient marginalization and stigmatization.

Conventional medicine predominantly employs an UR, hierarchal approach that seldom focuses on the needs of patients outside traditional practices. Cannabis use falls outside of this firmly established model for many reasons beyond its lawlessness. In comparison, a holonic model "claims that every physical event (UR) has at least four dimensions (the quadrants) and thus even physical illness must be looked at from all four quadrants (not to mention levels)" (Wilber 2000a, 91). Integrative medicine asserts a person's interior states (i.e., emotions, psychological state, imagery, and intentions) play a crucial role in both the *cause* and the *care* of physical illness, as well as the *cure* (Wilber, 2000a, p. 91; 2007, p. 92). Alternative health practitioner Dr. Andrew Weil is one, among many, who espouses the belief that mind, spirit, and *community*, as well as body are important factors that influence health, wellness, and disease; a fact conventional medical providers fail to recognize as they ignore an "entire panoply of effective treatments across all quadrants and dimensions of human health and illness" (Wilber, 2007, p. 92). Wo/men's Alliance for Medical Marijuana (WAMM) and Harborside Health Center (Harborside or HHC) are ostensibly integral organizations and model cannabis programs. Both are founded on a belief similar to Wilber's (2003) notion of Integral Medicine that calls on medical practitioners "to utilize as complete and as comprehensive an approach as possible in treating any illness," believing it necessary for healthcare organizations to follow the same premise, thus treating the whole patient. Both organizations offer services that span the Integral framework, concentrating on safe patient access, education, and support issues (in contrast to many cannabis and traditional healthcare organizations).

Future research may find that the ability to span the full spectrum of the Integral model is at least partially responsible for patients stepping into leadership roles, sharing their personal stories publicly, as well as supporting Harborside's struggle with federal authorities that seek to close a well-respected healthcare provider (David, 2012; DeAngelo, 2012). As important as both the UR and UL quadrants are for seriously ill patients, "individual consciousness does not exist in a vacuum; [it exists] inextricably embedded in shared cultural values, beliefs, and worldviews" (Wilber, 2000, p. 91). Wilber points out, "How a culture (LL) views a particular illness—with care and compassion or derision and scorn— can have a profound impact on how an individual copes (UL) with that illness, which can directly affect the course of the physical illness itself (UR)" (p. 91). Arguably, cannabis patients are marginalized not just by how society views (LL) their illness (chronic pain, PTSD, AIDS, among others), but also by how society views the use of an illegal drug as treatment. Compassionate care policies require patients demonstrate that conventional treatments have failed to provide relief before one can apply for consideration as a potential cannabis patient; patients must also obtain a physician's recommendation. The decision to become a cannabis patient is not about "getting high" or intoxication, as the media and dominant narrative would have us believe; instead, for most patients, like me, it is about the chance of living a better quality of life and seeking wellness. Regardless, experiencing, witnessing, or fearing potential stigmatization causes numerous patients to conceal their use of cannabis; many are unable or unwilling to defend their choice or themselves when confronted by others armed with a narrative that cannabis patients just want to "smoke pot" or that "all illicit drugs are bad." It is an act of leadership to stand against social conventions challenging healthcare providers with one's own embodied experience—an experience often sought in desperation when conventional methods fail to provide relief. As a cannabis patient, I frequently face these charges from the uninformed, including my own physicians establishing that there is still much work to be done to remedy issues like this.

Encounters like those above cause fear, stigmatization, and feelings of oppression, and they will remain a dominant part U.S. culture until as a society there is a better understanding of cannabis patients and marijuana use. For, as culturally acceptable as it has become over the past two decades for cancer patients to use cannabis to relieve symptoms brought about by chemotherapy treatments, very few patients fall into this category.

The chronically ill, who from quick observation may appear physically healthy, have been the target of MMJ detractors and are the most affected. Skeptics, politicians, and medical professionals frequently stand on the premise that the Schedule 1 classification of marijuana "affirms" there is no medical benefit provided by its use, mimicking the dominant narrative that "all illegal drugs are bad" and labeling those who use cannabis as misguided souls or addicts. This type of stigmatization, compounded by a lack of support, causes patient stories to remain concealed and the knowledge they might share silenced. In contrast, the Integral framework provides a space for the marginalized to share their stories, first with each other and then with others who may benefit from their knowledge.

An informal survey of several MMJ specialty physicians revealed that more than 95% of cannabis patients were "self-medicating" prior to the receipt of their recommendation, leading Mikuriya and associates (2007) to conclude that physicians were really "approving" the medical use of marijuana as opposed to "recommending" it. This statement is important because it illustrates a situation cannabis patients recurrently face: a lack of knowledge and understanding by their primary care or specialty physicians compounded by a shift in role redefining an experienced cannabis user as knowledge agent (in contrast to the culturally acceptable passive patient who relies on the clinical expertise of the medical provider). Passive cannabis patients are those who have little or no experience with cannabis but who may benefit from its use. These same patients find little assistance and a general lack of ability to answer medically relevant questions regarding cannabis use from traditional medical providers. As a new cannabis patient it is often more productive to access other patients or cannabis providers (dispensary personnel) than to seek advice from one's primary care physician or even a specialist (oncologist, endocrinologist, etc.) because knowledge is often not exchanged between those who know (cannabis patients and providers) and those who need to know (conventional medical practitioners).

Integral organizations offer patients and physicians a variety of opportunities to bridge this communication gap. Time and observation will help us assess their success, but certainly several integral MMJ organizations are making strides in changing public perception. Leadership scholar Boas Shamir and colleagues (2005) contend, "Telling the biography is an important leadership behavior." Sharing one's personal story, as a cannabis patient, is then an act of leadership within itself. Contrary to popular belief, medical cannabis users seldom medicate or use cannabis with other patients (Hathaway, 2004); therefore, patients need to understand the experience of others in order that they may evaluate and validate their own relationship with cannabis (Becker, 1997). It is also necessary for others to understand why MMJ patients choose cannabis as medication and how they perform the act of medicating with cannabis, so that they can evaluate their views about this controversial medication.

A rare few MMJ organizations have embraced an integral approach that encourages patients to share information and thus personal narratives in this manner. As mentioned, Harborside Health Center proffers a model that concentrates on safe patient access, education, and support issues that fit the AQAL model. I visited Harborside while in the San Francisco Bay Area, and for the first time since I became a patient, I walked into a dispensary that not only offered cannabis medications in forms I prefer and typically cannot find (salves, tinctures, and oils); but also allowed me to engage with perhaps the most knowledgeable MMJ staff I have encountered in three years of cannabis research. In addition to increasing my knowledge, I was encouraged to accept literature for myself *and* my physician that would facilitate a discussion about my cannabis use, medical condition, and care. Harborside and other integral MMJ organizations recognize this type of empowerment is critical to the average cannabis patient knowing that patients are placed in the uncommon position of being the bearer of medical knowledge (instead of the receiver in their physician-patient relationships).

Given this unique position, it is critical to have structures that support and empower patients to share their stories, first with each other and their own physician, and eventually more publicly, perhaps sharing their story with non-cannabis using family or community members.

In Integral Medicine, the importance of the LL quadrant lies within the "intersubjective factors" that are "crucial in any human interaction—such as the shared communication between doctor and patient; the attitudes of family and friends and how they are conveyed to the patient; the cultural acceptance (or derogation) or the particular illness (e.g., AIDS); and the very values of the culture that the illness itself threatens" (Wilber, 2000, p. 91). All of these factors are to some degree causative in any physical illness and cure (simply because *every* holon has four quadrants) (Wilber, 2000, p. 92). When taking a holonic approach to the needs of cannabis patients, one can see that they are affected by physical health condition as well as economic, insurance, and social delivery systems (with social delivery systems currently being the greatest area of focus in this movement); public policy; environmental issues and toxins that affect the quality of medication; and the expectations of traditional medicine. Physician, family, and community attitudes and perceptions are important factors in the acceptance or degradation of a patient. Terminal and chronic health conditions have causes, treatments, and cures that include emotional, mental, and spiritual waves, and as Wilber demonstrates, when "adding these levels to the quadrants, a much more comprehensive— and effective—medical model begins to emerge" (Wilber, 2000, p. 93). When considering cannabis patients in relation to an Integral model, we begin to understand that our nation's cannabis patients suffer incredible injustice and marginalization because their whole- person status is not considered in public policy, conventional medicine, or even a majority of the very organizations that advocate or provide services for MMJ patients.

Public policies supporting medicalized *access* to cannabis arguably fail to consider the needs of patients— individually or collectively—across quadrants. In New Mexico, the state in which I first became recognized as a licensed medical cannabis patient (MCP), this singular approach is inadequate. The MCP program is weak because it neglects to consider the needs of the whole patient, preventing it from meeting the needs of the population it is implicitly designed to serve. Five years after its inception, for example, state licensed producers are unable to meet even the basic access demands of the 7,000+ enrolled patients; given that many patients, like me, are driven to an illegal market due to medication shortages illustrates a need for integral responses to tackle complex problems. Integral models empower patients to take action, sharing their voice and making their individual and collective needs known so that policies are developed in relationship with those they are designed to serve.

In just a few short months, my own personal experience as a cannabis patient has resulted in a number of transformational learning experiences. In large part, these experiences are attributable to interactions with other cannabis patients, not "experts" as physicians are regarded in our society, but *experts* nonetheless. For the past three years, I have been researching the medical cannabis movement from a wide variety of perspectives that span the AQAL model, and while I still have much to learn, I consider myself a knowledgeable person within this domain. Yet the personal perspectives and knowledge other patients have shared with me through their stories have been the most instrumental factors in my success as a patient and scholar. Each patient I encounter has greatly broadened my understanding of this complex movement, the medication itself, and the people who individually and collectively are recognized as cannabis patients. Because I am concentrating my research on topics within this community, I seek out patients to speak with and place myself in situations in which I am able to interact with cannabis patients. For instance, I visit locations where state-licensed MCP patients purchase cannabis medications from state-licensed producers; I hesitate to call these providers "dispensaries," although this is the commonly used term. In New Mexico these healthcare sites are not permitted to perform as "storefront" healthcare centers, but only as "limited hour pick-up locations" or delivery services. In this patient's opinion, these organizations are *cannabis healthcare centers* and should be both operated and considered as such; delivery options may be convenient, but they are inadequate as a sole option for patients buying whole plant cannabis remedies. As legitimate, state-sanctioned businesses offering a critical service to marginalized citizens—sick and dying members of our society—these organizations should not be forced to conceal themselves forcing cannabis and cannabis users to remain hidden from others and forcing patients to make complex medical decisions over the phone or online. Reinforced stigmatization of this type denounces cannabis patients by supporting the dominant narrative that silences their voices, so their true needs remain unknown, and therefore cannot be addressed. It also silences conversations critical to cannabis patients like the need for whole-plant treatment centers, such as Harborside and WAMM, as well as the necessity of research focused on cannabinoid medications with conventional application like cancer treatment. Integral approaches, on the other hand, legitimize cannabis patients' needs, as well as the knowledge they embody.

Existing policies also continue to hide cannabis and cannabis use from the mass population, exacerbating the stigmatization of patients. What few outside the MMJ community understand, including the medical providers who often support these patients' healthcare in traditional ways, are the various forms cannabis can take as medication beyond simply "smoking marijuana"—a major detractor of medical professionals and citizens in relation to cannabis use. Many, many times over the past three years I have heard a health professional say, "The FDA will never approve a drug that patients must smoke." Although many patients continue to smoke cannabis, and do so with what studies consider minimal health risk (Pletcher et al., 2012), the majority of patients use cannabis in other forms (capsules, tinctures, oils, waxes, and other whole-plant formularies) that do not require smoking. Further, oncologist Dr. Don Abrams finds smoked cannabis as a preferred option to pharmaceutically derived and dosed cannabis, as included in the legal and FDA-approved cannabinoid drug, Marinol (Abrams et al., 2007). This is only one example of the knowledge disconnect between practitioners and cannabis patients that the Integral approach could contribute to resolving.

In contrast, when operated transparently using integral approaches, organizations like WAMM and Harborside are becoming deeply immersed in cannabis research, not quite as one would expect from a pharmaceutical company like cannabinoid leaders GW Pharmaceuticals (which markets Sativex, a cannabis-based throat spray available by prescription in Europe, New Zealand, and Canada), but they are working on solid community-based research. In understanding patients' needs, because nearly every person involved is a cannabis patient or hands-on caregiver, an organization like Harborside is able to research and offer improved whole-plant cannabis options for patients as young as five years old ("Jayden David's Story," 2012). Jayden David has a rare form of epilepsy called Dravet's syndrome, which once inflicted persistent daily seizures that left him unable to eat solid food, walk, play, or even hug his parents. However, a year after his father, Jason David, approached Harborside leadership seeking a treatment for his son without the psychoactive effects cannabis is known for; Jayden is now eating, running, and attending school seizure-free. After exhausting conventional medical routines, parents have much to lend this discussion regarding the alternative treatment cannabis provides for their children.

This case also highlights the importance of reclassification and the expanse of beliefs versus knowledge that Integral Research must address. For instance, arguably cannabis is improperly classified in the Schedule I category; in contrast, cannabis patients and healthcare providers stand on the conviction that cannabis may in fact be closer in relation to herbal therapies such as St. John's Wort. St. John's Wort is not regulated by the Controlled Substances Act; instead it is an over-the-counter (OTC) medication with labeling that attests it is only a *dietary supplement* and has no *confirmed* medicinal value. Perhaps the removal of cannabis from the Controlled Substances Act in totality is an unachievable rescheduling goal for advocates at this time, as it runs counter to dominant notions that demonized this plant-based medication; however, whole-plant remedies like "Rick Simpson Oil" are being used widely and successfully in the United States for a wide variety of treatments, suggesting not only that a Schedule 1 classification is unwarranted, but also that FDA approval is unnecessary for cannabis in whole-plant forms. That said pharmaceuticals like Marinol or Sativex represent only the beginning of what should become a burgeoning field of cannabinoid medicine, offering measured, precise treatments for chronic and terminal healthcare conditions in addition to the alternative therapies patients now rely on. Further exploration in medicine, public policy, and leadership related to this population will only improve our understanding of cannabis and cannabis patients.

I have only recently begun sharing my story with others, an action I feared, but which I now find empowering. For as much as cannabis patients have united online through social media like Facebook, few have a sense of community with other patients that they can interact with face-to-face. For this reason, developing a patient-centered support group seems like a good starting point in any MMJ community. However, after discussing this idea with a number of patients and considering their responses regarding individual and collective needs, I have come to realize that unless an organization is structured using AQAL concepts, its chances of resolving issues that patients experience is slim. Community development scholars John McKnight and Peter Block (2010) postulate, "The idea of co-creation...becomes possible when we join our neighbors to live and create a community that nurtures our family and makes us useful citizens." The process of co-creating can only take place when the collective knowledge and wisdom of the community are engaged. Figure 1 lists a number of patient needs uncovered since I have entered the MMJ community. Unquestionably, this chart does not represent a complete accounting of cannabis patient needs or desires, but it highlights the value and necessity of the Integral approach in attempting to meet these needs.

Table 1: AQAL
Overview

UL	UR
Interior Individual	Exterior Individual
Consciousness	Behavioral
Subjective Learning	Objectified Learning
LL	**LR**
Interior Collective	Exterior Collective
Cultural	Social
Intersubjective Learning	Interobjectified Learning

Starting in the UL quadrant, this realm is where patients determine whether they are willing to share their private voices publicly or accept a leadership opportunity. Fear of being labeled and stigmatized, fear of federal prosecution, or any other number of concerns may prevent a patient from participating collectively as a cannabis patient while concealing their individual needs and concerns. Integral concepts expand the leadership potential within an organization; therefore, a primary objective is for patients to learn to recognize leadership opportunities across the four quadrants. Further, they must be empowered to act upon these leadership opportunities from within their community.

Development in the UR quadrant focuses on behavior, and as mentioned physical health is located in this quadrant. Individually and collectively, patients have the opportunity to influence conventional medicine by engaging in this quadrant. Currently, a majority of patients who seek to use cannabis find themselves in the peculiar position of educating their personal physicians about the medical efficacy of cannabis. At the Seventh National Patients Out of Time (POT) conference, Abrams (2012) explained most physicians graduating from medical school before 2007 have not been formally educated about the endocannabinoid system. This lack of knowledge deepens the stigmatization potential that current cannabis patients experience as it relates to their ability to interact with their primary or specialty medical providers. The physician's lack of knowledge combined with a marginalized patient's fear squelches meaningful conversation about cannabis use. As a patient, physicians have dismissed me more often than questioned me in further detail about my experience as a cannabis patient. Some medical professionals express a fear of committing "career suicide" by engaging with medical cannabis and MMJ patients or becoming known as a "pot doctor," but these beliefs seem to be based on fear of stigmatization and not knowledge of the endocannabinoid system, cannabis, or cannabis patients.

Issues of institutionalized stigma, like these, demonstrate a need to focus on issues within this quadrant. There is value and empowerment in supporting patient development and growth, especially among a marginalized and physically weak population; the key is to consider patient needs from an integral perspective. Public policies that support or prevent patients from using cannabis as medication fall squarely within the LR quadrant and have been a primary focus of advocacy groups related to patient *access* to "safe, legal" medication. Policymakers seem to pay little attention to cannabis patient needs outside of this realm and notably fail to consider cannabis in forms beyond smokeable products, which drastically limits cannabis patients' choices once the policy has been implemented. Yet, humans want and need shared and deliberative decision-making in healthcare, public policy, and other aspects of their lives. Leadership in the medical cannabis movement has a great deal of knowledge to share that could offer improvements across dimensions, not just in social delivery systems. The AQAL model supports growth and development in all quadrants and advances the notion that in looking at issues from a single quadrant perspective, advocates and policymakers are missing the bigger picture and failing to develop the structure required to support patient initiatives and organizations.

Finally, common language, signs, and symbols that are understood and shared with others characterize the LL quadrant. If we are to successfully rescript cultural beliefs about what it means to be a cannabis user in U.S. society, this realm requires reflection. Until the taboos, rituals, and shared meanings about cannabis use are demystified, leadership within the MMJ movement will continue to be dismissed by the dominant cultural script and media as radical messengers. The ability to shift social perspectives in this way is a daunting task and one that can only be achieved if MMJ patients are willing to share their private voices, in the medical cannabis community, with medical and other service providers, and with others outside the community. Research concentrating on stigmatization of cannabis patients would increase our understanding of this marginalized population from an integral perspective that considers the internalized experience of patients (UL), as enacted through their individual behaviors (UR), while taking into account the cultural phenomenon cannabis patients experience at this time, as well as how stigma has been institutionalized through (LR) structures such as organizational policies (pre-employment drug testing), public policy (compassionate care policies), and laws (the conflict between state and federal laws), for example. Integral organizations encourage growth and development that benefits the individual as well as the collective across these dimensions, facilitating societal shifts in thinking that will in turn help cannabis patients overcome current societal stereotypes.

Integral Diversity Maturity: Its AQAL Benefits

I have discussed the ways leadership opportunities may present themselves in each of the quadrants and across dimensions; however, I have yet to discuss the importance of Integral Diversity

Maturity (IDM). Scholars Toni Gregory and Michael Raffanti (2009b) posit diversity maturity as "a developmental process…achieved through transformative learning" (p. 43). These two scholars build upon the work of Roosevelt Thomas who also justifies the need and the importance of analyzing diversity dynamics from multiple perspectives. Thomas (as cited in Gregory and Raffanti, 2009b) elucidates:

> Diversity maturity signifies a deep clarity
> about the fundamental concepts of
> diversity…
> We can acquire the conceptual clarity and
> learn the diversity principles through

*Table 2: MMJ Whole
Patient Needs*

UL - Interior Individual	UR - External Individual
	Initiate changes within traditional medical practices including improving practitioner/patient relationships
Understanding one's own story	Ability to affect the course of physical illness through "whole" patient practices
Empowerment	Clinical training that highlights the patient experience
Compassion	Enhanced familial relationships
Enhanced coping with physical health and stigmatization	Reassess cultural values and norms/achieve cultural acceptance
Be positively influenced by sense of community	Safe and legal access to cannabis products and the ability to cultivate/produce privately or in collective/cooperatives
Assess one's social support	Share perspectives about the taboos, myths, rituals, and shared meanings associated with cannabis use
Leadership opportunities	Leadership opportunities
Learn/share diversity principles	Learn/share diversity principles
LL - Collective Interior	**LR - Exterior Collective**
Develop a greater sense of community	Expansion with other affinity groups: cancer support, industrial hemp, et al
Patient support groups	Public education and increased general knowledge about cannabis use/users
Community gardens	Increased cannabis research/clinical trials
Community outreach and educational programs	Develop model cannabis programs for states/federal/international communities
Rescript the dominant narrative regarding what it means to be a cannabis patient	Shared and deliberative decision-making in healthcare, public policy, and all aspects of one's life
Cultural acceptance of cannabis use	Address economic, insurance, and social delivery system issues
Leadership opportunities	Leadership opportunities
Learn/share diversity principles	Learn/share diversity principles

education (formal and
informal) and personal reflection. Maturity
comes through putting these principles into
action on a daily basis. (p. 43)

Gregory and Raffanti (2009a) demonstrate the
effectiveness of IDM in their article, "Climbing a Great Hill,"
which is framed by an AQAL approach. In the article, the
authors demonstrate how an "individual's level of
development and openness to transformative learning
determine not only how an individual will respond to
diversity tension, but also the number of options available for
responding" (Gregory & Raffanti, 2009a, p. 44). Both
Malcolm X and Nelson Mandela provide illustrations of "the
transformative learning that occurs as individuals
reconceptualize diversity beyond traditional categories and
dualities to recognize diversity as unlimited creative
possibility" (p. 30).

Although the authors discuss their theory in relation to
prominent leaders, they also demonstrate how "extraordinary
situations" can become "fertile ground" for the development
of "transformative and integral learning experiences and
opportunities to lead" for anyone (p. 30). Cannabis patients
are currently experiencing "extraordinary situations" by
choosing to medicate with cannabis in spite of federal (and
often state) laws that deny them that ability. In many ways,
this makes them a prime population of potential leaders and
research participants (co-researchers), and there is also an
opportunity to use IDM as an impetus for leadership
development efforts within the MMJ community. The IDM
model avoids "quadrant absolutism" and "recognizes that
diversity dynamics...are generated as a result of the complex
process of integration and differentiation in which similarities,
in addition to differences, play a key role" (Gregory &
Raffanti, 2009b, p. 45). Within IDM, "the four quadrants
represent a co-enacted field of probability waves and
potentiality/creativity out of which multiple, complex events

emerge in each quadrant and interact with each other within and between quadrants" (p. 45). The authors move diversity "beyond race and gender" and "beyond winning and losing," which increases the understanding that "diversity is everywhere and in every context, and that its dimensions of expression are unlimited and have unlimited combinations" (p. 46). Largely, adversity could be lessened in the MMJ community if the use of cannabis as a drug became normalized in our society, and although the paradigm is shifting, much work remains to be done. Susanne Cook-Greuter (1999) explains, "Much suffering is alleviated when the automatic habits of mind and heart are unlearned and uncoupled from memory (what was) and desires (what ought to be) and replaced by mindful, non-evaluative attention to what is—now" (p. 35).

Gregory and Raffanti (2009b) provide readers with multiple examples of diversity maturity in action (case examples of a service manager, salon owner, etc.), each performing leadership "now" based on the context of the circumstances and time they were experiencing, much the way cannabis leadership is acting "now." By structuring a patient-centered organization using an Integral frame, not only will the diversity maturity within the MMJ movement exponentially increase, but that change will also have an effect outside the community, helping us redefine what it means to be a MMJ patient in American society. As patients share their stories with others, they engage in experiences that force the type of self-reflection and analysis Nelson Mandela and Malcolm X presented in Gregory and Raffanti's findings. Patient empowerment, diversity maturity, and leadership across the AQAL spectrum are each primary benefits of this type of leadership frame. There is a significant opportunity to learn more about IDM in relation to leadership development by engaging in research with this population.

Conclusion

As a researcher concentrating my studies in the medical cannabis movement, I have a much clearer understanding of the needs of patients because I have now walked a mile in their shoes. My fear in being labeled a "stoner" because I am a cannabis patient has receded as I find personal relief from suffering, acceptance among other patients, and empowerment from sharing my story with others. Given the right context and circumstances, I believe other patients can have similar experiences. Filling this need within my own community motivates me to consider patient needs with a broad interdisciplinary lens that encompasses the whole patient—an Integral perspective. Based on my observations, organizations founded on the Integral model best serve patients as whole persons and their communities. Using the Integral model to develop a patient-centered organization supports (individually and collectively) an avenue for knowledge exchange, the potential to develop a sense of community, increases diversity maturity, and offers leadership opportunities. As patients become empowered and develop post-conventional emotions, there becomes a tremendous capacity to reach beyond the MMJ community with a message of care and compassion that is worldcentric. For this reason and many others, I posit that integral models are critical in our society; it is time we reconsider Western medical traditions in patient care and explore how integral approaches can assist in reframing what it means to be a patient in our society.

While it may not seem like embracing the Integral approach will change the world, it just might. If we consider leadership as an architecture that facilitates the collective genius of people, instead of a singular hero, we can learn much from the leadership patterns that integral organizations encourage. If we consider the patient as a whole and very important part of the physician-patient relationship, instead of a checklist of symptoms to be diagnosed and treated by protocol, we can also make great strides in healthcare. If we challenge evidence-based medicine with an Integral Research approach, perhaps even greater strides can be made as it relates to cannabis and its purported medical efficacy. This notion could allow us to consider the embodied knowledge of a large population while we wait for the U.S. government to reschedule cannabis, releasing restrictions on cannabis research. The Integral model as described and used as a frame for a research program goes beyond the limitations of current leadership, medical, or research inquiries and persuades us to consider the knowledge cannabis patients hold in each of these subjects. Furthermore, it highlights how little we have inquired about cannabis, cannabis patients, or the organizations and systems designed to serve their needs. A model based on an Integral frame can help us understand more about other marginalized populations and may well have global healthcare and public policy implications.

Chapter 4
July 2012 –December 2012

My fourth semester is a bit of a blur. Due to financial pressure and a desire not to become homeless, when my lease was up in Albuquerque I put my keepsakes into a 5' x 5' storage unit and packed my other belongings into a used truck I'd just purchased and headed to San Diego to stay with my youngest daughter, Stephanie and her family until the end of the year. The move was good for several reasons besides being with my daughter and granddaughter, it gave me the ability to travel up and down the California coast to events, seminars, and to meet patients, and the 5-minute drive to the beach afforded me some much needed peace of mind. Besides my classes—I was trying to get on top of my health issues and find a way to survive—I was in revisions on "Framing Integral Leadership in the Medical Cannabis Community," trying to scope out research opportunities, applying for teaching jobs, and from an attorney, I had a gut feeling I should not trust, I was also being offered the opportunity to start a patient-centered organization. I wasn't getting paid by anyone, but I was working my ass off!

I survived much of this year because my mother loves me. Every few weeks she's been sending me a nice little card and a check (and a few cash dollars). She keeps me in food and medicine, and better yet, I know she respects what I am doing and wants me to know she's proud of me. It would take a whole other book to explain to you how important this is to me—not just to my survival, but to who I am. (Mom, I love you! Saying Thank You for all you're doing at this time in my life, well it can never be enough...Thank you!). When my paper published her disappointment that I was not being paid for the work was palatable, she was really worried about her little girl and the tough journey I am on—the ambiguity is more than her linear thinking can handle at times. I tell her that everything is okay, reassuring myself that everything will be alright, but sometimes I wonder about my own willingness to withstand so many obstacles. I'm tired and if it weren't for my daughter, I would be homeless at this point. I have no idea when relief will present itself, but I try to remain optimistic.

My kids, at this point, are confused—no idea really what I am doing (And why would they? I am riding an ambiguity wave that's tsunami-sized and rarely have the time to chat. I am not performing my role as mother or grandmother very well, but knowing what I know now I persevere because I want to leave the world a better place for my grandchildren; each and every one perfect in my eyes). For the first time in my life I am casually dating—and enjoying it. Plus, I am meeting with people like Steve DeAngelo, Dr. Donald Abrams, and others who've already made history with their contributions in cannabis, am being sought out by patients and caregivers, and being asked to speak at national conferences. Yet, I really wonder what will become of me...where am I headed? And, will I ever find a paying position in this industry—anywhere? The attorney and a new partner try to convince me, "they'll take care of me"—this does not feel right, but I am desperate and hopeful. It's through him and his connection to another very well-known cannabis organization that I learn too well that even those known in this industry are typically not trustworthy and will use a person at any opportunity—this was an exhausting lesson to learn!

My truck gets stolen, my financial situation is bleak, and revisions on the article are driving me mad, so one night I take my scooter to the beach to relax, smoke a joint, hopefully let go of the chaos and find a little order...some clarity. After parking the scooter, I walk past a homeless woman, pushing a shopping cart and muttering to herself. Now, mind you, her mutterings weren't crazy, or loud, she was just talking to herself about life and the insanity of it all. I could relate all too well!

I walked about a mile up the beach and as I was headed back I caught another glimpse of that same woman as she crossed by the pier...and I started to laugh...then I started to swear! I exclaimed to the world and whomever was listening, that her path is not mine---I can and will do this—I will find a way to make a living helping cannabis patients...I will find a way to finish my PhD...I will not succumb to homelessness even though I am jobless, penniless, homeless in days, and without transportation...I will not succumb to pushing a shopping cart and muttering about how I could have changed the world, I will press on—damn it all!

I stared at my fear, faced the reality of it, and decided I could and would fight back. Sick and without healthcare? Doesn't matter. Sick and without income? Doesn't matter. Sick and without transportation (beyond the scooter I am now selling because I desperately need the money, my daughter's lease and marriage are both about up and I need to find a place to land)? Doesn't matter. I let go of my fears as best I could in that moment and put one foot in front of the other and continued riding the wave of ambiguity that had lead me here. I left with determination. When I returned home...

There was an empty shopping cart sitting in front of the gate at my daughter's apartment complex.

I laughed a big 'fuck you' kind of laugh and pushed it out of the way...I will be damned I will succumb!

Regina Nelson

Case Study: Forfeiture Policies & MMJ Organizations: A Clash
December 2012

It seemed every conference call for this course was met by me with some sort of drama---from airports, the backseat of a friend's car, and huddled in coffee shops and rest stops, I think I made every call, but wasn't the least bit prepared for one. The politics of California Medical Cannabis influenced my studies as I was now a patient in what some believe to be the mecca of medical cannabis, and while I was hoping it was as well, what I found surprised me. Dr. Nancy Boxill's course, "Women, Leadership & Public Policy" made me consider the voice of patients differently as I considered my own plight and that of other California cannabis patients watching powerlessly as the feds shut down their apothecaries. I don't think this particular case study was what Dr. Boxill had in mind, but again, it was a paper I was compelled to write. (Thank you Nancy for allowing me the space; and know that taking this course while revising my article definitely helped slant it toward Integral Public Policy {As did the critical feedback of fellow student, Jon Ross—Jon, know I appreciate you so much}).

The focus of this case study is on the impact federal forfeiture notices, which frequently result in the closing of medical marijuana dispensaries, have upon cannabis patients, particularly female patients. This case specifically considers the how the civil forfeiture notices served upon the Harborside Health Center's locations in Oakland and San Jose, California and the threat these actions present to cannabis patients. In considering only this one dispensary, which has managed to stay open (at least thus far) despite federal threats, we can understand how patients of other medical cannabis organizations may be impacted. From viewing videos from the "Save Harborside" campaign and local media coverage in newspapers we begin to understand the impact federal action have on state certified cannabis patients, particularly women and attempt to answer the following questions: How does the federal government's actions—forfeiture notices—affect patient's rights that are granted via the state? Specifically how are women responding and taking leadership to address this violation of medical cannabis patients' state rights?

History: California's "Prop 215"

California became the first state to legalize cannabis for medicinal purposes when voters passed Proposition 215 (aka Prop 215) in 1996 through voter referendum. Since then, seventeen additional states (including the District of Columbia) have implemented medical marijuana (MMJ) policies as well. In California alone, the medical cannabis industry has prospered into a profitable industry generating more than $100 million in tax revenue each year in some estimates (American's for Safe Access). Regardless of the will of the people, the economic benefit to the cash-strapped state, or the compassion Prop 215 put forward for medical cannabis patients, the state law remains in violation of the Controlled Substances Act (CSA), the federal law that explicitly prohibits the possession, cultivation, and sale of cannabis for *any* reason. The CSA classifies cannabis as a Schedule 1 drug with "no accepted medicinal value" and the penalties for violating this law are steep, as witnessed by the fact the U.S. incarcerates more of our citizens than any other nation in the world (Alexander, 2010).

In contrast, Prop 215 and California Senate Bill 420, signed into law on October 12, 2003 and designed to clarify the intentions of Prop 215, are "compassionate care" policies that allow qualified patients, under the recommendation of a physician, to possess, cultivate, and use cannabis as treatment for cancer, anorexia, AIDS, chronic pain, spasticity, glaucoma, arthritis, migraine, severe nausea, cachexia, seizures, and persistent muscle spasms (regardless of whether they are associated with multiple sclerosis) or "any other illness for which marijuana provides relief" under California

State law ("Proposition 215," 1996). In fact, this final clause under California policy provides broad coverage for the conditions under which patients may qualify for MMJ certification. In an effort to provide better guidance to Law Enforcement agencies, SB 420 also allows patients and primary caregivers to possess up to six mature plants (or 12 immature plants) and eight ounces of cannabis. However, it does not clarify nor grant approval for a dispensing model though it does allow and encourage cities and other municipalities to set policies in their own communities (S.B. 420 Medical Marijuana, 2003). This lack of clarity has given the federal government room to harass California cannabis businesses and patients, often further than the law should extend.

During his 2008 campaign, President Obama committed to ending federal raids, which frequently include forfeiture actions, stating, "I would not have the Justice Department prosecuting and raiding medical marijuana users. It's not a good use of our resources (*Chester, VA*, 2008)." Statements such as this were welcome among the medical cannabis community after the Bush administration aggressively raided and prosecuted medical cannabis patients and organizations and Obama received much political support from this population. Shortly after Obama took office, the Department of Justice (DOJ) issued the "Ogden memo," which directed U.S. Attorneys not to target medical marijuana providers "whose actions are in clear compliance with existing state laws," producing a sigh of relief in the medical cannabis community that led to expansion of patients services significantly increasing the number of medical cannabis businesses (Freedom is Green, n.d.). However this reprieve was short-lived, as more states implemented medical cannabis policies the Obama administration shifted its stance. Taking an incongruent position to the Ogden memo, the "Cole memo" issued in June 2011 informs U.S. Attorneys that they may target medical cannabis providers *whether or not* they comply with state laws. This memo stands in opposition to statements both President Obama and AG Holder have made publically ensuring the public and medical cannabis patients and cannabis organizations that "only providers out of compliance with state laws" would in fact be targeted for enforcement.

Confusing the medical cannabis community are public statements by AG Holder, who in September 2009, when asked if raids on medical cannabis providers would continue, stated, "No. What the president said during the campaign you'll be surprised to know, will be consistent with what we'll be doing in law enforcement...What he [Obama] said during the campaign in now American policy" (US Attorney General Eric Holder..., 2009). At the time this statement stood in sharp contrast to actual happenings in the medical cannabis community, which continued to face federal raids as well as forfeiture actions. Earlier this year, in June 2012, AG Holder made a similar statement that upheld the position of refraining from enforcement in sworn testimony before a House Oversight Committee, stating "We limit our enforcement efforts to those individuals, organizations that are acting out of conformity with state law". Just one month later, in July 300 dispensaries, including Harborside Health Center (HHC) a "model MMJ organization," became targets of federal forfeiture notices. The Cole memo addresses the federal position:

> There has, however, been an increase in the scope of commercial cultivation, sale, distribution and use of marijuana for purported medical purposes. For example, within the past 12 months, several jurisdictions have considered or enacted legislation to authorize multiple large-scale, privately-operated industrial marijuana cultivation centers. Some of these planned facilities have revenue projections of the millions of dollars based on the plant cultivation of tens of thousands of cannabis

plants...The Odgen Memorandum was never
intended to shield such activities from federal
enforcement action and prosecution, even
where those activities purport to comply with
state law. (Cole Memo)

As you can see, the federal government does not agree that
dispensaries, especially large dispensaries, like Harborside
(patient collectives or co-ops) comply with California state
laws. Yet, in my experience, few patients can access the
medication and the advice that they need unless they have
access to dispensaries like Harborside. Certainly, this has
been my own experience and it's a common topic of
conversation among patients, who are afraid to ask for what
they need and the increased fear in the medical cannabis
community caused by the federal intervention in state medical
cannabis policies has effectively silenced patient voices.

Administrative forfeiture is the process by which
property may be forfeited to the United States without
judicial involvement. The authority for a seizing agency to
start an administrative forfeiture action is found in 19 U.S.C.
§ 1607 which states, "Civil forfeiture is a proceeding brought
against the property rather than against the person who
committed the offense. Civil forfeiture does not require
either criminal charges against the owner of the property or a
criminal conviction." In other words, if law enforcement
suspects a person(s) is in violation of federal drug laws they
may seize their property *without ever charging the person with an
actual crime.* This means that licensed medical cannabis
businesses operating within the laws of the State, in this case
California, are subject to raids, as well as property seizure by
the federal government with or without judicial involvement.
(Note: The federal agency shares proceeds from these asset
forfeitures with state and local police departments—the same
departments the state and local citizens expect to support the
state medical cannabis policies within their state. While this
case study does not address this issue it is certainly a topic
that must be explored further, for it is contrary to not only

good public policy, but common sense). Occasionally charges are filed against medical cannabis business owners and employees, such as in the case of Chris Williams, a Montana medical cannabis business owner (Volz, 2012), but often, as in the case of seven Long Beach, CA dispensaries (Stoltze, 2012), no charges are filed at all against a person, the property is simply seized and in some cases violently (Jauregui, 2012).

In cases of federal forfeiture, federal agents routinely 'seal' the case in federal court, usually within 24 hours, and the property (buildings, vehicles, cars, business supplies—and, in this case lights, other growing supplies and equipment) remains in federal custody, except for the cannabis which is destroyed. In federal court, it is up to the owner to prove that the property was not engaged in a crime and state medical cannabis laws may not be offered as a defense in federal court, thus the property is remanded to and sold by the federal government—the owner loses their property regardless of their compliance with state laws.

Civil forfeiture remained a relative backwater in American law for many years, modern civil forfeiture expanded greatly during the early 1980s as governments at all levels stepped up the "war on drugs." Because of shrinking budgets, police departments (local, state, and federal) have been forced to develop "creative budgeting strategies," and asset forfeiture assists in the budgeting realm by helping to offset the costs associated with fighting crime (Worrall, 2008). Currently, forfeitures such as those described in this paper, financially support local and state SWAT Teams and other specialized law enforcement efforts that otherwise lack public funding. Forfeiture power applies to a broad range of crimes but the vast majority of forfeitures currently executed impact licensed medical cannabis businesses (Worrall, 2008, p. 2).

On July 9, 2012 Harborside Health Center (Harborside or HHC), perhaps the largest medical cannabis dispensary operating under Prop 215, was served with a forfeiture notice -- or rather their landlord, Ana Chretein, dba

Concourse Business Center and ABC Security--was served with notice that *her* property was subject to forfeiture. This means that not only could Ms. Chretein lose two of her properties in Oakland and San Jose, but that action would also led to her to lose other businesses she owns that share the facility with HHC in San Jose (in a business park), and, which employ over 250 local Californians in indisputably legal business ventures (Kuruvila, 2012). Although over 300 of these notices have been served on businesses in California in the last six months alone, HHC and Concourse Business Center are the first to challenge what this means in court. Most other businesses that've faced eviction from their landlord in response to such notices have simply moved on to other facilities or closed altogether before the federal government can seize their property.

The opening statement to the "Asset Forfeiture Fund and Seized Assess Deposit Fund Annual Financial Statements Fiscal Year 2011," specifies: The primary mission of the Department of Justice (DOJ) Asset Forfeiture Program (AFP) is to "prevent and reduce crime by disrupting, damaging, and dismantling criminal organizations through the use of the forfeiture sanction. This is accomplished by means of depriving drug traffickers, racketeers, and other criminal syndicates of their ill-gotten proceeds and instrumentalities of their trade" (*AFP Fiscal* Report, 2011). In fact, congress and state legislatures created asset forfeiture laws to target large-scale narcotics trafficking operations, but since created these policies are repeatedly used against small-scale offenders. In the case of many California based medical cannabis organizations they are habitually being used against businesses that are in compliance with state law and licensed under local and state business policies. It appears to some observers that the purpose of the federal forfeiture campaign is toppling these systems of state and local cannabis regulation.

On July 9, 2012 notices of Property Forfeiture were taped to the front doors of both HHC locations (Oakland

and San Jose). This situation is unique in several ways from past DEA and DOJ actions that used this method of enforcement. First, HHC is a model of professional and responsible cannabis distribution with the medical cannabis community. Additionally, the notices taped to HHC's door were not threats, but formal notices that legal action has been filed without prior warning. Further, there is no allegation by the federal government that Harborside is either within 1000 feet of a school (it is not) or not in compliance with state law (it is). When questioned about the departure of targeting primarily dispensaries in close proximity to schools, California Attorney General, Melinda Haag stated that HHC is a target not because it is not in compliance with state law but because of its large size. In the media Haag repeatedly states, "The larger the operation, the greater the likelihood that there will be abuse of the state's medical marijuana laws, and marijuana in the hands of individuals who do not have a demonstrated medical need" (Kuruvila, 2012). Not only does HHC have a spotless record of legal compliance, with no allegations that it has provided cannabis to any person not legally qualified to purchase it, but it is a licensed business that has garnered great support from the City of Oakland.

HHC was issued a medical cannabis dispensary license by the City of Oakland in October 2006 and its owner, Steve DeAngelo, a long-time cannabis advocate, has used this opportunity to develop a medical cannabis dispensing model that brings "professionalism and integrity to the industry" (ASA). HHC quickly gained recognition for its free (no cost to patients) holistic care clinic, laboratory tested medicine, and low-income care package program, plus HHC has a wide-array of other patient services. DeAngelo's biography on the Discovery Channel website (2011) that offers a description of HHC during the short-lived reality show, "Weed Wars" states, "Out of the shadows and into the light epitomizes Steve's mission. His work to expose the myths created about cannabis, and to promote the positive science that is starting to emerge about it, aims to enlighten the public on the many benefits of the cannabis plant." While it is easy for the media to single out one leader at HHC, especially given that DeAngelo is a public figure in the medical cannabis community, HHC became a model cannabis dispensary model only in part because of its owner. Instead, DeAngelo himself credits much of HHC's success to its patients (Discovery Channel, 2011) and it is his patients—and primarily his female patients—who've come to HHC's defense in a public manner.

Federal law allows the government to forfeit real estate from owners or landlords who let it be used for marijuana distribution or cultivation. Since 2007, the DEA has sent letters to hundreds of California dispensary landlords warning them that their property is subject to forfeiture. So far, no forfeiture suits have been filed pursuant to these letters. Nonetheless, in Santa Barbara, the DOJ successfully forced landlords to evict their tenants by warning them that they would otherwise face certain forfeiture in 45 days (August 2008). The DEA successfully invoked forfeiture after raiding the Los Angeles Cannabis Resource Center (LACRC) in 2001. The LACRC's building was actually owned by the City of West Hollywood, which had bought it as a gift for the club. The government had no trouble forfeiting it from the city, effectively closing the LACRC after seizing its West Hollywood property that the City of West Hollywood had lent $300,000 to help purchase (American's for Safe Access).

Reform geared towards correcting current asset forfeiture law deal most directly with seizures of property that can happen before charges are filed or whether or not any charges are actually filed against the owner of the property. In forfeiture cases, the accused (the victims) face a manifestly unjust legal process where they have to prove the innocence of their property. The normal burden of proof shifts to the accused and they have to prove they have a legitimate claim or interest in the property that the government has seized and that that property has not been involved in a crime. This is unquestionably contrary to our constitutional protections. Perhaps our congressional leaders should consider bolstering the due process protections afforded victims, which will force the government to obtain a criminal conviction *prior to* acquiring property that it alleges, is party to a crime.

In a public response to the forfeiture notices served on HHC, California Representative Barbara Lee has initiated HR 6335 the "Medical Marijuana Property Rights Protection Act," which would prohibit the Justice Department from using civil asset forfeiture to go after properties so long as the tenants comply with state law; those in violation of state law would still be open to federal [or state] prosecution (Richman, 2012). Affirming that, "We should be protecting and implementing the will of voters, not undermining our democracy by prosecuting small business owners who pay taxes and comply with the laws of their states in providing medicine to patients in need," Lee has taken action on behalf of those she represents (Richman, 2012). But, who are these medical cannabis patients that not only Lee represents but whom HHC serves?

Seemingly, cannabis patients are likely to be located, "with lesser or greater degrees of social visibility, all over the map" of actors and institutions (Hathaway et al., 2011; Pederson, 2009; Smucker Barnwell et al., 2006). Demographics suggest that most patients are male and over the age of 40, but the number of women and particularly minority women becoming medical cannabis patients is increasing (American's for Safe Access). Both the arguments 'for' and 'against' medicalization, and even the legalization of marijuana, have historically been the arguments of white men and until recently this had not changed a great deal. However, when HHC reached out asking patients to come forward and help protest this injustice "the majority of patients who stepped up to help were women" and they did so not so much "to support legalization, but to end the war on drugs" (S. DeAngelo, 2012).

As represented in a commercial sponsored in the

"Save Harborside" campaign, each patient introduces themselves, discusses their debilitating health issue as well as the relief they find with cannabis use, and then asks the question, "Where will I get my medicine?" bringing this discussion to the focal point of this clash between federal and state marijuana policies and its impact on women who are cannabis patients (*Where will I get my medicine?*, 2012). The language of compassion is tucked within these women's narratives and represents an ethic of care from the standpoint of "suffering seen as the kind of thing that could happen to anyone, including oneself (Blum, 511)." These commercial or video messages are of care and concern for fellow citizens, because none of us knows when we may suffer equally to the other. When considering a care perspective, Carol Gilligan (1987) elucidates, the conflict between self and others recedes and places "the self as moral agent" able to perceive and respond "to the perception of need (p. 35)." Whether the viewer has suffered from pain or illness, or known someone who has, she is able to perceive the need of those represented in the commercial and empathize with their plight.

In the immediate aftermath of the forfeiture notification on HHC properties, not only did female patients from Harborside come to the dispensary's defense publically by offering to take part in the "Save Harborside" online commercial, many also took part in local protest rallies (*Where will I get my medicine?* , 2012). When interviewed for the *Huffington Post*, Evelyn Hoch stated that she was participating in efforts to support HHC because she has been caring for a friend, "a victim of stomach cancer, for 23 years" ("Protest in Oakland," 2012). For two decades, Ms. Hoch's friend's was prescribed pain medication that "turned her into a zombie," but after trying cannabis her friend was able to significant cut down on pain medication—a result quite common among medical cannabis patients (Holland, 2010). And, as this caregiver declared, "She's not a well person, but she's so much better. She has a little bit of a life again ("Protest in Oakland," 2012)." So while cannabis is not necessarily a "miracle cure" (though some will argue) it has been established as a "treatment" well worth the risk for many patients. Over a hundred Bay Area activists and patients, the majority of which were female, joined the demonstration Hoch participated in. These patients each suffer or love someone who suffers from illnesses and chronic health conditions and claim medical cannabis is the best therapy. Certainly each of these patients prefers the safe, quality-tested, and effectual products offered by a reputable business like HHC over black-market marijuana hence their decision to participate in "Save Harborside" events such as this protest is based upon this ethic of care.

One of the greatest concerns regarding cannabis in our society regards the availability and use of it among minors. However, in contrast to forfeiture actions, which until recently focused on medical cannabis businesses near schools, parks, or churches, mothers interviewed said they "wished federal officials would focus their attention elsewhere" rather than on dispensaries like Harborside. For example, Dale Sky Jones, a cannabis activist, stated, "As a mother, I demand our Justice Department focus on child predators, gun violence, and human traffickers...The action by the U.S. attorneys is tragic for the victims and families of violent crime that do not have the full attention of law enforcement; tragic for schools and emergency services that depend on millions in tax dollars from medical cannabis ("Protest in Oakland," 2012)." It is especially tragic that given that Oaksterdam, Ms. Jones employer and another notable Bay Area dispensary and school (teaching cannabis related courses such as cultivation) was raided by federal authorities this year though they were and remain in compliance with California law, while at the same time across town a gunman killed seven people (Gardner, 2012).

I spoke with Ms. Jones at the 2012 NORML (National Organization for the Reform of Marijuana Law) Conference in Los Angeles a few weeks ago and during our conversation we spoke about the federal forfeitures and the effects on female patients. Both of us have notice a marked difference in the medical cannabis community, in that patients who had ventured out of the closet appear to have re-entered concealment as one notable effect of these actions. Ms. Jones states that the greatest effect on the medical cannabis community in her opinion is the silencing of women's voices. Much as described in "The Grandmothers of the Plaza de Mayo and The Disappeared Children of Argentina," the actions of our government exacerbate the "conspiracy of silence" that shrouds the women of medical cannabis (Arditti, 1999). Much as the military leaders of Argentina "intended to modify, by any means necessary, the social, political, economic, and cultural structure" of their country by exporting the children of others, our government seeks to do the same by silencing the voices of women who've are just beginning to come forward publically with stories that rescript what it means to be a cannabis user in our society. Civil forfeiture notices are a strong arsenal in battle between federal forces and state certified medical cannabis patients and their caregivers.

Compassionate care acts like Prop 215 were designed to provide patients with *access* to cannabis in a safe and effective manner. HHC provides just this type of service and does so in an effective, safe manner at a much lower cost than many other dispensaries simply because they are larger than most and have the ability to invest in the production of superior cannabinoid products. There are reasons HHC boasts over 100,000 patients; it did not burst onto the medical cannabis scene as a top dispensary, since 2006 it has slowly grown and expanded as more and more patients have supported their efforts to offer continually improving cannabinoid medicines. Much of this growth is documented in local media as the City of Oakland has been among HHC's biggest supporters. Further as represented in local media and on the reality TV show, "Weed Wars," HHC is deeply immersed in cannabinoid research that offers improved options for patients as young as 5 years old ("Jayden David's

Story," 2012) without the psychoactive effects cannabis is known to produce. Parents, particularly mothers, have much to lend this discussion for the alternative treatment cannabinoid medicine provides for their children, who have typically exhausted normal medical routines.

Over the past year more and more mothers have taken to social media with their stories; however, as a medical cannabis patient and researcher currently in San Diego, California I have been unable to access a local patient support group, because the medical cannabis community has gone back underground due to the federal forfeiture actions. Even inquiries in the largest and most reputable medical cannabis collective in this city did not prove helpful in this search. Additionally, the first eight dispensaries I attempted to visit as a patient were closed and the few remaining open had limited options in comparison to HHC. Certainly, my personal experience, as well as the experiences of patients throughout California, stand in opposition to media representations of California as the pinnacle of cannabis consumption. Instead when I do find a dispensary that is a grassroots project, much like Harborside, that meets my needs as a patient I find patients much like Cornelia Grunseth and Eileen Levin two of the women who participated in the "Save Harborside" videos (*An Appeal*, 2012; *Where will I get my medicine?*, 2012). The conversations I've had with perhaps a hundred women reflect the sentiments expressed in these video clips. For instance, women in particular speak of the need to have "safe" access, which encompasses more than just access to medication but feelings of personal security. Several HHC patients mention "feeling safe" at the HHC facilities, one even equates HHC to a "Four Seasons" resort. Personally, I call it an "oasis" when I entered an HHC facility. Perhaps more importantly each woman shows her vulnerability to the former black-market that can supply/has supplied their medication, when as a black woman in her mid-60's says, "I am an older woman, I can't be going to the streets for my medicine. Help me!" (*An Appeal*, 2012) with a cracking voice, viewers begin to understand the impact of the forfeiture notices on patients in a very real way.

Dispensing collectives provide an incredibly important service both to medical cannabis patients and to the community at large, which has an interest in caring for its sick and dying members. Without dispensing collectives, many of California's estimated 500,000 cannabis patients would have no way to get their legally sanctioned medicine and would be left without relief. Renting facility space to dispensing collectives also assists in implementing both California law and *the will of the people*, yet as these forfeiture notices demonstrate people who use or provide medical cannabis are at risk of federal prosecution even if their conduct is legal under state law and sanctioned by local government, as are the facility owners who lease property to them. Observing that, asset forfeiture "revenue has increased nearly 350% since 2003, from $500 million in 2003, to $1.8 billion in 2011" demonstrates the increase in use this program has experienced at the expense of cannabis patients and the cannabis healthcare services they rely on (American's for Safe Access).

Federal agents claim Harborside's scale of operation goes against the "spirit" of Prop 215 but for patients like me HHC represents *hope*. I visited HHC for the first time this week while in the Bay Area for business, and for the first time since I became a patient a year ago in New Mexico (I am a registered patient in California now that I have relocated), I walked into a dispensary that not only offered cannabis-based medication in forms I need (salves, tinctures, and oils) but one that also allowed me to engage with the most knowledgeable staff I have encountered in three years of medical cannabis research; plus, the medications I purchased were affordable (at least in comparison with other dispensaries in California). It appears that federal authorities don't think economies of scale are good things when it comes to helping severely sick people deal with their pain—at least not as it relates to cannabinoid medication offered by non-pharmaceutical companies, but in HHC the advantage of having large scale medical cannabis organizations is demonstrated—better medication, safe access, quality tested products, knowledgeable staff, and a holistic health approach were just a few of the benefits I noted as a patient within minutes of entering the HHC facility in San Jose. Had I been a cancer patient seeking treatment I would have been quite shocked to find the medication I needed in stock, as well as discover that it had not only been quality tested but costs 75% less than it does in the state-licensed dispensaries in New Mexico. Certainly as a patient these are the services I desire but I cringe when considering that availability could be gone in just a few short weeks.

During his 2008 campaign, President Obama said he would not use Justice Department resources to try to circumvent state laws that legalized medical marijuana and earlier this year he indicated he had not changed his stance in an interview for *Rolling Stone* magazine; however, he also commented that he "never made a commitment that somehow we were going to give carte blanche to large-scale producers and operators of marijuana (Wenner, 2012)." It seems our President, like the majority of our citizens, have little understanding of cannabinoid medicine beyond "pot smoking." Organizations like Harborside Health Center are vital to medical cannabis patients, especially terminally ill patients who require forms of cannabis that should only be provided by licensed, reputable "patient-driven" organizations that act as apothecaries in this community. Personally, I moved halfway across the country, from another medical cannabis state, in order to access cannabis in the form I need to combat the health issues western medical remedies have failed to treat effectively, only to find the federal government has interfered with my ability to access these products here as well.

Our government's law enforcement agencies have a financial incentive to maintain the status quo. When a United States District Attorney looks at the rapidly expanding medical cannabis industry, she can see a politically vulnerable industry where a lot of money is trading hands. Further, our federal government is invested—deeply invested--in the notion that they can fund their agencies through the exploitation of cannabis users and producers. The black market which was formerly outside public view is slowly moving into the mainstream and is openly visible in many California cities, like Oakland, much to the chagrin of the federal government (and sometimes local citizens and city councils). In response, federal authorities are engaged in actions that will certainly hinder the progress medical cannabis advocates have gained since 1996. If forfeiture notices are successful in closing a dispensary as large and valued to the medical cannabis community as Harborside the situation for patients becomes much bleaker. As DeAngelo mentioned during our discussion, "Folks like the grandparents in the video will simply go without. People as young as five years old and as old as 90 visit these dispensaries because of the wide variety of medicine available; not simply different tasting or smelling strains, but a topical rub that's non psychoactive, or a cannabis-based sleep aid" (S. DeAngelo, 2012). My own experience as a cannabis patient mirrors this belief. I moved to California in large part because I had difficultly accessing cannabinoid medications through the state-licensed producers in New Mexico and believed that dispensaries like HHC in California would offer the services I need as a medical cannabis patient—as well, as have patient groups or activities available where I could interact with other cannabis patients. During my visit to HHC this past week I found that not only can HHC meet my needs, but they are able to do so at a lower cost than I had anticipated. My relief at finding such a service was palpable as I made my first purchase at Harborside, but it was short-lived when I realized that in just a few short weeks this service could be lost to all California medical cannabis patients—and I remembered that in returning to San Diego, I too have no local access to medicine like this. Perhaps the

key to ending federal action against state licensed
organizations such as HHC is in changing the attitudes of our
society. As Tostan demonstrated in "Grassroots vs.
Treetops," empowerment "is contagious, accomplished
person by person and spreading village by village (Kristof &
WuDunn, 2010, p. 228)." The women patients of Harborside
attempt this same route by sharing their stories with others so
that we can all understand the impact of these actions taken
by our federal government.

The case with Harborside and Concourse Business
Center remains undecided at this time. In September,
Concourse Business Center asked the Northern District of
California to "enjoin Harborside from growing, possessing,
and selling marijuana on its property," representing the first
time in history a property owner has taken such action. This
request for injunctive relief claims the property owner,
"mistakenly believed that one could lawfully operate a
medical cannabis dispensary in the state of California" when
the property was leased to HHC. The dispensary's response
to this motion cites multiple federal cases to show that federal
courts that have examined this issue have overwhelmingly
found that private parties lack any standing whatsoever to
enforce the CSA. The hearing date originally scheduled for
November 1st that will bring a resolution of some kind to this
issue has been postponed, but the outcome of this case will
set a precedent that will cause us to consider this issue
further. Additionally, entering this discussion the City of
Oakland has filed suit against the federal government alleging
that the DOJ knew about Harborside for years and exceeded
the legal deadline for taking action against it. The lawsuit
"also claims federal officials are overstepping their authority
by interfering with the process Oakland has established for
licensing and monitoring dispensaries to make sure they
operate in accordance with state law (Leff, 2012).

In closing to a panel she participated on at the
NORML Conference in October, activist and hospice
caregiver and cultivator, Valerie Corral of Santa Cruz, CA

stated, "All movements come at great cost, we don't live separately from others or nature and the way it affects us. We have to serve each other, as well as cook our meals, raise our children, pay our bills…we must think of what we have to give because what we take is more than we receive." Sometimes all we have to give is our voice, but we must not forget, that alone holds great power.

Note: HUGE Thank You to Tom (A Bagel Extraordinaire), who not only took me to Harborside on the back of his scooter for the first time and let me crash at his house many times—but who also never feared a healthy debate - Tom, know you hold a special place in my heart—and you showed me good men still exist.

My Journey into Medical Cannabis Leadership

At this point in my journey, I was still okay with the ambiguity of it all, each day was an adventure—I'd started receiving offers for potential projects from people well-known within the industry. My networking seemed to be paying off—but I find myself still floundering around without income because no one in the cannabis industry really wants to work with you or partner with you unless you have a briefcase and bank accounts full of cash and a great credit line, but they all do like to pick your brain, steal your ideas, throw money at the wrong people to take on a project you'd be perfect to lead…but really, I am not bitter, I have to thank most for showing me who they were long before I got hurt by them personally, and truthfully, the warnings one gave me about another— well, those were valid and appreciated on both sides! The last few years' experiences would make a heck of reality TV show!

Though money seems to come when it's needed, it's certainly not security—and I long for some security. Around the end of this term I believed that security to be imminent—it's now nearly two years later and I'm still longing for some security, I've been used and abused in this industry and by people who appeared patient-centered and simply are not. I've learned a lot of lessons that benefit me greatly now, but that hindsight, well it's been expensive—or cheap, since I'm broke—but I proceed just as I did then: One foot in front of the other, determined….determined! What I find during this term is that it's not money that I need for security, but health and community. I need others—more than my Cohort, and more than my family, I need to find my place in the cannabis community so that I might possibly find health. Dr. Bob Stilger, despite the drama-filled course he led, helped me see that what I needed was simply to belong.

I've spent much of the last six weeks of this term traveling up and down the California coast chasing opportunities, making new friends, and expanding my knowledge of my new community. I've suddenly and unexpectedly entered a new "neighborhood" so to speak, in the medical cannabis community. I have been welcomed through a series of introductions that still has my head spinning days later. Tonight, however, I sit in a hospice room in New Mexico with a family I didn't know a year ago; in a few short days I will lose a friend, a community member, someone who has had a great influence on my life and who will remain in my most beloved memories. I am not even quite sure how I ended up here, I have no money and even less available time, but as new friends listened to stories about others in our community they offered suggestions and assistance to help bring together not only ideas but people. So here I am, holding the hand of a woman I love and admire as she says goodbye to her mate. I lay exhausted in the recliner thinking how much this woman has in common with a new friend as I reflect upon the last few weeks. My new friend from the Santa Cruz Mountains has quickly become not only my champion but also my partner and co-creator in an exciting project, and even a spiritual mentor of sorts in the span of less than two weeks and it is partially her doing that I am here consoling my friend and her family. I innately knew when I met each of these women that we would be interconnected—I wasn't quite sure why at the time, but today the picture is starting to become clear: Together we are going to build a national medical cannabis patient support network.

These are two of the most caring, compassionate women I've ever met but only two among many that I've come to know just this past year. Each seems to embody C. Otto Scharmer's (2009) notions of "open mind, open heart, and open will." In fact, I would describe each of these women as a powerhouse of energy, intellect, and perseverance—as well each has an incredible story that brings them into the medical cannabis community; perhaps they would describe me much the same but in hearing each of our stories you'd see that our paths to this place vary greatly as do our life experiences, there is no reason necessarily our paths would have crossed, except for cannabis.

Each of us brings with us a dynamic community of supporters who have already begun to intersect and interconnect via social media, it's now time to introduce them all and ask for their assistance. Demographics do not begin to capture the diversity of the cannabis women who will participate in this project; they are of many races, a wide span of ages and come from every social class. Quite honestly, I would have a hard time trying to assemble a group as diverse as these who've become my closest of community. Tears of joy and absolute amazement fill my eyes as I recognize how truly blessed my life has become in the middle of the most chaotic time of my life.

When I began my Ph.D. journey at Union Institute and University, I did so with the intent on focusing my studies on the topic of medical cannabis not because I was a patient—I was not—but because in educating myself about cannabis and its use as medication I recognized that the criminalization of this plant was damaging our society and negatively impacting our social systems (way beyond our healthcare system). Taking this journey was simply the right thing to do, I had no idea where it would lead, but I knew deep within myself that there was no doubt it was the right thing to do. To this day I can't explain exactly what called me to this particular public policy battleground. However, I know without a doubt what keeps me on this path; the stories each of these amazing women have shared with me—and those shared by many hundreds of other patients. Collectively our life experiences, our stories have power, much more power than my story has alone.

Over the course of this term my peers have gotten to know more about my background in community development and human resources, as well they have witnessed my exploration as a cannabis patient into a community that is new to me. Over the past two weeks I have discarded four nearly complete essays that each more or less met the final requirements for this course and which were much more scholarly and far less personal narrative, but those just didn't fit where I am today as it relates to my growing knowledge of community and my recent experiences in the medical cannabis community—they fit where I was yesterday or the week before—I just could not bring one to completion. This paper is an attempt to not only meet course requirements, but also explore how paradox influences my engagement in and commitment to the medical cannabis community, as well as explore my own journey into medical cannabis leadership.

Over the years I have come to participate in a great many communities, some based on geography (neighborhood or local communities), others family, work, education, or even personal interest; leadership has varied greatly between these communities. Some are clearly hierarchal (for instance, corporate communities), offering titled leadership opportunities for some and few opportunities for others to stretch their leadership wings (although this is often true in other types of communities as well). Other communities function more holonically; for instance, I am finding medical cannabis communities seem too engage holonically regardless of geography, allowing for more opportunities for shared leadership among members. With the primary emphasis of my studies focused on the medical cannabis community and having spent time in the past several years in community in Texas (a non-medical cannabis state), New Mexico, and California (both medical cannabis states), I have witnessed the need seriously ill patients have for community and last year became one of those in need.

In New Mexico, it has been five years since the *Lynn and Erin Compassionate Care Act* was implemented as public policy. Community among medical cannabis patients is at the very beginning stages of forming as patients begin to cautiously leave concealment and publically share together in community. Over the past year, I observed as a new Patient Alliance formed and grew from a handful of patients to well over 300 members; today, I humbly observed as many of my fellow community members united to support other patients impacted by threats to limit patient access to cannabis at a public hearing in Santa Fe demonstrating the power of community and the need patients have for support. That said, for many New Mexico Medical Cannabis Program (MCP) patients, local support and thus leadership for are still sorely missing.

In Texas where no such legislation exists to protect patients from prosecution for medicating with cannabis, the medical cannabis community is deeply hidden from public view. In contrast, and based on expectations from the media I was optimistic regarding the medical cannabis community on the West Coast. In fact, I anticipated finding several patient groups and organizations shortly after relocating. However, since arriving in August I have been deeply disappointed. Recent actions by the federal government in the way of "civil forfeiture notices" have all but forced medical cannabis patients back into concealment. In a city the size of San Diego, California (population 1.3M per google public data), I have been unable to locate even a single patient support group or regular gathering of medical cannabis patients after more than 90 days of searching. For this reason and many others in late October I launched a 'crowdfunding project' on indiegogo.com attempting to raise funds to begin a patient organization that would build to a national level and offer support for patient groups across the country. The week after I launched the fundraising project a national organization, or rather a Board member of, Patients Out of Time (POT), offered the opportunity to work within their organization to launch just such a national patient's network and assistance funding other community development projects that are in the works, where I sit today the future looks promising.

Although I am recognized as a leader within the medical cannabis communities I have lived, this marks my foray into leadership in the larger medical cannabis community—a community filled with members I have never interacted with, sometimes never heard of, or only read about as I have explored the history of the cannabis legalization and medicalization movements—it is a community within a community. In the past six weeks my cannabis community has expanded considerably and I sit here amazed and perhaps even a bit confused by the outpouring of support and resources—so dumbfounded in fact I am not sure where to focus first as we begin this community development project. It is entirely possible that my brain is truly spinning around inside my head.

So, how did this course help get me to this point? Well, it is no secret to anyone who has participated in our class forums that throughout this course I've been overly preoccupied with sense of belonging. As I have explored various medical cannabis communities, I am continually confronted by the fact that paradox runs rampant in these communities; just the notion that patients medicate with cannabis in eighteen of our fifty states and the District of Columbia represents a significant public policy paradox of its own (that two states passed voter referendum's that tax and regulate cannabis like alcohol further muddles medical cannabis issues, even though it is a significant victory in most advocate and patient opinions). In their book, *Paradoxes of Group Life: Understanding Conflict, Paralysis, and Movement in Group Dynamics*, Smith and Berg (1987) elucidate, "Membership in groups simultaneously creates fear and hope—fear that the group will be either overwhelming or isolating and hope that participation will be both personally and collectively enhancing—both of which come from the power of the collective and the associated potential strength that emanates from the mutual interdependencies of members" (15). When I became a patient and began engaging in the medical cannabis community I had to consider what this particular group membership will mean for me—and how it will affect my personal identity *and* other group memberships. In fact, even before I became a patient, when deciding whether I should focus my studies in this arena I had concerns in this area. While I had used cannabis, my use had been isolated and few people in my life knew about that portion of my identity. I struggled at lot, in isolation; with these concerns because I did not know where to find and engage in a medical cannabis community and few resources were available in New Mexico. In short, there is an obvious need and it's time to take action on filling this need in our communities, but it isn't just my need, it is a community need so the solution must be created within and by the community it will serve.

The social stigma associated with using cannabis in our society still gives many patients pause as to whether they choose to be identified, as a member of this community invariably assuring patients will wrestle with the paradoxes associated with group membership. I had to confront fears and emotions "around both belonging and not belonging" and the "ever-present relationship between the two 'opposite' conditions" (Smith & Berg, 1987, p. 90). It is for this reason that our readings regarding a "sense of belonging" spoke so strongly to me. The "paradox of identity" suggests, "when individuals approach a group, they invariably struggle with what they are going to have to give up in order to belong" in addition to fears of being accepted by others (Smith & Berg, 1987, p. 90-91).

Research also shows that cannabis patients are particularly concerned about "losing status" (Hathaway, Comeau, & Erickson, 2011). Identifying as a member of the cannabis community opens one up to societal stereotypes and causes one to contend with what it means to be a cannabis user in our society, for women and seniors, concerns of being stereotyped in this way produce fear frequently leading to concealment of a part of identity. For me personally the shift in my identity has until recently seemed more like a series of lurches and lunges instead of a linear course in personal development. Like many other medical cannabis community members, I find strength and empowerment in sharing my story with others and in taking this step and finally leaving concealment and engaging with other medical cannabis patients I have found a community—a place where I belong. Again, this is why our readings regarding "sense of belonging" spoke so strongly to me and I returned to them time and again this term.

Block and McKnight's (2010) notions about small groups mirror my own recent experience and provide us with one of the strongest reasons for supporting community engagement and community-based leadership initiatives when they point out that "the most effective means of changing behavior is local small groups" (p. 20). In small groups within community we get to know one another and "discover that our own concerns are more universal than we imagined. The discovery that we are not alone, that others can at least understand what is on our mind, if not agree with us, is what creates the feeling of belonging (Block, 2008, p. 95)." It is within this type of community space that I have found support and encouragement to share my gifts with others and it is an important aspect of belonging to any community. In my case, as in many others, during the course of sharing one's gifts community leadership is initiated as the individual benefits the community. The support and empowerment received from community empowers me for instance to act on the ideas and notions we share—and I am amazed at how many of us share the same ideals, if not experiences—and how strong we are when we act together.

Community is a place where one can go and safely share her stories. Block (2008) calls it "a place we feel among friends" and this certainly mirrors my experience. As cannabis patient finding this sense of belonging was crucial to my ability to find my voice and embrace my own identity. If one is to leave concealment and begin sharing a private voice publically she must be empowered to do so, and the support of community helps bring this to fruition. This empowerment comes in part from being accepted for who one is. If we fail to acknowledge the power of community in helping members build personal strength and commitment to community values too many citizens will remain isolated and uninvolved in issues of great importance.

As cannabis users, patients must find a way of changing our relationship with the past so that we may co-create a new future. Block (2008) elucidates that this is best accomplished when we realize, "through a process of reflection and rethinking, how we have not completed our past and unintentionally keep bringing it into the future. The shift happens when we pay close attention to the constraints of our listening and accept the fact that our stories are our limitation. This ultimately creates an opening for a new future to occur (p. 15)." In providing members a place to share their stories of past or present cannabis use and discover truly who they are and what gifts they have to contribute, we provide a space for leadership opportunity to be born. Community provides the possibility for ordinary citizens to become leaders and create the change necessary for a societal shift.

Medical cannabis patients and advocates have been waiting for this shift and politically it seems we are finally at a tipping point—just this week, two states agreed via voter referendum to "decriminalize" and "tax and regulate" small amounts of cannabis like alcohol, but these policies still violate federal law, so what actual ground has been gained by cannabis advocates is yet to be determined. However, this societal shift in opinion has been brought about in large part because of growth within the medical cannabis community and the willingness of patients to share their voices publically. A leader is not a special person, but as Block states, is "a citizen willing to do those things that have the capacity to initiate something new in the world (Block, 2008, p. 86)." The best place to build opportunities for this type of leadership is within communities where opportunities to lead are abundant. So many things need to be done in the medical cannabis movement; within this community everyone's gifts are valuable and together they create a significant force. For this reason, it is critical that we invest in community development and initiatives to build leadership; this can be best achieved if patients become active in developing their communities based on the needs of local patients.

In my opinion, the "paradox of disclosure" is also closely connected, and of similar concern to members, as is identity. Smith and Berg described this paradoxical circle stating, "for members to learn who they are going to be in and to the group, they must be willing to disclose; to self-disclose, members need to know about the group to which they belong (111)." Many medical cannabis patients—and even more potential patients (those who may qualify within their state to be recognized as a medical cannabis patient but who refuse to be labeled as such, so they conceal their use even from the state that offers them some legal protection and access to legal medication)—are fearful of sharing this particular aspect of their identity in groups where it is not accepted as normal or with groups that marginalize cannabis users. Further, patients with little or no experience with cannabis may fear being labeled as a 'stoner' by others who do not share this membership; in fact, this fear keeps people who may benefit from cannabis from considering its use even if their state affords them the opportunity through compassionate care policies. "To know oneself in a social context, one may reflect on one's inner experience, but one also needs to know how one is experienced by others (Smith & Berg, 1987, p. 12)." If one believes others will oppress or marginalize her she will often avoid the confrontation. In groups outside of the medical cannabis community I must decide whether I want to expose this particular part of my identity to others and risk being marginalized; however, this learned behavior influences how I behave in groups within the medical cannabis community as well. For instance, I question whether I can contribute to a group that I am not always comfortable representing or that I represent in a manner that some community members may find to be other. I believe many patients experience this same concern. For these reasons, the need for a patient support network that is patient-led and patient-driven is vital for medical cannabis patients; a place they can assimilate with other patients and a space for co-intelligence to develop. Few ill, vulnerable patients have the energy to expend looking for community members in hiding—but given a space to share their stories with others and to learn not only about cannabis but also about themselves is vital.

Social spaces where community members meet and share ideas are the places that co-intelligence is generated. Community development scholar, Tom Atlee (2003) describes co-intelligence as "simply intelligence that takes the wholeness of life fully into account (p. 10)." Although this definition appears straightforward and uncomplicated it is actually quite complex. Life is a complexity, as Atlee describes:

> [W]hen we ask What is Life? we don't get a simple answer. We know that life manifests in such wildly different phenomena as birds, grass, reproduction, human consciousness, natural selection, suffering, love and vitality among many other things. The word "life" allows us to usefully consider these diverse phenomena as expressions of one larger category—life. (p. 3-4)

Further, Atlee elucidates, "*From the inside of a whole*, inclusion and creative process look and feel like participation (PART-icipation)" (Co-Intelligence.org). To participate one must play a role or take an active part in something with others—a co-creative, interactive, interconnected, part of the whole. For it is within community (with others) that we co-create a new whole from which a new co-intelligence arises. Today, I find myself contemplating the new whole I find myself a part of and from which I am overwhelmed with possibilities. This co-intelligent network I now belong is made up of a group of people with gifts and talents that complement my own and each other in such a way anything feels possible at this moment. Everything moves us forward because the goal is action and action releases the story structure in a way that allows us to share our gifts toward the greater good.

As I mentioned in a paper earlier this term, one of the biggest obstacles to developing co-intelligence in our communities is the conflicting notion of individualism that permeates our nation's dominant discourse. Ingrained in our society is the notion to "think of intelligence as something we either have or do not have, and to link intelligence with economic success (Atlee, 2003, p. 10)." While co-intelligence favors the gifts of each individual it also acknowledges the importance of collaborative intelligence. Atlee (2003) posits, "When people align their individual intelligences in shared inquiries or undertakings, instead of using their intelligence to undermine each other in the pursuit of individual status, they are much more able to generate collective intelligence (p. 55)."

Perhaps one of the reasons I have connected with Atlee's work so strongly during this term is because in reading *The Tao of Democracy* and then exploring his other works I've found Atlee clearly articulates many of the beliefs and values I've held about community but until recently I had not considered in quite the same terms or experienced in the same way that I have in the past. However, what I did not recognize until just this past week is how my own notions of individualism have kept me just on the brink of community, as an outsider looking in, not quite allowing me to fully experience community, good for the researcher in some opinions, but lousy for the patient. This week through an avalanching cascade of events and periods of self-reflection, much as I experienced in my friend's hospice room, I got it. I recognized the obstacles I was placing in my own path and I recognized that in order to fulfill my needs as a whole patient I have to allow myself to fully experience community.

These personal observations and new understandings of myself came to my awareness because of the interconnectedness I have experienced in this community. Perhaps Atlee's (2003) most compelling argument in favor of interconnectedness is there really is no other option because "[w]e cannot individually comprehend the range, depth and detail of the consequences we are collectively generating for ourselves (p. x)." The need for interconnectedness as part of a co-intelligence approach should not come as a surprise, because connecting with others is a normal part of the human dynamic for creating knowledge. The most powerful means to generate knowledge is with others, as Weinberger (2012) noted, "Knowledge always has been social (p. 51)." Individuals simply cannot achieve alone what they can achieve together, as Atlee (2003) observes, "As a culture, we have abundant insight and know-how that just needs to be pulled together and aligned so our whole society can see and think and feel and dream more effectively together (Atlee, 2003, p. xii)." Although I have had dreams, ideas, and even begun taking action, my own thoughts take on a greater dimension when shared with others who add value and who begin co-creating with me immediately through conversation. The plans I am ruminating over today look quite different than a few days ago—but then they aren't my plans anymore—they are ours—our community's.

Perhaps the greatest lesson I've learned this term has to do with "the dance of order and chaos" which Atlee posits is inherent in a co-created reality (Atlee, 2003, p. 32). Since no one is actually in charge, thus leadership is shared, I've had to learn to let go of attachment, certainty, and my need for control and just be at peace with a chaotic situation and to be open to the potentialities it possesses—live in ambiguity. However, I've learned to ask for what I need, which for me was a daunting obstacle—it's been the last to fall. Now that my real needs have been made known this community—my community--has stepped up and shown me that the value of my work is exponentially more than I ever expected multiplied by each person whose values and gifts are also made known to me.

For the majority of my life my community has primarily centered around one of three things: my family, my job, or my education. Not only was I raised in a family in close proximity of extended family, I have successfully raised six children to semi-responsible adulthood and now have six beautiful grandchildren. These responsibilities kept me tied closely to local communities; however, because my employment required relocation my family did experience many types of communities to varying degrees of success for our family system. Corporate communities and travel greatly expanded my notions of community and offered me many opportunities to co-create and interconnect in co-intelligent groups for a wide variety of purposes. Through these experiences I gained a greater sense of my global citizenship and a deeper understanding of others; however, the interdisciplinary communities I continue to belong are those that have most challenged, expanded, and blessed my life experiences. In posts on our discussion board a few weeks ago I commented in relation to a question posed by a peer group:

> Embracing ambiguity and uncertainty may be one of my best skills. The only constant truth is that things are going to change. My dad has always said that changing horses in the middle of the stream and doing it gracefully is one of my best traits. Well, I think he only adds gracefully because I do end up on my feet— but I wouldn't say I am usually or even occasionally graceful about it (I hear my cohort chuckle from afar). But, he also wonders why I am willing to change my mind mid-stream (he is a much more linear thinker than I)…I'd say, at least for me, it's because it is within the wave of ambiguity that things become certain…or at least the next step becomes certain. Leadership requires considering all options and if one appears to be better than another, not being afraid to change plans…ride the wave, go with ambiguity! Take a risk!

At the time I wrote this I was confident that I had a clear vision of where I was going, I had some structure coming to my future dissertation work and overall I felt I was surfing ambiguity quite well—then I was hit by a tsunami-like wave of new possibilities after an invitation was extended that brought me deeper into an often closed and fearful community. I am transcending the situation and learning while I go, but I know I am not doing so gracefully; however, I've found many outreached arms to catch me when I trip up.

This community differs so much from others I have belonged—the warmth and compassion I have been extended is familial. Meeting another patient is very much like finding a long-lost cousin because unless you're really searching for others it is still a rarity. Patients have to seek out community, it is not readily available—a safe place for marginalized citizens to gather and discuss issues important to their needs—their health related needs, as well as their social, cultural, and political needs (and spiritual needs, et al). Each interaction I have with these women and other community members, and many more will be involved in this project, our connection moves us forward closer to the shared future we see—a future in which cannabis patients come together openly sharing their stories, thus taking action. Much as we are doing now and will do together in community throughout our lives.

Note: In the time since I wrote this piece, I've ended my friendship and professional relationship with one of the women mentioned—as I mentioned, the cannabis industry is full of users and I've found most of them over the course of the last few years. It's hard to really "belong" in a pioneering new industry that is leaving the black market for more formal terms and legitimization it seems like all the bad folk come out—some good ones too—but it's rough on patients to know who to trust and everyone wants a place to belong, so often trust is misplaced and people get hurt. So far, I have encountered many more opportunist than leaders when I look at the politics and business of cannabis. Where I see leadership is among patients. It is the patients that educate me and help me understand the right way to turn, for my own health or to understand the limitations of each and every medical cannabis policy, to see how they are affected (few really have access to the cannabis medicine they need know due to… well too many reasons to expound on here). At this point, I remain uncertain of most individuals in this industry and even less in those involved in policy, but each and every patient I met teaches me something new and helps me continue along this ambiguous path. I hold tightly to faith and hope that in time we'll all—each and every human with an endocannabinoid system—find the respite we so desire and real legalization of a plant that should never have been treated as more than the food/medicine it is—then we wouldn't revere it in such an undeserving fashion.

Note: This essay still reflects the hope I have and the investment in Cannabis Patient Network Institute (www.CPNInstitute.Org) is the outcome of my desires—though it's still a work in progress. In just over a year Cannabis Patient Network Institute has reached out to help thousands of patients, and personally Mark and I have accumulated a mountain of personal debt (for more about Mark keep reading). CPNI has never been able to pay its own expenses, even when sizeable industry donations were received, they never meet the full financial requirement of an event, or covered even basic office costs—instead we've have struggled after returning and/or walking away from several sizeable investment offers that just didn't meet our ethical standards regardless of the holes in our wallets—we've reevaluated a thousand times and still do—we take our commitments to patients seriously and despite the firestorms we've endured CPNI persists—and after a bit of reflection 2015 is looking to be a year full of exciting announcements! Despite some of the hurdles we've had to jump and the toll the whole experience has taken on our personal relationship

Mark and I are both devoted to CPN Institute and in time we hope to have a national organization to be proud of—one that focuses on developing patient leadership!

An Integral Frame for Challenging
Evidenced-Based Medicine
May 2012

So this is where my dissertation work seems to be leading…or so I am convinced at this point on this ambiguous path, it certainly may change—now in 2014, I have taken three terms off to deal with my own health issues and to try to survive in this industry. I worked on this paper as part of my Interdisciplinarity course with Dr. Kirsten Piep and then reworked it a bit with Dr. Jennifer Raymond as part of an independent study course- so it's really a two-term project thus far. And, the argument it contains—well, it's not yet where I hope it to be…but I am determined to further the debate any chance I get.

Just as this book is entering the final preparation for printing, I have been selected to present, "Integral Frames: Interdisciplinary Tools Supporting Medical Cannabis Research" at the International Cannabinoid Research Society 2014 Symposium in Baveno, Italy (June 2014). Shocked is not a strong enough word for how I felt when my abstract was accepted for presentation at this renowned clinical conference. To be able to take the patient story to those who hold our research needs in their hands is an honor and it just astounds me that it's me taking this information to this forum, little ol' me—Regina Nelson from Oklahoma. Y'all, more research is so desperately needed in this arena!!

The majority consensus among medical practitioners is that advocacy is a poor substitute for the dispassionate analysis of evidence-based medicine (EBM), and that popular vote should not prevail over scientific evidence in deciding whether cannabis is an appropriate pharmaceutical agent for the masses. The reasons for research into the medicinal efficacy of cannabis are numerous, and beyond the scope of this paper, but include increasing anecdotal and clinical study reports of potential benefit, advances in understanding of the endocannabinoid system upon which cannabis acts, as well as growing public acceptance that cannabis should be available as a medicine if a physician recommends it. Further research emerging from other countries and even a small amount in the U.S. has recently supported the use of cannabis as treatment for a number of conditions. Additionally, nineteen states and the District of Columbia have medicalized cannabis in the sense that via public policy (compassionate care policies) each recognizes cannabis as medication and provide some legal protection for patients who choose to medicate with cannabis (with the recommendation of a physician). Estimates place the number of recognized medical cannabis patients at over 1,000,000 across our nation—over a million patients whose treatment relies little on 'accepted' medical knowledge. My research will consider ways of gaining valid medical knowledge besides those represented in the evidence-based hierarchy, which places Randomized Controlled Trials (RCT) as a superior form of knowledge in relation to how medical practitioners actually gain knowledge.

Seeking an interdisciplinary approach to this problem, one that plagues a community membership who have an intimate understanding of cannabis based on their bodily experiences as medical cannabis patients. This concept paper will explore how medical practitioners gain knowledge as well as the importance of narrative based research in developing knowledge that can be validated both qualitatively and quantitatively by medical practitioners or interdisciplinary research teams.

      Broken down, EBM requires clinicians to define a clinical question, assemble the evidence, appraise the evidence, and apply the evidence while considering their experiences as a medical practitioner and their patients' individual circumstances ("Evidence based medicine: what it is and what it isn't," 1996). Presented in this manner EBM appears a reasonable, ethical guideline to understanding patient needs and increasing practitioner knowledge. However, there are many flaws within this system that the western medical establishment is built upon. It is difficult to challenge the notion that physicians and other medical professionals need the best evidence available to make good decisions in practice but this particular hierarchy of evidence is ingrained and consider unchallengeable among many medical professionals. At the top of the EBM hierarchy of evidence, designed to free medical research from bias, are Randomized Controlled Trials (RCT) with narrow confidence intervals, as well as systematic reviews of RCTs. The hierarchy descends from the Level I status of RCTs to the Level V, an expert opinion. At Level IV is a Case Series, (i.e. a case series is study of patients treated one way with no comparison group of patients treated in another way) suggesting the information gleaned in these types of studies are less valid, more biased, and less likely to increase knowledge among a medical audience (AAOS, n.d.). Most EBM practitioners concede to this hierarchal system although they themselves, as studies show, gain knowledge best through the study of individual cases or a narrative based understanding of how the patient is affected by treatment (Greenhalgh, 1999).

As I've journey through the medical cannabis community as an interdisciplinary researcher and a medical cannabis patient, I've come to question the authority of this belief as well as the rationale. It seems to me that when I hear ten or more patients, who often don't know one another, live in different geographical areas, and have other diverse factors but who experience much the same relief from using cannabis, I begin to believe that there is something to this. Now that I have seen hundreds of cancer survivors, for instance, I have a conviction of belief that cannabis may well an effective treatment for cancer, and as I meet more parents medicating their autistic or epileptic children I have come to believe cannabis may be a great alternative for some pediatric patients. Physicians who practice cannabinoid medicine have similar convictions of belief, but with a lack of "acceptable" medical science to prove the validity of this claim, our medical establishment is unable to move forward and come to understand the affects patients experience with cannabis. How can this be when each and every human being has an endocannabinoid system?

In short, we can preserve the status quo or look for ways to help medical practitioners gain valid knowledge about the endocannabinoid system and cannabis as a therapeutic agent. My research will follow the course of thinking that there are other ways of gaining valid medical knowledge that may prove to be more beneficial as a learning tool for practitioners, as well as the masses, than EBM. After all, much of the knowledge is based in the bodily experiences of patients, whose medical experience can be validated both qualitatively and quantitatively by medical practitioners and researchers. Further, two RCTs do exist for Sativex, a cannabis based medication available in Europe and Canada…a comparative quantitative study focused on how physicians glean information and come to understand more about cannabis as medicine and about patient needs could be a significant tool. As well, I'd like to engage in interviews with several practitioners to compare their experiences (moving from skeptic to believer—there are many such physicians practicing in the cannabis community who might participate in such a study) to the quantitative data. So although I am not thoroughly outlining my methodology at this time, I expect to use mixed methods.

In the U.S. RCTs are not being conducted in significant numbers at this time if they relate to cannabis research that may validate these patients' experience; this has been the case for nearly a century due to prohibition of cannabis and its later classification as a Schedule 1 Controlled Substance. Although this situation may change in the near future it's time for cannabis patient voices to sing and share their embodied experiences in a way that can benefit medical research and provide practitioners with a practical understanding of how cannabis may work in their patients. There is much to be explored: side effects, symptom relief, dosage, and, alternative delivery methods, to name just a few areas of concern. These issues can be fettered out and understood if our medical establishment will seek to gain knowledge from those that have knowledge—there is no better example than the medical cannabis population as a base of knowledge that has gone virtually untapped in "acceptable" medical research: patients.

Reasonable people overcome reasonable fears—and medical research that includes the narrative perspective of patients would go far in alleviating fears in our society regarding 'stoner' stereotypes. My own physician had no knowledge of raw cannabis juicing when I began consuming cannabis in this manner earlier this year. In fact, at the time I tried this particular therapy I had little knowledge of how it would work either, but I believed it would do no harm and I proceeded based solely on my own research and knowledge I had gained from interacting with other cannabis patients and caregivers. During the appointment following my initial juicing experiences, my doctor and I spoke about several incredible benefits I had experienced—the ending of a 3-year long stomach ache and a notable improvement in my anemia. Afterwards, she made the following comment, "It so great that you don't just sit around getting high like my other patients but actually have learned to use this drug well." The conversation continued because I do "get high" each day, in that I consume cannabis in both psychoactive and non-psychoactive ways throughout each day, but that aside the larger problem is that medical cannabis use is still greatly associated with "getting high" and not with these sometimes incredible medical benefits.

My physician is not afforded much education in this arena, except through me—as her patient, because she is employed within a government healthcare facility that forbids she even recommend cannabis for patients and would not most likely support the furthering of her education in the cannabinoid sciences or of the endocannabinoid system, though it is a major endocrine system in every person's body (every mammal, in fact). My experience with my personal physician is not greatly different than experiences I've heard many cannabis patients relay publically when they share their personal stories. The reliance on EBM and its hierarchy of "valid medical knowledge" short-circuits many conversations between uneducated care providers and patients whose embodied experience differs (often greatly). I posit that research that embraces a mixed methodology of both qualitative and quantitative approaches will help medical practitioners understand the practical applications of cannabis as a therapeutic agent with much broader applications than expected, largely because they will come to understand the effect and benefit to the patient. Those who readily embrace cannabis as medicine accept the fact that it may well replace many conventional treatments. This is easily witnessed in the cannabis community where patients readily attest to large decreases in need for prescription medications like opiates, narcotics, anti-depressants, and many others. Yet, this knowledge is not readily available to practitioners or patients because it cannot be verified, published, or disseminated via typical evidence-based channels—instead, much of the current knowledge, including my own knowledge, comes from narrative research or talking to patients.

In the absence of medical research I could argue that narrative based research is simply better than no research at all, but in fact, narrative improves upon the CRT and evidence-based hierarchy in large part simply because it stands the chance to increase the knowledge about cannabis and how patients experience treatment. Research like this will pose questions and offer windows into possibilities that will lead more traditional researchers down perhaps more focused research paths that will help us understand why patients report and physicians can often verify dramatic health occurrences when cannabis is used therapeutically. Yet, the complexity of cannabis is such that even if medical research became legal and of prominent importance in the U.S. immediately, there it might still takes years, decades even for us to begin to understand how cannabis works within the body, but cannabis patients can attest and practitioners can verify symptom relief, cancer remissions, or other changes in patient health (many years' worth of work has been done by patients). In fact, repeatedly cannabis recommending physicians tell me that they note observable differences in a majority of their patients seeking annual certification renewals (All states require at least annual updates for cannabis patients to maintain their status under state laws). There appears to be no good rationale for not including qualitative methods as a portion of this research—in fact, certainly CRTs are validated in part by patient narrative—their description of the treatment received—even if this dialogue is not made an official part of the disseminated research.

If the real goal of medical research is the weigh the risk versus the benefits of particular treatments for patients and do so in a way that presents the least amount of risk or harm to the patient, then surely considering the embodied knowledge of a large population of patients who already treat with cannabis would surely increase our knowledge. Much is already known about the potential addiction potential of cannabis and science has proven there is no lethal toxicity factor (Holland, 2010), but much more could be known if we would simply take action on a theoretically sound, but alternative approach to medical research. New Hampshire just became the 19th state to support citizen driven "compassionate care" initiatives allowing the medical use of cannabis for patients residing in their state (This subject, the medicalization of cannabis is separate and aside from the cannabis legalization initiatives passed in Colorado and Washington). It is time that we learn about and come to understand the embodied knowledge that resides in the medical cannabis community.

Patients should not have to give up a medicine that appears to be working among a large population just because it has not been proven valid by the status quo; given the context of the medical cannabis situation we must consider alternative sources of information. This is not a new drug coming to market but a food/drug many consume each day, millions in fact. It's time to move the knowledge of cannabis as a therapeutic treatment from self-help based to valid evidence-based methods that embrace mixed methodologies. It's time to empower patients by validating hypotheses that they experience as truth. When a patient is suffering from a treatable condition (even something as non-life threatening as lower back pain), it is intolerable to allow that human being to continue suffering when some treatment somewhere exists that can help. Bridging the divides that separate physicians from patient narrative offers fresh opportunities for respectful, empathic, and nourishing medical care based on sound knowledge.

As a frame for the research and study this concept paper requires to move forward, I will be utilizing Ken Wilber's Integral Theory as my framework. Throughout his vast work on integral theory, Wilber (2000) describes his labors as an endeavor to "honor and embrace every legitimate aspect of human consciousness (p. 2)." The AQAL model, the foundational structure of an integral approach, has two axes: the horizontal axis denotes a continuum between "interior" and "exterior" realities; the vertical axis signifies a continuum between "individual" and "collective" realities. Together, the four quadrants are the fundamental domains in which change and development occur in individuals and collective groups.

By its title, the AQAL method effectively supports an Integral approach as the interaction of these dimensions produces the fundamental domains through which all developmental change occurs. Further, Integral approaches maintain that understanding any social phenomenon requires that at least two fundamental dimensions of existence be considered.

Table 1: AQAL
Overview

UL	UR
Interior Individual	Exterior Individual
Consciousness	Behavioral
Subjective Learning	Objectified Learning
LL	**LR**
Interior Collective	Exterior Collective
Cultural	Social
Intersubjective Learning	Interobjectified Learning

An Integral understanding of cannabis patients might include, for instance, a phenomenological analysis on the subjective meaning to individual patients (UL); observations of individual behaviors (UR); promoting tools and processes to be used at the collective level (LR), and the uncovering of the social and cultural characteristics that affect patients (LL). Using Wilber's AQAL model and interdisciplinary methodologies, one can study the perspective of each quadrant from their complex interconnected relationships.

"Individual consciousness does not exist in a vacuum; [it exists] inextricably embedded in shared cultural values, beliefs, and worldviews (Wilber, 2000, p. 91)." Wilber points out, "How a culture (LL) views a particular illness—with care and compassion or derision and scorn—can have a profound impact on how an individual copes (UL) with that illness, which can directly affect the course of the physical illness itself (UR) (p. 91)." Arguably, cannabis patients are marginalized not just by how society views (LL) their illness (chronic pain, PTSD, AIDS, among others), but also by how society views the use of an illegal drug as treatment. Compassionate care policies require patients demonstrate that conventional treatments have failed to provide relief before one can apply for consideration as a potential cannabis patient; as well patients must obtain a physician's recommendation and apply for state authorized approval. The decision to become a cannabis patient isn't about "getting high" or intoxication, as the media and dominant narrative would have us believe; instead, for most patients, like me, it is about the chance of living a better quality of life and seeking wellness. Regardless, experiencing, witnessing, or fearing potential stigmatization causes numerous patients to conceal their use of cannabis; unable or unwilling to defend their choice or themselves when confronted by others purporting the institutionalized, dominant narrative that cannabis patients just want to "smoke pot" or that "all illicit drugs are bad." It is an act of leadership to stand against social conventions challenging healthcare providers with one's own experience—an experience often sought in desperation when conventional methods have failed to provide relief. As a cannabis patient, I frequently face these charges from uninformed others, including my own physicians establishing that there is still much work to be done to remedy issues like this and the scope of this article allows only for a glimpse into a few of the motifs that yearn for exploration and Integral solutions.

Note: At the end of semester four, I'm still not really sure where I am headed but determined to continue I enroll in semester five, hopeful that this journey will get easier. On many levels, it seems I'm moving in the right direction, but deep in my gut I know parts aren't quite right...I am on an adventure that I am not totally prepared for, but one that teaches me many lessons that I needed to learn but the self-reflection is often painful and what seems easy never is...such is life, right?

Chapter Five
January 2013 – May 2013

I left San Diego just about two weeks after the bag lady incident, leaving part of my belongings behind or giving them away, and packing what was left into two suitcases, and shipping one box of books to Mark Pedersen. Mark and I had begun talking by phone just a few months prior, he was living in Missouri and going through hell as a cannabis patient and an advocate who'd begun Cannabis Patient Network while living near Saint Louis. And his work, literally hundreds of patient interviews he shares on YouTube, had become a staple of my research diet. In addition, a friend of his—the crazy attorney, I'd met along the path—was offering us an opportunity...an opportunity to start a national patient organization. At this point, I didn't trust the attorney, but his Santa Cruz friend still seemed sane, and Mark is among the most honest people I've ever known. I had to take a leap of faith and see where it would go...I had no idea what I was in for...

During just the first six weeks of the term, Mark and I traveled through 16 states, my trek beginning immediately after residency when I headed to Missouri to cajole him into joining me on this journey. Storms blew all around me but I had a basically clear path forward...I landed on his doorstep and three days later we were off to begin a new life, whether we recognized it or not. The next few months were spent in and out of Denver, moving Mark from Saint Louis, where I hoped to find some stability and get caught up on my suddenly very overdue school work...But, just as we were packing his things into a moving truck, all the shit hit the fan (literally) with the attorney and his minion (who now had gone stark raving mad).

Survival took precedence to my studies, the journey Mark and I set out on almost ended abruptly with our walking away from funding and these two insane partners. We thought we had support from Patients Out of Time, another organization Mark's forthrightness saved during this same time, but little support has been received (And over the next two years, I'd learn the support was only verbal in nature; again, another cannabis organization that cared little about patients or sadly even about friends). Virtually penniless, every day became about survival and about starting over—our goal was still to build an Integral patient organization and to survive in Colorado despite the odds against us. We had no idea if we could make it or not and the stress it put on us both began to erode the personal relationship we'd just begun to build.

It helped that one of the courses, as I mentioned earlier, was an independent study course, with Dr. Jennifer Raymond as my guide and mentor. She stuck with me and helped me through, though I can't say I furthered my thinking as much as I had hoped during the term. By early May when the term ended, I took an incomplete in the other course, "Social Movements" with Dr. Lois Melina; a first for me—but I was not defeated. I struggled on, certain I could continue but my health was poor and so was my pocketbook.

When I arrived at my sixth and final residency, Mark was with me, and we were both well beyond normal exhaustion. Midway through a cannabis oil treatment program that had already "got rid of" two breast tumors, I was determined to finish the treatment though it was daunting, especially with Mark and I back on the road—traveling through 12 states in less than a month. Several of my Cohort brothers and sisters took me aside to assure themselves that I was "okay"—sick, tired, broke, desperate…I was anything but okay. About a month into the term, when Mark and were working the first cannabis education booth ever allowed at the Colorado State Fair, I realized I simply could not give my education the attention it needed, I was nearly homeless, sick, and all my time was devoted to building CPN Institute. Survival was key…I was at the bottom of Maslow's Hierarchy and something finally had to give. With many tears I took a medical leave of absence from Union Institute and University, hoping to gain some ground health-wise and find a way to survive while avoiding homelessness for not just myself, but for Mark too. Though our personal relationship was becoming more and more strained, we were and still are, in this together!

Despite the odds, Mark and I worked hard to receive sponsorship from several well-known cannabis dispensaries; however, personality conflicts between owners and endless promises with no action (and often no funding) left us with a bad taste in our mouths. We learned quickly that most owners prefer to steal the ideas from non-profits like ours and then fund their own non-profit without the oversight of a Board of Directors or even basic business ethics. In fact, owners were working public policy out their back doors in order to change the Colorado Amendment 64 and Amendment 20 Regulations—assuring patients have no opportunity outside of the highly regulated market to legally purchase their medicine—assuring they alone can produce the medicine most patients can produce in their own kitchens—this was and continues to be very eye opening, particularly after we became Caregivers and watched the industry 'leaders' work very hard to take away the rights patients have work so hard to gain. CPNI was burned so many times in 2013 that in 2014 we stepped away from seeking sponsorship from within the cannabis industry simply because we couldn't find anyone to trust…We quietly begin working directly with patients, mostly children with terminal diagnoses—had we not taken this action, I truly don't believe either of us would remain in Colorado—but these tiny little miracles began to change our lives.

Case Study:
Victory Deferred: How AIDS changed life in America
December 2013

Throughout the term I mourned my loss at leaving school, but kept moving forward...scheduling events, meeting with industry execs, counseling patients, and building organizational structure. Somehow, I managed to write the long overdue paper for the Social Movements course—another paper I was not directed to write, but somehow felt compelled to write (a definite pattern has emerged). Lois, again, I appreciate your support! While it wasn't what was requested of me, somehow understanding the struggle AIDS activists, like my friend, Dr. David Ostrow, has experienced help me make sense out of the struggles I'm experiencing here in the trenches of the war on drugs. (David, thank you for supporting my research and for allowing me to room with you in Baveno—someday I hope to repay you—in full and with interest).

As I Ponder'd in Silence
By Walt Whitman

As I ponder'd in silence,
Returning upon my poems, considering, lingering long,
A Phantom arose before me with distrustful aspect,
Terrible in beauty, age, and power,
The genius of poets of old lands,
As to me directing like flame its eyes,
With finger pointing to many immortal songs,
And menacing voice, What singest thou? it said,
Know'st thou not there is one theme for ever-enduring bards?
And that is the theme of War, the fortune of battles,
The making of perfect soldiers.
Be it so, then I answer'd,
I too haughty Shade also sing war, and a longer and greater one than any,

Waged in my book with varying fortune, with flight, advance
and retreat, victory deferr'd and wavering,
(Yet me thinks certain, or as good as certain, at the last,) the
field the world,
For life and death, for the Body and for the eternal Soul,
Lo, I too am come, chanting the chant of battles,
I above all promote brave soldiers.

**"... love, concern, and the drive for survival eventually
win out over fear and even the need for approval." John-
Manuel Andriote, *Victory Deferred: how AIDS changed
life in America***

A historical account of the AIDS movement from the pre-
AIDS 1970's "coming out" celebrations and protests through
the post-AIDS gay community of the late 1990's is provided
in John-Manuel Andriote's book, *Victory Deferred: how AIDS
changed life in America*. Through the personal narrative of
AIDS-era activists and leaders interviewed by Andriote for
this account, the reader comes to better understand how
individuals and organizations were affected during the course
of the AIDS movement and how this movement changed not
only the gay community, but also America. This paper is a
case study of *Victory Deferred* and the AIDS social movement
as represented by its author. In particular, this paper will
focus on the experience of AIDS movement leaders and, at
the time, new physicians, Drs. David Ostrow and Donald
Abrams, whose personal testimonies are a central part of
Andriote's discussion of gay medical providers and their
leadership during the AIDS movement. This paper will
consider the personal commitment, education, organization
and resources activated to mobilize the gay community to
make major changes in healthcare practices involving research
and experimental drug treatment that serve as models today.

Through dozens of personal testimonies, Andriote
demonstrates to readers that "the solutions gay people forged
have served as models for the nation and the world (p. 1)."

The models, leaders like Ostrow and Abrams, established during the AIDS movement are vital today in the medical cannabis movement. As well the healthcare experiences of the affected population have amazing similarities: doctors and patients both afraid to enter discussions regarding serious healthcare decisions. At the onset, AIDS patients, caregivers, and early activists did not recognize that their battle would be fought, "at the juncture where culture, medicine, morality, and politics intersect," a place medical cannabis activists like myself find ourselves now, "as volatile, even dangerous, a battlefield as ever existed (Andriote, p. 4)." Andriote intended for Ostrow and Abrams's personal stories, as well as the others included, to help readers recognize his book as, "… the story of how the members of one community—an "army of lovers"—were conscripted into service in a war that neither they nor any other human being ever chose to fight (p. 4-5)."

Social Movement Scholar, Myra Ferree establishes that most social movement participants appear to be what Hirschman (1970) calls "loyal"—that is, they care about the outcomes enjoyed by the group as a whole, whether or not they personally share in all of them" or in other words, they have a "moral commitment" (Ferree, p. 32). As will be demonstrated in this case study, Ostrow and Abrams both felt a moral commitment to AIDS patients and the movement that would begin to help alleviate some of the suffering their patients were experiencing. In the pre-AIDS work, *The Plague*, Albert Camus states, "the essence of heroism is caring for others as "a matter of common decency," (Camus, p. 3) echoing the sentiment of care ethics theorists like Carol Gilligan, Joan Tronto, and Richard Rorty, among others. When considering a care perspective, Gilligan (1987) elucidates, the conflict between self and others recedes and places "the self as moral agent" able to perceive and respond to the perception of need (Gilligan, p. 35). In considering the personal narratives of those affected by AIDS, when a patient shares their personal story of suffering from pain or illness, others are able to perceive the need of the other and empathize with that patient's plight. For gay physicians like Ostrow and Abrams, each day they looked directly into faces they cared for and understood the need to care about bringing relief to those suffering. Further, they gain some knowledge and understanding of who AIDS patients are and why the personal moral commitment of others is important. For this same reason, patients individually and collectively show leadership when they share their stories with others. In fact, gay pioneer, Harry Hay—founder of the nation's first "homophile" organization, The Mattachine Society—believed, "gay people had something special to teach non-gay people about human life (Andriote, p. 19-20)." During the AIDS movement, gay people taught many heterosexuals about what it means to care "for" and "about" others (Tronto, 1989).

Tronto's (1989) theories regarding *caring about* and *caring for* are valuable in this debate. In short, she elucidates that, *caring about* refers "to less concrete objects: it is characterized by a more general form of commitment;" while *caring for* implies, "a specific, particular object that is the focus of caring." In this sense, in the AIDS movement, citizens cared about public education and research, because many were caring for dying AIDS patients. When AIDS emerged, researchers had no precedent or guide in dealing with this catastrophic collapse of their patients' immune systems. Without an identified causative agent, no treatments could be devised. Doctors, like Ostrow and Abrams, "were forced to pioneer treatment protocols, resorting to trial and error exploration of off label prescriptions for never-before-seen maladies such as opportunistic infections with Toxoplasmosis gondii and Cryptospodidium parvum (Werner, p. 2). Abrams recalls, "We didn't have anything to offer them. [Patients] died, and the deaths they died, I recall were very terrible deaths; they were deformed and disfigured and wasted away, Kaposi's sarcoma lesions all over their bodies (Werner, p. 20)."

Tronto maintains that "the practice of care describes the qualities necessary for democratic citizens to live together well in a pluralistic society, and that only in a just, pluralist, democratic society can care flourish (Tronto, 1993, 161-162)." Yet as Ferree also shows us through the works of other scholars, including Curtis, this care ethic (or perhaps the lack thereof) may be "a reflection both of structure (the current uncertainty of resources) and of culture (the group's history of reliance on communal networks) (Ferree, p. 46)."

To understand the uneasy relationship between gay people and the American medical establishment, one must look at the medical specialty of psychiatry and its shifting views of homosexuality over the years. From the time psychiatry emerged as a discipline, in the nineteenth century, it offered medical explanations of human behavior that, in earlier times, was explained and evaluated in religious terms. An increasingly secular society looked to psychiatry for guidelines on right and wrong. The religious language of sanctity and sinfulness was translated into the terminology of science. But the moralism of earlier times carried over into the translation, as psychiatrists spoke of behavior in terms of "normal" and "abnormal." ....Homosexuality, however natural it was for some people, was not merely labeled abnormal, but its difference from the heterosexual "norm" led psychiatrists to condemn it—in terms that may have seemed scientific but that would prove to have less in common with the rationality of science than with the irrationality of prejudice (Andriote, p. 27-28).

Early gay activist, Frank Kameny believed "psychiatry's designation of homosexuality as a mental illness was the prop holding up society's disdain of homosexuals. Remove it, kick it out, he reasoned, and the walls of discrimination would come tumbling down (Andriote, p. 28)." In 1973 the American Psychiatric Association (APA) removed homosexuality from the official list of mental illnesses, but it took until 1990 for the World Health Organization to discard its definition. "Today there are gay-affirmative theories and therapies and hundreds of openly gay and lesbian psychiatrists who enjoy voting representation with the APA's governing bodies. But it hasn't been this way for long (Andriote, p. 28)."

> Despite the shift in the American Psychiatric Association's position on homosexuality, "modern medicine," as it was often called with a note of awe, seemed unassailable in the seventies. The medical establishment was at the apex of a self-confidence tilting toward cockiness when it came to infectious diseases that had long plagued humanity. In the 1950's and 1960's, a number of deadly diseases were successfully treated and controlled, including polio, influenza, and tuberculosis. By the end of the seventies, modern medicine could claim an astounding success in the complete eradication from the world of smallpox, an ancient scourge that had killed and disfigured millions. It was a time of great optimism that medicine would eventually solve every biological affliction of humankind. As Pulitzer Prize winning health reporter Laurie Garrett puts it, "Few scientists or physicians of the day doubted that humanity would continue on its linear course of triumphs over the microbes (Andriote, p. 35)."

The first hints of the coming AIDS epidemic appeared in the late 1970's when doctors in larger cities, like Chicago (Ostrow) and San Francisco (Abrams), began to see rare and unusual illnesses appearing among young gay men. Initially, the illness was referred to as Gay Related Immune Deficiency (GRID), but the appearance of GRID-related opportunistic infections among hemophiliacs, transfusion recipients, and intravenous drug users confirmed that the infectious agency lacked specificity to sexual orientation, and it was renamed Acquired Immune Deficiency syndrome (AIDS). In 1981 when AIDS was first recognized and publicly acknowledged most gay people were not aware of or even particularly interested in the political implications of their personal lives and they knew most within their community. Abrams recalls, "In the old days, … I used to know all of the patients in San Francisco by name. There was a time when all the people that were involved in caring for patient with AIDS around the world knew everyone by name too. It was a tightly knit group of investigators and people who were really committed and on the front lines in dealing with this total unknown. It was, as you mentioned, a challenge, but it was really exciting to think that you could actually do something that might make a difference. It was such a frightening time (Abrams)." This social network (della Porta, p. 117-121) that Abrams was a part would expand considerably throughout the 80's and 90's.

The 1970's had been a 'coming out' era activated by Stonewall and characterized by parallel increases in political activism and promiscuity in the gay community. Andriote states, "The revolution wasn't only in the healing of psychological wounds, but in the increasing boldness of the gay people to asserting their rights as American citizens (Andriote, p. 16)." The immediate interests of gay people were in feeling free to share who they were and establishing social and sexual connections with others. della Porta elucidates, "Trying to summarize various and not always coherent definitions, we suggest that participatory democracy is empowered when, under conditions of equality, inclusiveness, and transparency, a communicative process based on reason (the strength of a good argument) is able to transform individual preferences and reach decisions oriented to the public good (della Porta, 205)." So, how do we get to this type of public good? Empowered participatory democracy is inclusive; requiring citizens with a stake in the decisions to be taken be included in the process and able to express their voice, sharing a plurality of values and experiences, and where different perspectives on their common problems and explored (della Porta, 241). "Even as gay people with AIDS helped educate doctors and scientists about AIDS, they continued to share information with one another through PWA (People with AIDS) coalitions, in the gay press, and in town meetings (Andriote, p. 176). **Andriote states, "In the context of AIDS and other life-threatening conditions clinical trials cannot be considered solely scientific experiments. Access to clinical trials becomes access to therapy, access to quality health care, and for many, access to hope (Andriote, p. 193)."**

There were only a handful of political activists at the time trying to galvanize a very disjointed gay community—and as many have experienced, it's hard to pull together community in populations known to hide themselves from others. The AIDs movement pushed the lives of ordinary gay citizens into becoming part of public life; "Before AIDS forced open so many closet doors, gay life revolved mainly around circles of friends and lovers, and their interconnections with other similar circles across the country, even around the world. Despite the personal contacts, however, there was little sense of belonging to a 'national' gay community (Andriote, p. 2)." Forced "to be 'sexual outlaws' by an oppressive American society, many homosexuals defined themselves as society defined them, by the very trait that distinguished them from heterosexuals: their sexuality...But the question ultimately became, plainly and simply, whether sex was worth dying for (Andriote, p. 3)." Yet, as Jasper reminds us, "The prospect of one's own death, the death of a loved one, even the death of a stranger...all these can arouse intense, urgent emotions, can force one to affirm or reconsider basic values (Jasper, p. 95)," it can bring you into the midst of a social movement.

Even before the first AIDS cases among homosexual men were diagnosed, the gay community was already in the midst of an epidemic of sexually transmitted diseases (STDs). During the 1970s, STDs carried virtually no stigma within the gay community. The ritual of repeated infection and treatment had become part of the lifestyle; however, physicians treating these patients began seeing increasingly serious infections. First it was syphilis and gonorrhea; easy treatment with antibiotics had instilled the men with such a cavalier attitude toward venereal diseases that "many saved their waiting-line numbers, like little tokens of desirability, and the clinic was considered an easy place to pick up both a shot and a date (Shilts, p. 39)." Then came hepatitis A and the enteric parasites, followed by the proliferation of hepatitis B; "a disease that had transformed itself, via the popularity of anal intercourse, from a blood-borne scourge into a venereal disease (Shilts, p.39)." It was in fact, hepatitis B that brought Dr. David Ostrow from curious medical student to Principal Researcher for the first NIDA funded research. At that time many within the gay community avoided the "becoming known AIDS doctors," like Ostrow because they "did not want to be 'outed' themselves. And, it was even harder to get gay doctors involved, they didn't want to lose the bulk of their heterosexual patients, who might either suspect they had AIDS or leave for moral reasons, bankrupting their practices. Already on the front line in medical school I could not turn my back on so many kindred souls (Ostrow, personal communication, December 30, 2013)."

In 1974, while still a medical student at the University of Chicago, Ostrow helped to establish, what is now, the Howard Brown Health Center. When the center began, "there was a coffee pot, a portable kitchen table, a room above an old grocery market, and four medical students who were members of the Chicago Gay Medical Students Association (CGMSA), who had a desire to help Chicago's gay community (www.howardbrown.org)." Ostrow was among these students who "shared a passion for medicine and research and a philanthropic sense of community and caring. [Who] believed there was a need for a safe and confidential place where gay men and lesbian women could get empathetic psychosocial counseling and sexually transmitted diseases (STD) testing and treatment without political, professional, or personal implications or intrusions (www.howardbrown.org)." Klandermans and Van Stekelenburg say that there are three types of information that may concern people and affect their opinion about their social and political environment: material interests, emotional: sympathies and resentments they feel toward groups and ideological elements. In this case, Ostrow and many he cared for and about, were being overlooked by "the government and mainstream medicine...who were not adequately attending to the needs of a minority or otherwise marginalized community, it became our responsibility... the responsibility of the community to take those matters in hand by either forcing the mainstream to recognize those health disparities or organize and provide those services themselves. We began doing them ourselves; we had to become part of the AIDS movement in order to help our patients and, ourselves (Ostrow, personal communication, December 27, 2013)." A leader is not a special person, but as Scholar Peter Block states, is "a citizen willing to do those things that have the capacity to initiate something new in the world" (Block, 2008, p. 86). The best place to build opportunities for this type of leadership is within communities where opportunities to lead are abundant, as AIDS spread through the gay community both Ostrow and Abrams would have many opportunities to lead.

Scholars Peter Block and John McKnight posit that the opposite of belonging "is to feel isolated and always (all ways) on the margin, an outsider (McKnight, *xii*)." Undoubtedly when the gay rights movement first began, well through the peak of the AIDS movement, the majority of gays knew well what it felt like to be an outsider. To become engaged with a social movement, a person must have a *sense of belonging* within the movement—a connection to it and to the people it represents (people like them, on some level). "Citizens mostly get engaged when something threatens their backyard (Block, p. 45)." AIDS was a threat to all in the gay community, and many outside. Activist Dennis Altman shared that "one uniquely important benefit of people with AIDS taking an active role in their own care is that it provides medical science with firsthand information about the disease from those who actually have it (Andriote p. 176)." The willingness to share one's personal story has been particularly helpful to contributing to the understanding of AIDS because of the willingness of gay men to put themselves forward and speak forthrightly of their experiences (Andriote p. 176). They speak for others who are silent, and in that way they also speak for the whole.

Ostrow entered AIDS research early on; it was on his recommendation that the National Institutes of Health started the Multicenter AIDS Cohort Study (MACS), the largest and longest-running HIV/AIDS study in the world. This particular project started with Ostrow's work with gay men presenting with hepatitis B in the late 70's. The blood work samples he began with during that project were of significant value tracking the progression of AIDS through that same population when later a blood test to detect HIV was enacted. With colleagues at the University of Michigan, Ostrow later established the National Institutes of Mental Health–sponsored Coping and Change Study (CCS), which examined the behavior and mental adaptations of Chicago MACS participants over a 14 year period. Although Ostrow retired from the practice of addiction psychiatry in 2004, he continues to be active in sexual and drug use behavior research- most recently establishing multiple causal links between recreational drug use and HIV transmission- and patient advocacy issues. Since the late '90s, Ostrow has also been active in the medical cannabis movement hoping to help change failed national drug policies, such as cannabis prohibition, with more effective and compassionate policies, including regulation and legalization of cannabis use, integration of Cannabinoid Medicine training into the Medical Student curriculum, and the formation of a Community-Based Clinical Cannabis Research Network that can inform scientifically based Medical Cannabis treatment guidelines.

Across the country from Ostrow, Dr. Donald Abrams graduated from the Stanford University School of Medicine in 1977. After completing an Internal Medicine residency, he became a fellow in Hematology-Oncology at the UCSF Cancer Research Institute in 1980 and began seeing more and more gay men with swollen "reactive" glands, but who, at the time, did not present with serious infections. Puzzled Abrams began to biopsy the glands, but his findings were inconclusive, like Ostrow's early research with hepatitis B, later these early samples would prove beneficial in still early AIDS research tracking the progression of the illness. After completing his fellowship, Abrams returned to the clinical arena where he recognized many of the early AIDS-related conditions because of his experience in the lab. Abrams recalls, "In 1981, when we started seeing our first patients with Kaposi's sarcoma and pneumocystis carinii pneumonia, I began to wonder if the men with swollen glands two years earlier were now developing these more serious life-threatening manifestations. So I wrote a grant to the University of California...to do tests on patients with this syndrome. Because I was a member of BAPHR, Bay Area Physicians for Human Rights, the local gay doctor group, a lot of the gay doctors in the community knew that I was doing this, and they began to send me the increasing numbers of patients they were seeing with this swollen gland syndrome (Abrams)." The lymph nodes were "reactive" meaning that the men's immune systems were overcharged seemingly fighting off a severe infection though other tests did not reveal such an infection at that time. Since this time, Abrams name has become synonymous with the introduction of community-based clinical trials for AIDS therapies, which he pioneered in mid-80's at the height of the AIDS epidemic to find answers to these puzzling medical questions.

Abrams, like Ostrow, didn't anticipate upon medical school graduation that his medical career would place him in the midst of the gay community or a devastating epidemic, but to him, "It was a mission. I was a gay man, and this was my community that was being decimated, and they were having a cancer and I was an oncologist. It just seemed that I was where I needed to be. It was all very synchronistic." Abrams like so many others had personal reasons to care for and about this movement: "In 1989, I had a partner who died of AIDS after choosing not to take AZT – the only anti-retroviral drug available then – under my recommendation. I didn't think that it was very good. But he found benefit from smoking cannabis, which he did daily (TruthonPot.com)." It seems a cruel turn of fate that recent medical research suggests that cannabis may "weaken" HIV and its effects. In other words, it's probable that affected HIV patients who use cannabis may never develop AIDS, even without the use of antivirals which have atrocious side-effects for many patients. After all of these years and painful AIDS treatments, new researchers are following Ostrow and Abrams led and exploring the potential that cannabis, a non-toxic plant medicine, may hold an answer for AIDS patients (Ramirez, et al).

Due to the lengthy and involved Food and Drug Administration (FDA) drug approval procedure, when HIV and AIDS were first recognized there were no promising drugs to treat the unusual and painful symptoms so many in the gay community were experiencing. In fact, many thousands would die without treatment; there were a numerous problems getting medical research under way. At the time, there were only two possible paths to making a drug available for patients: through government sponsored clinical trials or by research funded by pharmaceutical companies in hopes of finding a marketable products. Further, neither the government nor the private pharmaceutical corporations were eager to develop treatments for AIDS patients; adversely affecting the ability of the nation's public health service, and physicians like Abrams and Ostrow seeing patients, to respond to the type of public health catastrophe that AIDS became (Shilts in Werner, p. 4). With no specific drugs to treat HIV, and very few available to treat the opportunistic infections that accompany the immune failure, AIDS patients and their caregivers were desperate. Andriote confirms that a significant number of the early AIDS-infected population included gay people who had pioneered the gay rights movement in the 1970's. This was a politically savvy group that was already growing a large activist network when the AIDS epidemic appeared. When the epidemic hit, gay rights activists became AIDS activists, fighting not just for equality, but for existence.

> Many members of the gay AIDS population were well educated and traveled, and used these privileges to their advantage. AIDS patients began researching promising treatments, unapproved by the FDA, but available overseas or across borders, where drug approval and distribution is less stringently regulated. Patients traveled to Mexico and other countries to buy the illicit medications and smuggle them back to the USA, frequently employing techniques developed by marijuana traffickers. In 1987 the first "buyer's clubs" were established in San Francisco and New York City, where they functioned as underground pharmacies for smuggled treatments and alternative therapies such as vitamins and herbs (Arno 1992).
> Werner p. 20

One of the most prominent Buyer's Clubs in San Francisco was run by gay activist, Dennis Peron, who operated his market in the predominantly gay Castro District and the majority of his clients were HIV-positive, among the alternative treatments sold by Peron was cannabis. Peron's home was raided in 1991, "During the raid, Peron and his housemates, one of whom was in the late stages of AIDS, were physically and psychologically abused being hogtied, threatened with weapons and taunted with homophobic and AIDS-phobic slurs." The only cannabis tied to Peron was a moderate amount of top-rate marijuana that he and his ill housemate, Jonathan smoked. Charges were dropped against Peron and Jonathan when they explained to the court that marijuana was an effective medicine against wasting. (Werner, p.21) Two weeks after the trial, Jonathan passed away; Peron (1996) recalls, "I kept thinking about how I was going to get even and I kept thinking that every AIDS patient needs pot and that is where I got the idea for a club." Peron's recognition that if he could sell cannabis with medical use as a legal justification and shield, "then he would be tormenting and humiliating the narcotics squad" while helping those he cared for and about. This realization was the impetus for Proposition 215 which led the way for California to become the first U.S. State to recognize the medical efficacy of cannabis and provide protections for patients using cannabis to treat symptoms of illnesses and conditions like AIDS.

A second arrest, forced the hands of Bay Area physicians like Abrams. San Francisco General Hospital's Ward 86, the AIDS ward, an increasing number of patients were reporting benefits from using cannabis. The ward's "Volunteer of the Year" for two years running, "Brownie Mary" Rathbun, had earned her nickname by baking marijuana-laced brownies for her "kids with AIDS." In June, 70 year-old Brownie Mary was arrested in the process of baking a large batch of the medicated brownies. After admitting that she not only baked them, but drove the brownies to San Francisco to give them to AIDS and cancer patients, she was arrested and charged with transporting marijuana, a felony. The arrest of a little old lady for baking marijuana infused brownies for AIDS patients was the ultimate human interested story and was picked up quickly on national news. Rathbun was defiant, vowing (San Francisco Examiner, 1992, p. A6), "My kids need this and I'm ready to go to jail for my principles...I'm not going to cut any deals with them. If I go to jail, I go to jail."

Abrams then Assistant Director of the AIDS Program at San Francisco General Hospital, was in Amsterdam attending an International AIDS Conference when he turned on the television in his hotel room and saw the story of his friend Brownie Mary's arrest. Also watching as the Brownie Mary saga unfolded was Rick Doblin, founder of the Multidisciplinary Association for Psychedelic Studies (MAPS), an organization which works to facilitate clinical research into the therapeutic potential of Schedule 1 drugs. Seeing that Brownie Mary was a volunteer at the world premier AIDS facility chaired by Abrams, Doblin sent a letter to the program suggesting that a clinical trial of cannabis as a treatment for AIDS wasting should be conducted at "Brownie Mary's institution" (Abrams 1995). The letter was forwarded to Abrams who would come to pioneer and direct community-based clinical trials for HIV/AIDS patients through San Francisco General Hospital's Community Consortium. Initially dismissed as "too novel and too community based (Andriote, p. 190), doctors, like Abrams and Ostrow, treating AIDS patients became researchers, providing the opportunity for the collection and assessment of clinical data in untraditional settings, rather than university hospital settings. Through AIDS and related cannabis trials conducted by Abrams, community-based clinical trials became the third avenue for drug approval in the US.

In an effort to move forward with research which would compare control patients with patients taking Marinol, (generically known as dronabinol, a synthetic THC provided through legal pharmaceutical means) and patients smoking marijuana, Abrams consulted with FDA researchers in designing a trial and ushered it through approval from hospital committees, state and university investigational review boards, and the FDA. However, he hit a roadblock at NIDA, and only NIDA could supply the marijuana required for the trial, given that marijuana is a Schedule 1 drug. While Abrams continued to navigate the NIDA obstacles, charges were dropped against Brownie Mary and Peron relocated his buyer's club to a larger facility "at one of the city's primary public transportation hubs and he invited the media in to see (Werner, p. 28)." By the time Abrams received approval to conduct the clinical trial in 1998 California's Proposition 215 was two year's into providing California citizens with a Compassionate Care Policy under which to use cannabis as medicine. Though little infrastructure supported cannabis programs, Peron's buyer's club had expanded and was servicing over 10,000 Bay Area patients with cannabis and other experimental HIV drugs. In early 2000, Abrams research found, "Cannabinoids, smoked or oral, do not adversely affect HIV RNA levels after 21 days exposure...Smoked marijuana and dronabinol lead to significant increases in caloric intake and weight in AIDS patients (Abrams 2000)." With this project, Abrams paved the way for more community-based research projects in the AIDS community, including investigating complementary therapies in patients with HIV including therapeutic touch, Traditional Chinese Medicine interventions, medicinal mushrooms, and distant healing.

Mark Orbe describes the objective of his article "An Outsider Within Perspective" as an "attempt to advance a co-cultural theoretical model to organizational communication—one that is situated in the lived experiences of those persons occupying an outsider within positioning" and in reaching this objective he draws on existing research on muted group theory, standpoint theory, and Black feminist thought by scholars such as Collins and Hartsock, among others. Orbe explains the distinctive contribution of a co-cultural approach is that it is "designed to speak to the issues of traditionally underrepresented group members as they function within societal structures governed by cultural groups that have, over

time, achieved dominant group status (Orbe, p. 233)." The
co-cultural model Orbe argues for is grounded in one of the
central tenets associated with standpoint theory that "research
must begin from a person's concrete lived experiences. Many
physicians, including Abrams and Ostrow, understood from
their personal experience with loved ones and friends
suffering from AIDS, as well as from seeing ever increasing
lines of young gay men at their clinics, that they had to help
share the experiences of these patients through the means in
which they were skilled.

Activist, Michael Callen notes that despite the
desperate need of AIDS patients for drugs to aid against
pneumocystis and the promise an inhaled drug, pentamidine,
showed when used off-label by physicians, "No one in the
AIDS establishment seemed to have any interest in the
clinical observations of the physicians on the front lines of
this epidemic (Andriote p. 191)." As physicians, gay men, and
often caregivers for loved ones with AIDS these researchers
had through experience critical knowledge vital to many
suffering people and their own medical establishment, yet
standard protocols disallowed this "too novel and too
community-based" knowledge. Two years after they'd been
dismissed through traditional routes, pentamidine was
approved by the FDA based solely on research conducted at
the community level. Although the research "wasn't as
'pristine' as traditional academic medical research used to
decide for or against a new drug, Ellen Cooper, a former
FDA official, said, 'I guess the lesson is, first, that important
information can come from rather primitive trials as long as
certain key elements are followed,' including randomization,
two 'arms' of the study that are different enough to detect
whether one was superior to the other, and reasonable
'endpoints' in this case the development of [pentamidine]
(Andriote, p. 191)."

Abrams and Ostrow led the way to setting models
outside traditional medical protocols and showed there are
alternative ways of conducting medical research; ways that

favor an integral approach to patient care. Such an approach encourages the recognition of an assortment of standpoints within and between cultural groups....[describing] the importance of incorporating the lived experiences of marginalized group members within the process of inquiry in meaningful ways...[allowing space for] alternative understandings of the world that are situated within the everyday/every night activities of co-cultural and dominant group members can be revealed (Andriote, p. 235)." The "essence" of the model revolves around the process by which co-cultural group members adopt various communication orientations during their interactions in organizational settings. To this end, Community-based clinical trials empowered patients to inform sciences by sharing their lived experience.

Going back to our discussion on care ethics, the models set by Abrams and Ostrow demonstrate that by putting research in the hands of the doctors on the front lines, and the patients who are receiving the care, scientific information can be balanced with not just *caring for*, but also *caring about* patients as human beings, friends, neighbors, and citizens. The active involvement of people with AIDS in community-based trials served—like support groups, coalitions, and buyer's clubs—to strengthen the patient's own will to survive. Additionally, physicians acting as researchers can evaluate experimental and alternative treatments that come through these routes and because community-based research "empowered patients and fostered strong ties with their physicians, community-based research offered, above all else, something whose value could not be measured: a sense of hope (Andriote, p. 192)." When considered from the standpoint of researchers like Ostrow and Abrams who began conducting community-based trials, it would seem patients would be "more likely to believe his or her personal health is a top priority with the community physicians than with the investigator whose first goal is to study the effects of the drug (Andriote, p. 192)."

Chapter Six: Conclusion
November 2014

My academic journey—complete with all its ambiguity—is still in progress, this is simply the conclusion to this book, not to my academic journey. I am finally gaining some ground health-wise though it's been a much slower recovery than I thought it would be—and truthfully, I am still not sure how much better my health will get. It is a day to day process but cannabis has been a saving grace. I hope to return to finish my final course load in one fell swoop—two electives, an independent study course, and a course to prepare me for written and oral comps in 2015, but it may take longer, who knows at this point. My fingers are crossed, I don't know yet if it's possible to return but it is probable. Like most things, this hinges on finances...student loan endorsement, Union's willingness to work with my overdue account (for a social justice institute they were sure quick to throw a sick, homeless student into collections), and more...But, I continue to have faith (Now that I've read this book, I think, perhaps I am completely crazy—but crazy good!). With good luck and good planning, I hope to complete my doctorate by 2016...we'll see.

Though, today, I remain penniless, things are changing. I'm working to build a 'for-profit' educational organization and CPN Institute is moving forward (also rather ambiguously—things don't ever seem to go as planned in this industry). I had hoped we'd all be moving forward and announcing our plans, but as with all business transactions, things always take longer than planned. I am not certain how I continue to hang on financially, but so far, I remain fed, housed, and medicated...though not without struggle as the months continue forward while plans and agreements still have not finalized...(Yep, perhaps, I am totally nuts or just a glutton for punishment, but I persist).

Mark and I focus a great deal of our time on building CPN Institute. In less than a year (but one that felt like 20 years), CPN Institute has gained some much needed attention and has grown to nearly 1600 members (worldwide—all 50 US States and 12 Countries are represented within our membership). CPN Institute has also made a lot of history, and begun to touch a lot of lives---nearly 250,000 each month by social media metrics. We're finally ready to add board members, an advisory board, and begin offering education and services to our members and the public. We're certain that 2015 will bring much growth. It's our hope that CPN Institute will be an Integral Organization, reaching out to patients across the country and finding new ways to meet their needs. Visit us at www.CPNInstitute.Org and learn more about CPN Institute, the use of cannabis as medicine, the endocannabinoid system, and how patients are affected.

Today I feel as if I am standing on the brink of my future, I just don't know yet if I can afford to step forward—after the humbling experiences, the struggle to survive, and the deep-seated exhaustion of chronic illness, I am a different person—and yet, I am not quite the person I am meant to be. With faith, I continue to step forward each day, hoping beyond hope for my dreams to come true—not so much for myself, but for many...never have I had the opportunity to help so many people. When I set out on this Ph.D. journey, I had no idea where it would lead, as I look back, I am a bit astounded by it all, and as I look forward, I see nothing but potential. My belief is that medical cannabis will not only change healthcare as we know it, but every system that affects our lives as citizens of the U.S. and the World. We're in for an awakening, sustainable living, and good health—We humans are in for dramatic change: to hang on for the ride, educate yourself. For as much as I've learned these past few years, the one thing I am certain of...I have much more to learn about the use of cannabis as medicine and the patients who use it—We all do!

I never dreamed that along this path I'd find myself labeled 'a theorist'—the idea is still rather absurd, but then I never thought I'd be 'a writer' either. Nor did I think I'd remain "at-large" quite so long—more lessons to learn than I first recognized. Now I can recognize my own privilege, as well my understandings of American systems and public policies designed to help those in need are much greater. There is much work to be done and I now understand one major societal key: the restoration of cannabis in society. I've pointed in many directions in this book to issues that need Integral Solutions—I am trying to focus on 'what I can do'— I hope you take the time to think about the many other pieces that need attending and focus on 'what you can do'— together we will accomplish more!

Someday, the ambiguity will clear, but today I remain at-large…(and in search of a scholarship and a post doc fellowship)…for I also remain hopeful.

I leave you now with one final piece, a short article I wrote after returning from Italy—the time I spent with researchers there connecting their work to my own was invaluable! (Again, huge thanks to all those who helped me make it there and survive the trip! I can never repay you for the experience you provided me!

This article is full of hope for the future of cannabis medicine—my life's mission and hope is that all humans come to understand they have an endocannabinoid system and that together we must right the egregious error our society made taking this plant away from us!!

Cannabis Beats Placebo
August 2014
As published by LadyBud Magazine

Earlier this year against the advice of many, I submitted an abstract to present at the International Cannabinoid Research Society's 2014 Symposium. Not only was this Social Scientist selected from among over 300 other doctoral students, the remainder having the required Endocannabinoid Science experience I simply do not have, but I was one also of the few in attendance that had experience working with live human beings. I was thrilled!! And, after some months of struggle I became the first Ph.D. student to crowdsource my way to this prestigious event to present "Integral Frames: Interdisciplinary Tools for Medical Cannabis Research." It was quite a financial struggle even with the support but well worth the effort! Although I made many connections to research projects that were presented and had many dynamic conversations with my fellow researchers, one particular study, "Role of 5HT1A Receptors on the Neuroprotective and Neurobehavioral Effects of Cannabidiol in Hypoxic-Ischemic Newborn Pigs," (yes, it's a laboring title, this was a clinical conference—you have no idea how hard some presentations were to follow for the non-scientist) found a way to open my eyes to the future of cannabinoid medicine in a way no other did—it made a personal connection to me and my own babies.
Let me explain...

Just over 21 years ago my life was blessed with the birth of my twins, Timothy and Bryan. Born at only 25 weeks gestation they weighed in at only 1 lb. 11 oz. and 1 lb. 12 oz. respectively, their feet were smaller than my thumbs, their legs no bigger round than my index finger—they were tiny and they were highly at risk for brain damage given their premature birth brought on by a kidney infection that sent me to the hospital a week before they were delivered. The list of potential health problems was long—pulmonary and coronary problems, retinopathy, and more daunting long-term conditions that I could fathom as a young mother. Perhaps the most worrisome was brain damage…so many varieties and forms of potential brain damage that each week their little brains were viewed via ultrasound for possible bleeds. Each week I held my breath and prayed…My husband and I were among the lucky parents, especially given the odds with a twin birth, neither of our sons faced a brain damaging bleed.

Since that time my children have all grown, Timothy and Bryan are the youngest of six and have become handsome, healthy young men. My three older daughters have all had children of their own and between them they've had four premature babies, all but one also escaped the worst case-scenarios of premature birth. Shane has not fared as well and has spent much of his life in the hospital instead of at home with his family. As well, the pharmaceutical medications provided over the course of his young life—he's only three years old—have left him as a pre-cancerous, pre-lupus, and pre-rheumatoid arthritis, and underweight, to name only some of the pharmaceutical side-effects. Although we're seeing children as medical cannabis patients it's still not socially acceptable for parents to take the leap to cannabis medicine…yet, what does the science tell us??

More than twenty-one years and many traumatic NICU visits since, I am where I never expected to be, in Baveno, Italy for the International Cannabinoid Research Society 2014 Symposium—when the lights come on, so to speak! Let's return to the study of those baby pigs. At one day old these piglets were robbed of oxygen to the brain to mimic hypoxic-ischemic conditions: the brain damage caused by the oxygen deprivation often brought on by severe apnea and/or cardiac stress events premature babies sometimes experience multiple times per day. Following verification of the induced brain damage the piglets were given Cannabidiol (CBD) Oil—one group received one dose of CBD oil thirty minutes after the event and another group was given only three very, very small doses over the course of six days. Later these piggy's brains were compared against those of normal, healthy piglets.

Here's where it gets interesting: In looking at each of the eight regions of each piglet's brain the researchers were "shocked and amazed" to report FULL RESTORATION and not just that but, "Full restoration in each of the eight sections of the brain AND evidence of neuroprotection in all cells!" (Jimenez-Sanchez, L., ICRS). As excited as Laura was to have found these amazing results, I was just as shocked to hear this good news! So excited I followed up after her presentation and during our conversation came to realize that when these piglets were dosed with CBD oil the amount given was considerably small! When I say small, I mean 1 mg of CBD Oil per kg of weight. What does this mean?? Well to me it means my sons would have had similar neuroprotective results at less than 1 milligram of CBD oil—Less than 1 mg!!! (Note: There are 1000 mgs in each gram of cannabis oil). And my grandchildren would have as well with only a little higher dose, given that their weights were considerably more at birth than a kg. However, they would not have needed much more than a one milligram dose as the research team also found that "There were no differences between piglets receiving one dose or three doses of CBD."

1 out of 8 babies born in the US each year is delivered prematurely and all are high risk for hypoxic-ischemic brain damage!! Many are not as lucky as my sons and granddaughters were in surviving their premature birth with little long-term effect. Most are like my grandson, Shane; they struggle to survive, sometimes for the rest of their lives, because of the circumstances of their birth and the pharmaceutical manner in which many of their conditions are treated. These babies are our most vulnerable and at risk citizens—and they are our future. Can any parent or grandparent sit idly by knowing there is a non-toxic, low-dose traditional medicine that is an option—a scientifically proven option—that's being overlooked because so few medical professionals and policy makers consider the science of cannabinoid medicine? I can't!! Especially, since I recognize that few of them have ever heard of the Endocannabinoid System (eCS) and its amazing ability to heal the body and protect, not harm, the brain.

Researchers have spent many decades looking for safe, non-toxic remedies for a wide-variety of illnesses and conditions; it's only been since 1988 that the eCS was discovered, much science must still be explored. Fortunately, we're beginning to see the stigma lift from this research arena. During the Symposium I was pleased to note the large number of young women conducting cannabinoid research, many Ph.D.'s under the age of 30 from all over the world, including the good Ol' USA. Once word got out that I work with human beings, not mice, rats, piglets, or even cells—but real, live people, I got quite popular and was able to help connect what these young researchers do in lab with what patients are doing at home without the interference of NIDA or the pharmaceutical companies these researchers contend with on a daily basis---you know, those looking to mimic Cannabis beats Placebo results with other, less effective and far more toxic substances and compounds than *cannabis sativa* contains.

There were a number of other research stories in which Cannabis Beats Placebo was touted with much amazement during this Symposium—Alzheimer's Disease, PTS Disorders, Neuropathy, Substance Abuse, Seizure Disorders, Memory Improvement, Psychiatric Conditions, and so much more! Pharmaceutical researchers aren't really used to these kinds of results; typically they just hope not to kill the patient too quickly, even if it is a laboratory mouse. (BTW: No cancer treatment currently marketed beats placebo in clinical trials—but cannabis does!). When you consider that we humans all have an eCS system which reacts favorably to the phytocannabinoids from this amazing plant it's somehow common sense that cannabis beats placebo in trials—at least to me, as a patient, social researcher, and more adept scientist than I previously recognized. But now this grandma is also really angry! When I first started exploring cannabis it was about my own health issues, and I just figured we didn't know what we didn't know yet—but now, this has affected my babies and my babies' babies (and so many, many family's babies)! It's time for the science to reach the masses so that we can understand we have a safe choice and options beyond hazardous treatments.

The science required to remove cannabis from the Schedule of Controlled Substances is far more than adequate, yet every citizen with an eCS (100%) and every citizen who supports the medicalization of cannabis (87%) wait for our government to take action. People from all over the country have come to Colorado as medical cannabis refugees seeking treatment for their child, themselves, or someone else they love dearly and yet there is not nearly enough cannabis oil, especially Cannabidiol rich oil to meet the current demand—and demand is growing far quicker than supply as citizens educate themselves by reading research studies just like this one! Yet, one small gram of CBD oil could potentially treat up to 1000 babies (1000 babies born under 2.2 lbs., unfortunately far too common these days) and "induce neuroprotection" that is so desperately necessary for these high-risk infants!

In my opinion, the educational chasm between endocannabinoid researchers and family physicians is greater than the gap between patient and doctor or even patient and researcher. Patients are self-educated and rely heavily on other patients for information, plus they embody a specific type of knowledge regarding the use of cannabis—one that still fails to reach researchers, medical professionals, policymakers, or the masses to significant degree, embodied knowledge. This seems to be where I fit in. With Cannabis Patient Network Institute (www.CPNInstitute.Org) and Integral Education and Consulting, LLC (www.IntegralEducationandConsulting.com) my primary goal is to bridge these communication gaps, to help patients share their stories, to engage patients in community-based research projects, and to spread cannabis education like wildfire through a network of trainers.

The birth—and possible death—of a premature baby has impacted nearly all of us in some way. Please share this information with others who can benefit from knowing. It's an easy way to be a leader in cannabis education! And, if you have the time send NIDA a Thank You note for sponsoring the ICRS 2014 Symposium and encourage them to continue acts of common good like this—it's so rare that a government agency does! And, to all those who helped me raise the funds to attend this conference I thank you from the bottom of my heart—this is but one "aha" moment I had during those 5 days in Baveno. I look forward to sharing more insights with you soon!

REFERENCES

Abel, E. (1943) *Marihuana: The First Twelve Thousand Years*. NY: Plenum Press (Reprinted 1980).

Aggrawal, S. et al (2009) Medicinal Use of Cannabis in the United State: Historical Perspectives, Current Trends, and Future Directions. In *Journal of Opioid Management*. May-June;5(3):pp.153-168

Alexander, B. (2004) *Black Skin/White Masks: The Performative Sustainability of Whiteness*. London: Sage Publications.

Alexander, M, (2010) *The New Jim Crow: Mass Incarceration in the Age of Colorblindness*. NY: The New Press.

American Medical Association. www.ama-assn.org Retrieved April 20, 2011

American Red Cross. (2011). http://chapters.redcross.org

Americans for Safe Access. www.safeaccessnow.org Retrieved April 20, 2011

Annas, "Reefer Madness—The federal response to California's medical-marijuana law." *The New England Journal of Medicine*, Vol. 337, No. 6, August 7, 1997, pp 1-4

Appiah, K. (2006) *Cosmopolitanism*. NY: W.W. Norton & Company

Arizona Election Results. http://azcapitoltimes.com/news/2010/07/30/statewide-voter-demographics/ Retrieved April 20, 2011

Babor, T. et al (2010}. *Drug Policy and the Public Good*. NY: Oxford University Press.

Baier, A. (1987) The Need for More than Justice. In Held, V (1995) *Justice and Care: Essential Readings in Feminist Ethics*. (pp. 47-58) NY: Westview Press.

Blum, L. (1980) Compassion. In *Explaining Emotions*, ed. Amelie Rorty. Berkeley: University of California Press.

Bourassi, M., & Vaugeouis, P. *Effects of Cannabis Use on Divergent Thought.*

Bourdieu, P. (1991) *Language and symbolic power*. Cambridge: Cambridge University Press.

Carter, J. (2011, June 16). Call off the global drug war. *The New York Times*. Retrieved from http://www.nytimes.com/2011/06/17/opinion/17carter.HTML

Couto, R. (Ed.). (2010). Creativity and Innovation. In *Political and Civil Leadership* (pp. 968-982).

Couto, R., Munley, A. E., & O'Neill, K. (2010). Leadership Cultures. In *Political and Civic Leadership* (pp. 498-506). NY: Sage Publications.

Cropley, D. H., Cropley, A. J., Kaufman, J. C., & Runco, M. A. (2010). *The Dark Side of Creativity*. London: Cambridge University Press.

Csikszentmihalyi, M. (1996). The Creative Personality. In *Creativity: Flow and the Psychology of Discovery and Invention* (pp. 51-74). NY: Harper Perennial.

Degenhardt, L. et al (2001) The Relationship Between Cannabis Use and Other Substance Use in the General Population. *Drug and Alcohol Dependence*. 64, pp 319-327

Department of Drug Enforcement Controlled Substances Schedules. Department of Justice. www.usdoj.gov Retrieved April 19, 2011

Feingold, P. & Knapp, M. (2006) Anti-Drug Abuse Commercials. In *Journal of Communication*, Vol 27, pp 20-28

Gamman, L., & Raein, M. (2010). Reviewing the Art of Crime: What, If Anything, Do Criminals and Artists/Designers Have in Common? In D. Cropley, A. Cropley, J. Kaufman, & M. Runco (Eds.), *The Dark Side of Creativity* (pp. 155-176). : .

Gilligan, C. (1987) Moral Orientation and Moral Development. In Held, V (1995) *Justice and Care: Essential Readings in Feminist Ethics*. (pp. 31-45) NY: Westview Press.

Global Commission on Drug Policy. (2011). *War on Drugs* (). Washington, DC: U.S. Government Printing Office.

Grinspoon, L. (April, 22, 2011) *Marijuana, Seniors and Aging*. NORML Annual Conference. Denver, CO.

Grinspoon, L. & Bakalar, J. (1997) *Marihuana: The Forbidden Medicine*. New Haven, CT: Yale University Press.

Hall, S. (2010). *Representation: Cultural Representations and Signifying Practices*. London: Sage Publications.

Hill Collins, P. (1998) *Fighting Words: Black Women and the Search for Justice*. Minneapolis, MN: University of Minnesota Press.

Hill-Collins, P. (2000) *Black Feminist Thought: Knowledge, Consciousness and the Politics of Empowerment*. NY: Routledge

Hilton, K. (2010). Boundless Creativity. In D. Cropley, A. Cropley, J. Kaufman, & M. Runco (Eds.), *The Dark Side of Creativity* (pp. 134-154). London: Cambridge University Press.

How Many People in the US Use Medical Cannabis? [comment]. (2009, March 11, 2009). Retrieved from http://medicalcannabis.procon.org/view.answers.php?questionID=001199

http://www.metacafe.com. (February 15, 2011). http://www.metacafe.com/watch/hl-50055155/the_green_rush_the_green_rush/

International Committee of the Red Cross. (2011). http://www.icrc.org/eng/resources/documents/misc/emblem-history.htm

Iverson, L. (2008) *The Science of Marijuana*. NY: Oxford University Press.

Jackson, J. (2011). It's time to end dismally failed 'war on drugs'. Retrieved from http://www.suntimes.com/news/jackson/5805266-417/its-time-to-end-dismally-failed-war-on-drugs.html

James, K., & Taylor, A. (2010). Positive Creativity and Negative Creativity (and Unintended Consequences). In D. Cropley, A. J. Cropley, J. C. Kaufman, & M. A. Runco (Eds.), *The Dark Side of Creativity* (pp. 33-56). Cambridge: Cambridge University Pres.

Joy, J. (1999) Marijuana and Medicine: Assessing the Science Base. Division of Neuroscience and Behavioral Research, Institute of Medicine, National Institutes of Health. Washington, DC: National Academy Press.

Mpofu, E., Myambo, K., Mogaji, A., Mashego, T. A., & Khaleefa, O. (2006). African Perspectives on Creativity. (pp. 456-489). Cambridge: Cambridge University Press.

Nelson, R. (2012). Framing Integral Leadership in the Medical Cannabis Community. *Integral Practice and Review*.

Noddings, N. (1984) Caring. In Held, V (1995) *Justice and Care: Essential Readings in Feminist Ethics*. (pp. 31-45) NY: Westview Press.

Nussbaum, M. (1995) Human Capabilities, Female Human Beings. In *Women, Culture and Development: A Study of Human Capabilities*, ed. Nussbaum and Glover. Oxford: Clarendon Press.

Nussbaum, M. (1996) Compassion: The Basic Social Emotion. In *The Communitarian Challenge to Liberalism*, eds. Frankel, Mills & Paul. Cambridge: Cambridge University Pres.

Nussbaum, M. (2001). *Women and Human Development: The Capabilities Approach*. London: Cambridge University Press.

Pope, R. (2005). *Creativity: Theory, History, Practice*. [Kindle Reader]. Retrieved from www.amazon.com

Sawyer, R. K. (2006). *Explaining Creativity: The Science of Human Innovation*. London: Oxford University Press.

Selzer, J. (). Rhetorical analysis: understanding how texts persuade readers.

Shujaa, N. et al (2009) Analysis of the Effect of Neuropeptides and Cannabinoids. *In Current Opinions in Pharmacology*. 2009 October 24

St. Pierre, A. (April 22, 2011) *Marijuana and the Media: Friend or Foe?* NORML Annual Conference. Denver, CO.

STATEMENT FROM COMMUNICATIONS DIRECTOR RAFAEL LEMAITRE ON GLOBAL COMMISSION REPORT ON DRUG POLICY. (2011). Retrieved from http://www.whitehousedrugpolicy.gov/news/press11/060211.html

Sternberg, R. J. (2004). Introduction. In *Creativity: The Psychology of Creative Potential and Realization* (pp. 1-9). : .

Sternberg, R. J. (2010). The Dark Side of Creativity and How to Combat It. In *The Dark Side of Creativity* (pp. 316-328). NY: Cambridge University Press.

Taylor, C. (1994) *Multiculturalism: Examining the Politics of Recognition*. Ewing, NJ: Princeton University Press.

Tronto, J. (1989) Women and Caring: What can Feminists Learn About Morality from Caring? In Held, V (1995) *Justice and Care: Essential Readings in Feminist Ethics*.(pp. 101-115) NY: Westview Press.

Tronto, J. (1993) *Moral Boundaries: A Political Argument for an Ethic of Care*. NY: Routledge.

Unknown (2011). *Medical Cannabis Logo* [Computer generated Image]. Retrieved from www.nmnorml.org

Welch, S.P. & Eads, M. (1999) Synergistic Interactions of Endogenous opioids and Cannabinoid Systems. Brain Research Institute. Nov. 27: 848 (102): 183-190

Cannabis Patient Network Institute

Cannabis Patient Network Institute (CPNI) has devoted its energy to passionately advocating for the politically under-represented members of our global family who suffer from illness and do not know about the Endocannabinoid System or understand the use of cannabis as medicine. Find out how you can contribute to a future in which cannabis is restored in our society as a food and medicine available to all people. Learn how you can support and participate in our educational events, future community research projects, and in other events in your area or online! Volunteer your time! Donate a few dollars—they go a long way to helping others!

www.CPNInstitute.Org

Integral Education & Consulting, LLC
Regina Nelson, CEO

www.IntegralEducationandConsulting.com

Join the Integral Speakers Network!

Integral Education and Consulting, LLC is currently considering Integral Speakers Network (ISN) agreements with patients, physicians and other medical professionals, veterinarians, lawyers, and former private and public leaders interested in entering the cannabis industry, whose skills and experience lend them to perform more optimally in an educational organization than in a dispensary or other ancillary business or even as an independent consultant.

IEC, LLC offers the unique opportunity of obtaining an educational investment in and owning one's own business while also engaged in the growth of IEC, LLC—collaboratively working and learning alongside a synergistic team of training professionals. Together the combined talent of the ISN will help achieve the goals of both IEC, LLC and you're own business endeavor! Networks accomplish more when they perform synergistically!! Contact Regina Nelson to see how you can become an Integral Speaker and Trainer!

ReginaNelson.IEC@gmail.com

Made in the USA
Middletown, DE
13 December 2018